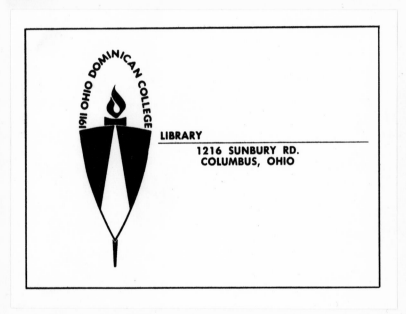

1911 OHIO DOMINICAN COLLEGE

LIBRARY

1216 SUNBURY RD.
COLUMBUS, OHIO

Will and Destiny

The publication of this work has been aided by a grant
from The Andrew W. Mellon Foundation

Will and Destiny

*Morality and Tragedy
in George Eliot's Novels*

by

Felicia Bonaparte

New York: New York University Press

823.88
E 42B
1975

TO MY PARENTS

ACKNOWLEDGMENTS

For many and varied kindnesses I am pleased to acknowledge my deep gratitude to: Professor William E. Buckler of New York University; Professors Alice Chandler, Barbara Watson, and Irene Tayler of The City College of New York; and Professor John Rosenberg of Columbia University. And to Dean Theodore L. Gross of The City College of New York I owe a very special debt.

Contents

Introduction

There is no question today of reviving George Eliot. The anti-Victorian reaction that began in the late nineteenth century, a reaction that subjected many Victorians to neglect and some to derision, yielded in the 1930s to a more disinterested reassessment. And few nineteenth-century writers have fared as well, as increasingly well, in the last forty years as George Eliot. Among critics, her standing is as high perhaps as it ever was in her own lifetime when many considered her the most important novelist of her age. And if the response of young students reading her for the first time is any indication, it may be that her popular standing will soon equal the general reputation she enjoyed a century ago.

But if we are no longer reviving George Eliot, we are still very much discovering her. It is not historical curiosity that attracts the contemporary reader but a growing awareness that Eliot speaks as immediately to the modern consciousness as the most current writer. In one sense, this awareness is nothing more than the recognition that the crises of modern man are essentially the crises of the Victorian, from whom, indeed, we inherited them. But Eliot is more modern than that, and the Eliot we have begun to discover, in another sense, especially in the last two decades or so, is one the general Victorian public neither knew nor could fully appreciate.[1] And this is not, as it is in some cases of reinterpretation, because we have returned to her novels a century later with the hindsight of some new expertise. The modern reading is not one that would have surprised Eliot as, for example, Mark Spilka's reading of Dickens, of novels whose sense of guilt and anxiety foreshadow Kafka, would probably have surprised Dickens.[2] We have found nothing yet that Eliot did not deliberately put in her novels; we know that from her letters, her journals, her essays, and above all from the novels themselves.

Indeed, the fact is we have not yet read in these novels all that Eliot wrote. We have not yet, for example, looked carefully at what Eliot had to say about women in society. Eliot was a great feminist, and her novels, although they never stoop to mere propaganda, urge a relentless war against the conditions by which women's lives have been restrained and wasted. We do not yet have an adequate understanding of the poetic element in Eliot's imagination, nor of the rich symbolic structure that informs her works. We have not yet probed the mythic imagery that echoes throughout her novels. There can be no doubt that we will have to revise many of our conclusions and judgments, especially of her achievement in *Romola*, when we have further examined these aspects of her work.

Similarly, we have felt perhaps but not yet explored the most thoroughly contemporary aspect of Eliot's novels, namely the existential, absurd universe Eliot perceived, a tragic universe in which man is born and dies for no purpose and with little hope of joy. This Eliot seems to resemble little if at all the novelist many of our mid-Victorian ancestors thought they were reading. In 1859, when Eliot's first novel was published, it was generally speculated that the author of *Adam Bede* was a country parson whose sweet portrait of rustic life was designed to confirm Christians in their faith.³ And for many readers, although the factual error was quickly corrected, George Eliot remained the author of essentially sentimental—and Christian—novels. It is easy to understand this phenomenon. Most readers found exactly what they looked for: more novels of the kind they had been reading, more novels that reflected their own vision. Had Eliot made radical changes in the form of the novel, had she violated more superficial conventions (as Hardy did later), her readers might have been jarred into recognizing a distinction, and some perhaps would not have continued to be her readers. But Eliot was quiet and subtle, and what in fact was something of a revolution in fiction passed largely unnoticed by the general reading public.

The response of the critics was another matter. Eliot's contemporary critics were of three minds. There were those who spoke virtually in unison with the general public, who thought Eliot was doing the same old thing but who praised her for doing it so well. Others, more perceptive but no less conventional, heard the new voice with some alarm. In October 1860, for example, the *Quarterly Review* published an evaluation of Eliot's first three novels. "The idea that fiction should contain something to soothe, to elevate or to purify seems to be extinct," the reviewer rightly discerned. But this is not an innovation he welcomes. "In its stead," he continues in a crescendo of repugnance, "there is a love for what would be better left in obscurity; for portraying the wildness of passion and the harrowing miseries of mental conflict; for dark pictures of sin and remorse and punishment; for the discussion of those questions which it is painful and revolting to think of."⁴

It was critics like R. H. Hutton, Leslie Stephen, and later Henry James, who were themselves intellectual mavericks, who were Eliot's best judges. But at least a partial recognition of Eliot's purpose and achievement was not uncommon among the better reviewers. Thus, the *Westminster Review*, although it did not rise to the demands Eliot makes on her readers in *Daniel Deronda,* softened its unfavorable notice of that novel with praise of Eliot's characterization of Hetty Sorrel in *Adam Bede* in remarks that show a very subtle understanding of Eliot's intention. "Never was the hapless simpleton, strange mixture of innocence and that self-love which is the root of ill, deserving of her fate, yet not deserving, in her lightness and reckless ignorance, of any such tremendous encounter with destiny and the powers of evil, so wonderfully set forth." "A lesser artist," the reviewer goes on to say somewhat later, "would have made this trifling country girl develop into a heroine in face of the terrible emergency; but genius knows better; and the tragedy gains in depth and solemn force from the helpless weakness of the central figure." We abandon, the reviewer concludes, Desdemona and Juliet to their fates feeling less pain than we do in watching "this poor, pretty, self-regarding fool crouch helpless and dumb before the awful fates."[5]

It is easier for us than for the general nineteenth-century reader to grasp the underlying convictions that inspired Eliot's novels. For Eliot was one of the Victorians who not only faced and welcomed the changing world but urged passionately that the old order give place to the new. It was always Eliot's purpose to write not in her time but for the future into which she attempted to take her readers. Although in many ways we have not yet arrived at the future Eliot envisioned, we are, far more than our predecessors, Eliot's contemporary readers. We have seen the absurdity and accepted the dilemma. What we have not yet done, what we are still very much struggling to do, is to imagine the implications and possibilities of this new reality. And here Eliot is somewhat ahead of us. She knew very well that every universe must make its own morality; and her morality, in which she encompasses the whole range of human life, like Camus's—and the analogy is not a casual one—can be understood only in the context of her dark, relentless vision. In it, Eliot probes what man must and may do in his tragic existence.

It is curious that, while we have read and loved Eliot's novels, we have refused, in some areas, to hear what she had to say about them, often in them. One of the claims we have seldom heard and never taken quite seriously is Eliot's assertion that her novels were, in the strictest sense, tragedies, and, moreover, Aristotelian tragedies. When we have considered the matter, we have generally concluded one of two things: that there may be some elements of tragedy in Eliot's fiction but that these are neither comprehensive nor central and that therefore she meant to call her novels tragedies in a very loose sense; or, since her novels conform to none of the conventional features of tragedy, that she was simply mistaken. But it is uncomfortable to rest on such conclusions, for Eliot uses terms with mathematical precision, and her interpretation of her own novels comes from an author who was not only a great writer but also a great critic, indeed, one remarkably well informed in all areas of knowledge and one of the few who had studied most of the great literatures of the world in their original languages. It is difficult to believe that Eliot meant something other than what she said.

My own conviction is that Eliot's novels are tragedies and that as such they may require an explanation but not an apology. And I believe that whether or not we read Eliot's works as tragedies is important, oddly enough for precisely the same reason that the question is in doubt at all. For the tragedy Eliot writes is to be found in the informing concept out of which the novels grow; like the causal connection between events which is so central a part of Eliot's fiction, the tragedy cannot be seen but must be inferred. It is there, in the novels, but it is there not as are the individual parts of the novels but as the order that binds them together. Indeed, it binds together all of Eliot's novels,[6] and as the unifying theme of Balzac's novels is suggested in their common title "The Human Comedy," Eliot's novels might well be called "The Human Tragedy."

It is with this shared informing vision that I will concern myself in this book. The bias of discussion will necessarily be on the intellectual side, both on Eliot's intellectual commitments and on the intellectual content of the novels. Some aspects of the novels will have no place in this discussion, and, more danger-ously perhaps, it will be impossible to take up the novels one by one. Something of the integrity of each work will undoubtedly be lost, but on this point I think Eliot would not have quibbled. In a letter to Elizabeth Stuart Phelps, Eliot wrote that "there has been no change in the point of view from which I regard our life since I wrote my first fiction" *(Letters,* VI, 318).

For Eliot the world was tragic from its beginning, although it did not always know it, or, at least, was not always able to face such knowledge. The Greeks faced it, and they are a constant source of perception for her; and modern man must face it, for he has no alternative. Thus, the subject of her novels, which is indeed modern man, is, at the same time, the human race as a whole, the compact tragedy of everyman. The question, which entails all others, to which Eliot addressed herself is the peren-nial riddle of the Sphinx: What is man? It was the question Sophocles asked in the mythological idiom of Greek tragedy and the question Shakespeare asked in the Elizabethan idiom of heroic tragedy. And in the characteristically Victorian idiom of what appear to be rather typical nineteenth-century novels, Eliot too writes another and very different form of tragedy.

At first, perhaps, it is easier to see Eliot's debt to novelists like Fielding and Gaskell, to works like *Pilgrim's Progress,* than to Shakespeare and the Greek tragedians. Certainly there is noth-ing like a traditional tragic hero in any of Eliot's novels. No one, in fact, comes close to that Aristotelian figure of great stature on whose fortunes depends a state or a kingdom. Quite the contrary. Most of Eliot's characters are, in the conventional terms of tragic judgment, insignificant, at best only aspiring to greatness, at worst unable even to imagine heroism. Mythology there is, espe-cially in works like *Romola.* But unlike Greek tragedy, Eliot's novels embody the myths in the concrete and often sordid fact; and as we focus on these petty scenes, as Eliot insists we must, the grander framework seems to slip away, or returns only to mock the commonplace events.

Yet, although it is clear that under no circumstances could Victorian England speak in the voice of traditional tragedy, for Eliot the nature of the novel she inherited and used largely without revision, the focus of fiction that inspired the prodigious production of novels in this century, was not a trap in which an alien concept struggled to find expression but the very substance of her tragic vision. In a sense, Eliot discovered modern tragedy, modern not only in the broad sense which encompasses the last two centuries but in the narrower sense in which Arthur Miller argued it in very recent memory in *Death of a Salesman,* both in his introduction to the play and in Linda Loman's cry to the audience as much as to her son:

> "Willy Loman never made a lot of money. His name was never in the paper. He's not the finest character that ever lived. But he's a human being, and a terrible thing is happening to him. So attention must be paid. . . . Attention, attention must be finally paid to such a person."

Linda's words are a clear challenge to Aristotle's definition of the tragic protagonist, and Miller is right to assume that even in our age we do not easily yield our conventional expectations of tragic stature. For magnitude, of course, is important, as Aristotle knew. It is perhaps a regrettable but nonetheless perennial truth of human psychology that we can be solemn only in the presence of something that seems to us larger than life. Melville made no mistake in building through so many chapters the physical size of Moby Dick; it would be difficult to take Ahab seriously if he were pursuing a sardine.

But size is also a matter of perspective. For Eliot who, like Miller, is concerned with asserting the tragedy of common life, the difference between great and petty is a difference in perception. Eliot was one of the first writers to wrest tragedy from the stronghold of elitism and concede it to the democratized future of the average man. There is a strong political radicalism in this act, but, even more, there is a stronger humanistic radicalism inspired by her deepest awareness of man's limitations and her deepest moral passion. The law to which every man's egotism invariably subscribes, Eliot held, is the absolute importance of self. From the perspective of egotism, nothing else is important, nothing else is real. But if we can imaginatively project ourselves into the identity of another, that same egotism that asserts the importance of its own self can recognize that to himself each feels equally important, however insignificant he may seem to outside appraisals.

This imaginative projection of self, which is at the very heart of Eliot's morality, is the cornerstone as well of Eliot's concept of the tragic protagonist. In this, Eliot is quite strictly Aristotelian. The catharsis in which Aristotle says the tragedy must culminate can be effected only through the audience's full identification with the protagonist. But Eliot takes Aristotle's argument one step further. Since every individual, Eliot held, secretly feels himself magnificent enough for tragedy, we can learn to accept as a fitting subject of tragedy whatever character the work of art makes us identify with. Art can give tragic proportions to the smallest living creature, even the squirrel whose heartbeat, as the narrator of *Middlemarch* says, is the roar on the other side of the silence within which each of us is locked.[7]

This is not clever artifice on Eliot's part, but the very truth of the case. The distinctions made by traditional tragedy implicitly claim some objective standard of judgment. But for Eliot what we commonly call the objective point of view is nothing more than the bias of someone's subjective angle of vision. There is no one in the universe whose objectivity is anything else. Protagoras, questioning the possibility of discovering absolute truth, concluded that man was the measure of all things. In a more modern version, Eliot, recognizing the empiricist doctrine that comparative judgments must be ultimately reduced to someone's bundle of perceptions, concluded that each individual must be the measure of his own importance.

Eliot's concept of tragedy is one that translates the universal symbol out of which Greek tragedy was made into the individual case. It is not an idle translation, and its interest is more than historical. The symbol predicates tragedy of the human condition, and this Eliot does too. The mythological, heroic, cosmic context is of great importance in the novels, reminding us that we all share in a common tragic experience, that the temporal unity that contains the tragic conflict is a perennial present. But the translation singles out each individual as a tragic protagonist whose tragic stature is achieved not vicariously, through Aristotle's paradigm man, but in himself, in his daily existence, in the very meanness of his redundant days. It asserts, therefore, something else too, that life is tragic not only in reflection but in fact. Tragedy is not something we discern only when we pause to consider the great questions of man's life; it is something we experience day by day, even if we do not know what our experience is called, even if we are powerless to articulate it. The symbol argues the proposition that life is tragic; the fact states that tragedy is what we live.

The translation from symbol to fact has enormous consequences in another, related, area as well, for it transfers tragedy from form to substance. While it is certainly not the case that those who have written tragedies have concerned themselves primarily (or sometimes at all) with conforming to certain rules of a particular aesthetic structure, it is true that we have come to think of tragedy as a literary genre. We do speak, at the same time, of the tragic vision of Herman Melville in *Moby Dick* for example; but we are a little reluctant to pronounce the novel itself a tragedy. There is a certain artificial distinction here of which criticism has taken too little notice. We grant tragic perception with relative generosity, but we grudge conferring the title of tragedy on works that do not fulfill certain formal requirements, and fulfill them, moreover, in a very specified way. Tragedy, in short, is a closed and possibly obsolete genre. Sophocles wrote it, Aristotle defined it, Euripides may have failed to grasp its essence, Shakespeare was ignorant of it but somehow achieved it nonetheless, Corneille regidified it, and, according to George Steiner in *The Death of Tragedy,* the language of the common man dealt it a fatal blow.

It is from this formal concept of tragedy that Eliot makes a radical departure. The modern tragedy, as I will now call it, that Eliot is writing is not in the structure of the work, nor in its content, but in the informing vision, a vision considerably more suited to the novel than the dramatic form. For if the perennial present is best contained in symbol and myth, as Eliot herself realized, and therefore in the concentrated action of drama, the actual present, which is life as it is in fact experienced, is the very lifeblood of the novel. Here, all the symbolic unities can disintegrate into their endless, repetitive parts which are the fragments of our daily lives.

In his recent book, *Architects of the Self: George Eliot, D. H. Lawrence, and E. M. Forster,* Calvin Bedient voices the rather traditional argument that indicts, in part, not only Eliot but the essentially modern concept of tragedy. Eliot, Bedient writes, "having made pity illogical, a mere indulgence, having reduced mystery to science, and having exchanged the metaphysical inevitability of the Greeks for the round of her own psychological needs . . . failed, failed utterly, to write the tragedy that she held to be implicit in the enduring conditions of social life." [8] Since a large portion of this book will be concerned with Eliot's notion of pity, I will not argue here what I think Bedient has misunderstood in Eliot's meaning and use of that term. But it will help to understand Eliot's position if we look at a few other assumptions in Bedient's summary dismissal.

It was not, of course, in the conditions of "social life" that Eliot found man's tragedy. In her essay "Liszt, Wagner, and Weimar," Eliot states that the core of tragedy is a "collision of forces," [9] and nowhere are the terms of this collision more succinctly or more clearly defined than through the narrator of *Felix Holt* who remarks that men have been inspired to "pity and terror" "ever since they began to discern between will and destiny." [10] *Will* and *destiny,* Bedient is quite right, are in no way metaphysical terms in Eliot. Indeed, Eliot abandoned metaphysics as she abandoned religion long before she began to write fiction. They are terms, and Bedient is right again, that arise in a very scientific concept of the universe. Eliot did reduce mystery to science, but it is by no means clear that science precludes mystery nor self-evident that this reduction closes the door on tragedy. Eliot thought quite otherwise.

It was in the nineteenth century that God died. In that same moment modern man was born, born of what has come to be known in our century as the existential anxiety of a creature adrift in an absurd universe. It is this modern dilemma that Camus's Caligula describes when he discovers that men die and they are not happy. Mortality, the finality of death in a godless universe, teaches us that there is no external purpose to our existence. That our lives have no intrinsic justification we learn from our own unhappiness. Either condition we might be able to endure; the secret of Caligula's revelation is that both are true. Man is trapped, purposeless and unsatisfied.

Not surprisingly, the Victorian world, while it felt very deeply the impact of this monumental transition, was to a large extent unaware that it was happening. Even among those whose profession was prophecy, writers and philosophers, many went on as before. Perhaps the most obvious example is Dickens, the giant of the mid-century, who sensed the need for change in innumerable social, economic, and political areas, but for whom the old truisms remained true. No less characteristic, for the century is defined through contradiction, are those other, fewer, voices who began living in the twentieth century while still in the nineteenth. John Stuart Mill was one, but Mill, who saw the hard empirical reality, never felt its tragedy. Toward the end of the century, in his later novels, Hardy was another. Hardy saw the reality, felt its tragedy, but never exonerated that nameless, metaphysical abstraction which condemned man, as Tess says, to live on this blighted star. Eliot shares much with both but resembles neither.

The answer to the riddle of the Sphinx, of course, has never altered. It was written on the temple of Apollo at Delphi when Oedipus consulted the oracle: "Know thyself." What those words meant to Eliot was essentially what they had meant to Sophocles. As the Chorus says in the second epode of *Antigone,* man is that being that has mastered the land and the sea, and the creatures of both; he has created the polis, with its arts, language, philosophy; he has probed the earth's secrets. Only death and his own blindness he has not conquered. Ultimate power remains beyond man's control; the laws of nature imprison his very identity and constrain his possibilities. Self-knowledge is the recognition of limitations.

At the center of man's tragic dilemma Eliot too found that same power of destiny and that same blindness of will. To the mind of the Greek poet, these cosmic forces, both within man and without, presented themselves in the metaphor of myth and ritual. And it is important to stress that myth and ritual are metaphors, and were so even to the Greeks. The literal reading of Greek tragedy yields a very different body of literature from the symbolic. Indeed, no literary work can be held to its literal content which must have, at best, a limited and ephemeral validity.

If this is a truism, it is one often forgotten. In one of his less perceptive moments, for example, Matthew Arnold pronounced in his 1853 Preface to the *Poems* that an "action like the action of the Antigone of Sophocles, which turns upon the conflict between the heroine's duty to her brother's corpse and that to the laws of the country, is no longer one in which it is possible that we should feel a deep interest." [11] It is a conclusion, certainly, which could be generalized to the detriment of much of our best literature. Since we no longer believe in Poseidon or his wrath, the *Odyssey* must equally fail to engage us; if we are not religious, indeed Catholic, Dante must seem to be babbling pointless fables; and in the age of contraception, the problem Dreiser dealt with in *An American Tragedy* has been solved. In "The Antigone and Its Moral," Eliot challenged Arnold's reading of Sophocles.[12] While the "dramatic motive" of *Antigone* is foreign to "modern sympathies," Eliot writes, it "is only superficially so." It is true that "we no longer believe that a brother, if left unburied, is condemned to wander a hundred years without repose on the banks of the Styx; we no longer believe that to neglect funeral rites is to violate the claims of the infernal deities. But these beliefs are the accidents and not the substance of the poet's conception" *(Essays,* p. 262).

This distinction, which makes clear that the gods are important not for what they are but for what they stand for, also makes clear the connection between Greek tragedy and Eliot's novels, a connection that is important both to Eliot and to us, for on it depend some of Eliot's chief aims as a novelist. Eliot wished to confront the modern world, to address herself, that is, to those questions which began to plague the modern mind in the nineteenth century and persist to this day. But she wished also to probe the essential, unchanging features of man's existence. Change was real to Eliot; man's world evolved and the modern age was different from all others in significant ways. But permanence was real too; the laws of nature remained the same; and modern man could recognize, even in his most remote ancestors, the same passions and aspirations. Together, these two facts begot a third: every age, although unique, was in another sense a new translation of the perennial story. The substance remained, the accidents altered. Precisely because Greek tragedy spoke in myth, it expressed that essential sameness for all ages. In her notes to *The Spanish Gypsy,* Eliot writes that the Greeks "had the same essential elements of life presented to them as we have, and their art symbolised these in grand schematic form." [13] Her own novels, then, translate this "schematic form" into the actual present of modern life.

What this translation meant for Eliot is just what Bedient regrets. Let me not dwell on Bedient's remark that Eliot substituted "her own psychological needs" for the "metaphysical inevitability of the Greeks." If true, the insight may be valuable for a biography, but it is surely unnecessary and unprofitable to read Eliot's novels as symptoms of psychic disorder. There is a vision of life the reader is asked to examine in the novels, and it is an important one. It is also a scientific one. In the modern world, Greek mythology becomes empirical science. Each age must answer the Sphinx in its own terms, and in ours, the self-knowledge Apollo told us to seek is available in the discoveries of astronomy, cosmology, anthropology, sociology, biology, psychology, and countless other disciplines which Eliot herself studied avidly, for she believed that through them we can come to know who we are and what kind of world it is we live in.

We have not lost the gods; we simply call them by different names. In our time, the destiny that Aeschylus called Zeus, Sophocles Apollo, and Euripides Dionysus has become the force of necessity—the natural laws we have come to know even to mathematical precision but understand, in an ultimate sense, as little and are as impotent against as Agamemnon, Oedipus, and Pentheus. Destiny still lurks, perplexing and ominous, in the shadows of our existence. And like the Greek protagonists, we are still born blind to the hard reality that contains us, still deluded by the natural instincts of our egotistic wills to imagine ourselves free and invincible and to challenge the universe in which we may be no more than an amusing and passing curiosity. The Greek gods and modern science, Eliot claimed, disclose the same absurd universe and the same tragic confrontation. The Greeks called it hybris and nemesis; Eliot calls it will and destiny.

The tragic collision of will and destiny was, for Eliot, a moral collision as well. The two were inextricably bound to each other and as inextricably bound to man's existence. And both, moreover, were as deeply inherent in the scientific as they had been in the Hellenic view of man.

The science that is often held responsible for the death of tragedy in the modern world is often also held responsible for the decline of morality. The historical connection between religion and morality that had obtained for nearly two thousand years in the Western world had come to be accepted as a necessary connection, and with the coming of the secular, scientific, age it seemed that morality too must perish. For many "moral" meant "religious," and those who did not espouse God, like John Stuart Mill, were, at best, morally suspect. Much of this connection, no doubt, can be attributed to a cultural habit of thought. But in the empiricism out of which modern science had developed, there was some cause for alarm for those who wished to retain the traditional morality or for those who could imagine no other.

For empiricism offered no substitute for the absolute, unassailable authority of God's word; there was no moral structure in the universe on which man's own moral law could be modeled. Worse still, empiricism acknowledged the ultimate subjectivity and consequent uncertainty of all knowledge. It seemed, since the definitions of good and evil were written nowhere in the cosmic scheme, that they must be merely matters of opinion—opinion, in fact, which had emotive but no cognitive value. Had not David Hume confessed as much? Without God, it appeared that the only alternative was moral chaos. Here was, obviously, the moral dilemma of modern man, the beginning of moral relativism which, at its best, might lead to liberation and liberal tolerance, as Mill urged and argued, but which also left a moral vacuum in which the best did often lack all conviction, and the worst, in the absence of some demonstrable moral criterion, could feel free to follow inclination.

Eliot understood and shared the dilemma. In *Romola,* she studied precisely such a case in Tito Melema, a character born in the Renaissance, a simlar period of transition. In Tito the dissolution of the religious cohesion of the Middle Ages has bred a

complete moral skeptic who paraphrases David Hume—the
anachronism is part of the connection Eliot makes between
fifteenth-century Florence and nineteenth-century England
—on the subjectivity of moral judgments to justify his narrowly
egotistic choices. Tito is a grim prophecy, and it is not surprising
that the Victorian world fought hard against it. But for the most
part the Victorians fought with the weapons of a world already
defunct. God was not to be resurrected. And the rigid dogma that
became the mark of the Victorian in the minds of many of his
descendants and critics (most notably perhaps, Butler and
Wilde) lulled the general sense of panic but failed to face the
enemy at the gate. Moral skepticism marched on.

The problem was the characteristic Victorian problem of trying to put new wine in old bottles. Without God, the old morality
could not be saved, for it was too thoroughly imbued with
religion, too dependent on the theological concepts of man and
his place in the universe. What many did not see was that other
moralities were possible. It was largely the empiricists, who
themselves saw the need for some moral authority, who attempted to build a new system out of the new truths, who argued
that science was not a threat to morality but a new and stronger
foundation for what must become modern ethics.

Eliot too was an empiricist. She too believed that science
must be the basis of the morality of the future. And, like John
Stuart Mill and Auguste Comte, she found in science the answer
to both relativism and skepticism. For it was science, Eliot held,
not God, that provided an inflexible authority for moral law.
God could be merciful, arbitrary, obscure, and, in the end, might
be a myth. Nature was real, inescapable, undeviating. It was no
Wordsworthian harmony with nature Eliot counseled. Nature
maintains its own harmony, whether we acquiesce or not. But in
the laws of nature Eliot found the definition of man's limitations, even as the Greeks had, the boundary of destiny beyond
which man's limitless desire could not step in safety.

Thus, the collision of will and destiny which revealed man's tragic condition also taught him what restraints he must put on his will if he hoped to make the best compromise he could with an indifferent but powerful enemy. Unlike the old morality, Eliot's claimed no intrinsic virtue. The laws of nature are not good, but they are compelling. Eliot's morality tells us to bow, when we have no alternative, to what Aeschylus had called the yoke of necessity; but it grants us the right, indeed urges us, to resent, and as far as possible resist, the tyranny of nature; for although morality is the best we can do, given the facts of existence, it remains always inimical to the full satisfaction of our will and is thrrefore itself imposed on us by the tragic condition into which we are born.

Notes

(I have attempted to make all references throughout this book more accessible by using, whenever possible, easily available texts.)

1. For one thing, we have more information about Eliot than has ever been available before. We have, most importantly, Gordon S. Haight's edition of Eliot's letters *(The George Eliot Letters* [New Haven, 1954-55], hereafter to be cited in the text as *Letters)* as well as Haight's biography *(George Eliot: A Biography* [New York, 1968]). Eliot criticism has always been somewhat uneven. When the Victorian revival began, for example, it was possible to find, side by side, such sensitive perceptions as those P. Bourl'honne offered in *George Eliot: Essai de biographie intellectuelle et morale, 1819-54* (Paris, 1933) and such uninspired studies as Lord David Cecil's discussion of Eliot, written in 1935, in *Victorian Novelists: Essay in Revalution* (Chicago, 1961). Partly because we know more, partly because so much has been done on which modern criticism can build, and partly, no doubt, because we can look back at Eliot now from the perspective of an age she foreshadowed, such current critical studies as Bernard Paris' *Ex-*

periments in Life: George Eliot's Quest for Values (Detroit, 1965) and George Levine's "Determinism and Responsibility in the Works of George Eliot" *(PMLA,* 77 [June 1962], 268-79)—to name the two I have found most indispensable to my own study—are in the constant process of seriously revising our reading of Eliot's works.

2. *Dickens and Kafka: A Mutual Interpretation* (Bloomington, 1963).

3. See Haight, *Biography,* pp. 280-295.

4. See Laurence Lerner and John Holmstrom, eds., *George Eliot and Her Readers: A Selection of Contemporary Reviews* (London, 1966), p. 21.

5. *George Eliot and Her Readers,* pp. 22 and 23.

6. Because the tragedy in Eliot is in the informing vision it is to be found not only in her novels but everywhere, even in many of her letters and essays. But I have chosen to limit my discussion to the seven novels that constitute the central corpus of her works. These are the works with which most readers of Eliot are familiar. While I have considered her other works in arriving at my conclusions, it seemed best not to multiply examples from her other fiction.

7. Edited with an introduction by Gordon S. Haight (Boston, 1966), p. 144. (All references to this edition will hereafter be cited in the text.)

8. Berkeley, 1972, pp. 38-39. I focus on this passage, an uncharacteristically hasty one I think in a very exciting study, because it is so much the prevailing view both of tragedy and of Eliot's claim to a place in the tragic canon.

9. *Essays of George Eliot,* ed. Thomas Pinney (New York, 1963), p. 104. (All references to this edition will hereafter be cited in the text.)

10. Edited with an introduction by George Levine (New York, 1970), p. 9. (All references to this edition will hereafter be cited in the text.)

11. Preface, *The Poetical Works of Matthew Arnold* (New York, 1949), pp. xxvii-xxviii.

12. Thomas Pinney is undoubtedly right in suggesting that Eliot is here answering Arnold's evaluation of the Greek play. Her familiarity with the 1853 volume is evident, as Pinney remarks, from her review of Arnold's *Poems: Second Series* in the *Westminster Review* in 1855. (See *Essays,* p. 262, n. 6.)

13. John Walter Cross, *George Eliot's Life as Related in Her Letters and Journals (New York: Illustrated Cabinet Edition, n.d.),* III, 34.

CHAPTER I

Destiny

The Artist's Method as the Novel's Subject

To be born, in Eliot's world, is to become an instant prisoner to an indifferent cosmic machine which grinds down with implacable certainty everything that opposes its unalterable order. It is to be trapped in destiny. This order, in Eliot's view, governs not only the fictional world but the real one as well; indeed, it is because it is the order of the real world that it must become that of the fictional one. The distinctions between the two were for Eliot largely formal not substantive.

At nineteen Eliot accepted the popular view of art. "For my part," she writes,

I am ready to sit down and weep at the impossibility of my understanding or barely knowing even a fraction of the sum of objects that present themselves for our contemplation in books and in life. Have I then any time to spend on things that never existed? *(Letters,* I, 23) [1]

At thirty-eight, on December 6, 1857, she wrote in her Journal:

"September 1856 made a new era in my life, for it was then I began to write Fiction" *(Letters,* II, 406).[2] In the years between Eliot found out what fiction was. Greater maturity and years of experience as a critic inspired an aesthetic which rejected the implied suspicion of her first estimate that fiction was the frivolous pursuit of those who wished to escape reality. Instead, art became for Eliot the ultimate and most intense confrontation of reality. The uninformed view, once her own, that the artist was a mere entertainer, distressed her constantly. "It is a comfort to me to read any cirticism which recognizes the high responsibility of literature that undertakes to represent life," she wrote to John Blackwood, one of her closest associates in the publication of most of her novels. "The ordinary tone about art is, that the artist may do what he will, provided he pleases the public" *(Letters,* III, 394). And many years later it is not without some personal passion that she refers to the popular notion of the novelist when she ironically describes Daniel Deronda as setting himself against authorship, "a vocation which is understood to turn foolish thinking into funds." [3]

It was not merely because Eliot had high seriousness (although she did, in the best sense of that term) that she expected the artist to see his work as a moral mission and to accept it as such with a deep sense of responsibility. It was more because she saw for him no alternative. Everywhere—in her letters, in her articles, in her novels—Eliot argues persistently that no one, artist or not, is exempt from that human interdependence in which whatever we say and do acts as a determining context for other people. The artist too is trapped in that destiny which, as I will discuss later, subjects, by its very indifference, every action to moral scrutiny. Long before she published her first novel, Eliot wrote to Sara Hennell, a friend for many years, that she thought " 'Live and teach' should be a proverb as well as 'Live and learn.' " "We must teach," she continues, "either for good or evil" *(Letters,* I, 242). By precept, implication, or example, every action is a moral paradigm. All the more, then, must the artist be aware of his moral obligation to the degree that his influence extends far beyond the personal. The claims of pure aestheticism—if indeed they justify exemption from such responsibility—Eliot had little patience with. Writing to Edward Burne-Jones, Eliot remarks that it "would be narrowness to suppose that the artist can only care for the impression of those who know the methods of his art as well as feel its effects. Art works for all whom it can touch" *(Letters,* V, 391). The "man or woman who publishes writings," Eliot elaborates in "Leaves from a Note-Book,"

> inevitably assumes the office of teacher or influencer of the public mind. Let him protest as he will that he only seeks to amuse, and has no pretension to do more than while away an hour of leisure or weariness ... he can no more escape influencing the moral taste, and with it the action of the intelligence, than a setter of fashions in furniture and dress can fill the shops with his designs and leave the garniture of persons and houses unaffected by his industry. *(Essays,* p. 440) [4]

Thus, the fictional world becomes for Eliot bound to the real one in two vital ways. The influence of the fictional world was "inevitably" in the real one. But, since in the real world few actions were morally neutral, the artist could not avoid adding to the good or evil of human existence. His effect, moreover, could be achieved only indirectly, through the reader. It was the reader whom the artist had to return from the pages of fiction to the real world with the sharpened perception that inspired a keener moral sensibility, and it was essential, for this reason, that the fictional world allow the reader no possible escape from the reality of his own life; quite the contrary, in fact, it was necessary that it reflect that life so intensely that the reader could not ignore in fiction what he might have managed to ignore in fact. It was thus that Eliot concluded that since fiction had its effect in real life, real life had to be the subject of fiction. Indeed, it became for Eliot the greatest burden of the artist to concern himself with understanding the reality from which no one was ultimately exempt. Life, the world, human existense were tragic for Eliot not in fiction but in fact. It was not the artist but nature that brought about the conflict of will and destiny; if the artist was a creator, he was so in a very qualified sense and not free to create at will, for he came upon a pre-defined condition which he might pervert but never alter.

Yet the artist was not merely a translator in the strict sense; he would have been far less necessary to the world than Eliot thought him had he had no larger function. Art was not a reproduction of life. Life was what the reader was already living, and it was the inadequacy of experience itself that made the artist necessary. Art must be a parable, a detour in reality through meaning. Between fact and fiction stood the artist as an intelligent, informed, and sensitive instrument of en-lightenment. What in life was obscure the artist could make manifest. What ordinary imagination could not grasp the artist could reveal. What blindness and egotism could not transcend the artist could compel awareness of. Paradoxically, it was life in fact that seemed illusory and fiction that could unmask the disguises of nature by penetrating and unifying the fragments of experience.

This taxing obligation which Eliot expected the writer to undertake required him to bring to his craft experience, know-ledge, and insight, qualifications which Eliot defined in a rather strict sense, for the three formed for her a continuum of per-ception. Experience the artist was by nature created to absorb in a more intense and meaningful manner than others. It is an important and rare talent, for, as Eliot shows throughout her novels, although experience is the invariable lot of all mankind, it is, at the same time, the very reality which human egotism is determined to avoid, as I will discuss in a later chapter. Neces-sarily, the artist too must struggle against the limits of his own subjectivity; but the very gift which makes him an artist has taught him to discern a far wider vision than nature grants to the ordinary man. Yet sensitivity, while essential, is insufficient. Precisely because subjectivity threatens always to question the truth of the artist's vision, experience must be refined and adjusted by knowledge, itself founded on experience but now reflected on formally and analytically. And this knowledge, in turn, must be deepened by the imaginative capacity which traces patterns suggested by but inaccessible to observation.

Clearly, in each of these three steps the artist is never free to escape the empirical fact. Gordon Haight dismisses far too lightly, I think, the insight that George Eliot's novels "seem to have been dictated to a plain woman of genius by the ghost of David Hume." [5] For there can be no doubt that Eliot was a thorough empiricist,[6] not in every specific philosophic point, but always in the large basis of her convictions. In her novels as well as in her letters and essays, Eliot seems, like Mill, to be often addressing herself implicitly to the rationalists and intuitionists and arguing against any criterion of truth whose basis is not in the solid fact. There is great danger, I believe, in ignoring this very deep commitment. Claude Bissell speaks for far too many when he states of Eliot that, regarded

> as a speculative thinker, she has, it is true, marked limitations. Her mind is not bold and adventurous; she is not impelled, as Meredith and Hardy were, towards the creation of metaphysics. She is at home only in those areas of thought where there is a solid basis in human experience—in the biological sciences, in religious and cultural history, in what today might be called sociology. But if this is a weakness for a philosopher, it may well be a strength for a novelist.[7]

Here Eliot's modernity seems to do her a disservice. The traditional identification of philosophy with metaphysics seems to subject her to charges to which Hume, Comte, and Mill would be equally liable. Not alone in her century but certainly among those who laid the foundations for the twentieth, Eliot is an empiricist with the characteristic empiricist's skepticism of metaphysics, religion, and similar systems of thought. Bissell is right—in fact if not in tone—that Eliot is "at home only in those areas of thought where there is a solid basis in human experience"—although these are far more comprehensive than Bissell suggests [8]—but this is no more than to describe Eliot's empiricist convictions to which, indeed, she arrived after long deliberation and not without some regret, as we are all too aware in her portrait of Dorothea. Eliot had been, roughly at the same age at which we first meet Dorothea, in a frame of mind very similar to that of her character, as one might suspect (even without biographical certainty) from the intimate and affectionate knowledge she has of her character's mind. Religious, then metaphysical, yearning for the impossible, intensely discomforted by the material, Eliot had begun her intellectual evolution in what August Comte had identified as the first and second of three stages of development in human and individual history. But Eliot had rapidly passed to the last (Comte's "positive") stage, that of empiricism and its formal expression, science.[9]

It is within the empiricist framework that Eliot's aesthetic judgments are invariably made. In "Silly Novels by Lady Novelists," for example, while discussing the *"oracular* species" of novels, to Eliot the "most pitiable of all," she writes that to "judge of their writings, there are certain ladies who think that an amazing ignorance, both of science and of life, is the best possible qualification for forming an opinion on the knottiest moral and speculative questions." [10] About the "Mind-and-millinery" novelists Eliot writes even more dirisively. These, "it appears, can see something else besides matter; they are not limited to phenomena, but can relieve their eyesight by occasional glimpses of the *noumenon" (Essays,* p. 310). The commitment to empiricism implicit in these remarks forms the first and most basic axiom of Eliot's own aesthetic and philosophic position. The foundation of the only meaningful and moral fiction Eliot can accept must be reality perceived without the prejudice of hypothesis and as accurately as possible. Lewes writes that Eliot was as "fidgety about minute accuracy as if she were on oath" *(Letters,* III, 263). This very point Eliot's narrator makes in her first novel, and in almost identical terms: "I feel as much bound to tell you as precisely as I can what that reflection [of the world on the mirror of the narrator's mind] is, as if I were in the witness-box narrating my experience on oath." [11]

As early as "Amos Barton," Blackwood and William George Hamley had been struck by Eliot's scrupulously accurate writing. "We alluded," Blackwood writes to explain the tone of their observation, "to a sort of precision of expression or illustration which gives us the idea that the writer was accustomed to scientific definitions" *(Letters,* II, 293-294). Although Blackwood does not cite the specific passages that called forth their comment, expressions of the kind he must have had in mind are so habitually Eliot's practice that almost any page of her works may provide a characteristic sample.[12] I choose the following passage from *Middlemarch* (a very typical one), not only because it makes its statement with scientific accuracy and through scientific analogy, but because it passes as well (also very typically) from mere illustration of a particular point to what Eliot considered the final and most important aim of such precise observation and knowledge. The narrator is probing Mrs. Cadwallader's motives. Disappointed that the match she had tried to effect between Dorothea and Sir James has been thwarted by Dorothea's preference for Casaubon, Mrs. Cadwallader revises her plans and prepares to offer Sir James to Celia. For Eliot the interest of the situation lies in discovering why it is a matter of such importance to Mrs. Cadwallader that one plan, if not another, succeed, and the narrator generalizes on the difficulty of reaching the fine basis of human action by relying on external observation only:

Even with a microscope directed on a water-drop we find ourselves making interpretations which turn out to be rather

7

coarse; for whereas under a weak lens you may seem to see a creature exhibiting an active voracity into which other smaller creatures actively play as if they were so many animated tax-pennies, a stronger lens reveals to you certain tiniest hair-lets which make vortices for these victims while the swallower waits at his receipt of custom.

A telescope following Mrs. Cadwallader through her daily business, the narrator had earlier remarked, could find no mo-tivation for her behavior. But the stronger lens of perception reveals "a play of minute causes producing what may be called thought and speech vortices to bring her the sort of food she needs" (p. 44). Here, with an observed fact of science, Eliot makes a thematic point about human nature, both specifically, in Mrs. Cadwallader's case, and generally. But she does more. Subtly but unquestionably Eliot establishes the continuum of organic matter, from the microscopic to the human, and urges, on that basis, the universal applicability of material laws. We are made aware not only of a disconnected fact, explained ana-logically, but of an informing vision which structures the thought of the entire novel. Moreover, it is a statement both of fact and of methodology. If the analogy reveals to us Mrs. Cadwallader's craving for relief from boredom, for importance, for the power to control lives, it reveals as well the manner in which Eliot arrives at the insight. It is the same method by which Lydgate hopes to arrive at the end of his research, the discovery of primal tissue, and forms, in fact, part of the con-tinuing theme in the novel for which Lydgate's investigations are the paradigm case. It is here that we discern the function of that insight which completes for Eliot the cycle of perception into reality. Transcription of phenomena is, as a foundation, necessary but alone insufficient. It is instructive that the the-matic focus is on the scientist of the novel but Lydgate's re-search, Eliot reminds us, is not limited to the organization of data any more than is the artist's. Where observation must necessarily end, imagination begins, imagination, that is, as distinct from fantasy. Lydgate, as Reva Stump points out, rejects the definition of imagination as the ability to invent at random, however vividly.[13] Rather, for him as for Eliot, imagination is something that "reveals subtle actions inaccessible to any sort of lens, but tracked in that outer darkness through long pathways of necessary sequence by the inward light which is the last refinement of Energy" *(Middlemarch,* p. 22).

That imagination is not a departure from knowledge but a necessary instrument in the acquisition of knowledge is a conviction which deepened as Eliot felt with increasing intensity the narrow limits and uncertain status of knowledge itself. In this too she is a thorough empiricist, caught between the purly analytic function of pure reason on the one side and the ultimately subjective perception of data on the other. In a very important section of *Daniel Deronda* Eliot takes up what is in effect a discussion of the subject. The argument is enacted in Daniel's mind. Pressed, by Mordecai's passionate urgency, to conclusions whose confirmation is yet beyond his factual knowledge, Daniel pauses to define for himself some acceptable criterion of truth. His English upbringing recommends the test of common sense, and Daniel is easily discomforted by Mordecai's visionary intensity. Yet what would he have done, Daniel asked himself, had Mordecai "introduced himself as one of the strictest reasoners?" Do such reasoners

form a body of men hitherto free from false conclusions and illusory speculations? The direst argument has its hallucinations, too hastily concluding that its net will now at last be large enough to hold the universe. *Men may dream in demonstrations, and cut out an illusory world in the shape of axioms, definitions, and propositions, with a final exclusion of fact signed Q.E.D.* No formula for thinking will save us mortals from mistake in *our imperfect apprehension of the matter to be thought about.* And since the unemotional intellect may carry

us into a mathematical dreamland where nothing is but what
is not, perhaps an emotional intellect may have absorbed into
its passionate vision of possibilities some truth of what will
be—the more comprehensive massive life feeding theory with
new material, as the sensibility of the artist seizes combinations which science explains and justifies. (p. 386)

In the first of the two passages I have italicized, Eliot, testing
pure reason to its ultimate possibility, discovers that it may
move from axiom to conclusion without ever touching the empirical fact. Self-contained, it may evolve a "mathematical
dreamland." Quite strictly, Eliot appears to be following Kant
(a philosopher she knew well, alluded to often, and on whom, in
fact, she wrote an article in 1855) in the function to which she
limits pure reason. But she follows Kant too in concluding that
we can have only an "imperfect apprehension of the matter to
be thought about." The empirical method yields knowledge but
knowledge which is uncertain and incomplete. It is with an
acute awareness of this difficulty that Eliot writes to John
Blackwood, who feared that *Scenes of Clerical Life* was taking a
depressing turn and hoped that mention of that fact would
improve its outlook: "I undertake to exhibit nothing as it should
be; I only try to exhibit some things as they have been or are,
*seen through such a medium as my own nature gives me" (Let-
ters,* II, 362). Virtually the same point is made in *Adam Bede*
where the narrator states his intention to "give a faithful account of men and things *as they have mirrored themselves in my
mind"* (p. 178). In the passages I have italicized above, what
Eliot suggests is that even the artist committed to realism could
not—were that his only purpose—give an objectively truthful
account of life or one, at least, which he knew to be objectively
truthful. That which we call "truth," the narrator of *The Mill
on the Floss* remarks, is rather a "complex, fragmentary,
doubt-provoking knowledge." [14]

It is not that Eliot here repudiates either the validity of the search for knowledge or the empirical, scientific, method, although that is a conclusion some have come to. Wagenknecht, for example, alluding to a quotation from Eliot—to which I will turn shortly—argues that Eliot "refused to reject human values and take molecular physics as her dominant guide." [15] Eliot's view, considerably subtler, does not require this disjunction. Wagenknecht, in fact, has misquoted, by implication, Eliot's letter to Mrs. Ponsonby who had complained that a belief in a determined world would paralyze her. It is in this important context that Eliot replies that "the consideration of molecular physics is not the *direct* ground of human love and moral action, any more than it is the *direct* means of composing a noble picture or of enjoying great music" *(Letters,* VI, 98-99; my italics). The word "direct," which Wagenknecht omits, and the nature of the analogy alter the meaning considerably, as does the specific argument of the letter. Clearly, Eliot accepts molecular physics—writes the letter in fact to defend it—but distinguishes it from its organic, far more complex manifestation in human psychology. Eliot's problem with the question of "truth," therefore, is not that science and the empirical method generally is wrong while something else is right. It is rather that all empirical observation, including science, can never be known to be knowledge of what is but only of what is perceived. It is in the full recognition of this limitation that the narrator of *Adam Bede* had proposed to speak not of what there was but of what he saw. The artist can never be a transparent glass—any more than can the scientist—but only a mirror. Noumena, things-in-themselves, the empiricist must concede, remain forever unknowable; man is granted only phenomena.

Thus, although Eliot is habitually called an aesthetic "realist"—not without good reason—it is necessary to qualify that term, for Eliot's realism becomes, of necessity, an attempt at objectivity that remains ultimately within the limits of subjectivity. This realism makes only a tentative and partial claim to accuracy in relation to fact. On the other hand, it refuses

to grant the criterion of intellectual honesty as its only justification. In the novels, as well as in her criticism, Eliot rejects visions
of the world held sincerely but, in her view, mistakenly. Rather,
somewhere between certainty and total skepticism, Eliot finds in
the inspired, informed, and imaginative study of the raw experience of life the possibility of a knowledge the artist may cultivate
in the reader. In Eliot's epistemology, the universe remains a
mystery, but a mystery man perceives through science. In a
passage Gordon Haight quotes from Herbert Spencer, one which
Eliot admired immensely, as she told Sara Hennell (*Letters,* II,
341), the inescapable connection between science and a sense of
mystery is made clear:

> After all that has been said, the ultimate mystery of things
> remains just as it was. . . . The sincere man of science, content
> fearlessly to follow wherever the evidence leads him, becomes
> by each new inquiry more profoundly convinced that the
> Universe is an insoluble problem. . . . He learns at once the
> greatness and the littleness of human intellect . . . its impo-
> tence in dealing with all that transcends human exper-
> ience. . . . He alone truly *sees* that absolute knowledge is im-
> possible. He alone *knows* that under all things there lies an
> impenetrable mystery. *(Letters,* II, 341, n. 1)

Not surprisingly, given the reciprocal relationship between art
and life in Eliot's view, the progression in knowledge by which the
artist comes to formulate his concept of reality is the same as that
through which Eliot takes her characters and readers. The artist's method becomes the novel's subject. For the process which
takes the artist from experience—fragmented, however intensely
perceived—through the analysis that structures experience, to
the imaginative knowledge which, as the narrator of *Daniel
Deronda* puts it, "pierces" "the solid fact" (p. 284) is the very
process which strains to grasp the order of destiny. Writer,
character, and reader are engaged, each in a uniquely synchron-

ized cycle, in the same search for a definition of the cosmic context which dictates to all three the terms of their existence.

"Undeviating Law in the Material and Moral World"

Mathilde Parlett does not exaggerate in saying that one may well look at Eliot's novels as expounding the "doctrine of consequences." [16] In man, in nature, in their interrelationships, the laws of causality define the process which, taken in its entirety, constitutes the fundamental nature of destiny. In her review of Mackay's *The Progress of the Intellect,* which appeared in January 1851, Eliot had enthusiastically explicated Mackay's thesis that the "master-key" to the revelation of reality "is the recognition of the presence of undeviating law in the material and moral world—and that invariability of sequence which is acknowledged to be the basis of physical science, but which is still perversely ignored in our social organization, our ethics and our religion. It is this invariability of sequence which can alone give value to experience and render education in the true sense possible" *(Essays,* p. 31). In her transition from her early religious to her later scientific views, Eliot arrived at the conclusion, as she wrote to Sara Hennell, that "the idea of creative design" in the universe was "untenable" *(Letters,* II, 306). What was left to her was a nonteleological, causal universe.

Few lessons are urged as intently and persistently in the novels as the conviction that every event, whatever its nature, is both causal and effective. And the class of events includes nonevents, on which in fact Eliot insists rather strongly, suspecting that the human mind is very likely to mistake their importance. "No errors are strictly speaking retrievable," she writes to Maria Lewis, adding "but those of omission more frequently appear to be so than the actual class" *(Letters,* I, 89). Indeed, in the novels, we see that characters often feel less responsible for omissions, regardless of the consequences, primarily because they feel that their deliberative wills are not, somehow, involved in them. This is the case—in a very complex psychological situation—with Bulstrode when he is caught between the conflicting desire for Raffles's death and his at least intellectual conviction of the sinfulness of murder. Murder outright Bulstrode can neither wish for nor commit, for he is not only a Christian but aspires to be an "eminent Christian" *(Middlemarch,* p. 386). It is with an agonizing, if egotistic, consciousness of sin that Bulstrode attempts to distinguish intention and desire (p. 516). Yet, immeditately after Lydgate prescribes moderate doses of opium for Raffles and repeats his order that no alcohol should be given him (p. 517), Bulstrode quite suddenly reconsiders Lydate's application for a loan. Earlier, he had suggested Lydgate become "a bankrupt," intoning piously that "trial" is "our portion here, and is a needed corrective" (p. 501). But rendering Lydgate indebted to him is a plan barely on the threshold of Bulstrode's consciousness. "A man vows," the narrator remarks, "and yet will not cast away the means of breaking his vow. Is it that he distinctly means to break it? Not at all; but the desires which tend to break it are at work in him dimly, and make their way into his imagination, and relax the muscles in the very moments when he is telling himself over again the reasons for his vow" (p. 519). It is in this frame of mind that Bulstrode instructs Mrs. Abel to administer the opium to Raffles but "forgets" to mention Lydgate's earlier insistence on the risk of not ceasing the doses at a specific point (p. 519). That the consequences he hopes for should come through an act of forgetfulness is essential to Bulstrode's conscience and illustrates the attitude Eliot believes man generally holds toward acts of omission. Had his unconscious will intruded more actively on his awareness, his failure to mention Lydgate's orders would have been an act of commission which not even his own self-indulgent religion could have interpreted as anything but murder. As it is, he can still convince himself that his intentions were good.

14

In the end, of course, Bulstrode hands Mrs. Abel the key to the wine-cooler (p. 520), thus violating the second of Lydgate's orders, but even here he must make a detour in responsibility. "And who could say that the death of Raffles had been hastened?" he asks himself. "Who knew what would have saved him?" (p. 521). Here we confront a different aspect of Eliot's concept of causal relations. The answer to Bulstrode's question is very obvious; Lydgate knew, not indeed with that knowledge that cannot fail of certainty but with the knowledge of the professional to whom these are not matters of absolute chance but of established probability. Lydgate, we are soon informed, "had not expected" this case to "terminate as it had done," and he is "uneasy" about it (p. 522). Bulstrode's question is virtually a key to his condition. He does not believe himself to live in a causal world. This is the characteristic fancy of the egotist. But it is one of Eliot's most persistent statements in the novels that no one is exempt from subjection to this causal destiny. No one may, by merely ignoring the unpleasant facts, resign from participating in the inevitable. The cosmic order is completely democratic, mercilessly just, in this respect.

Eliot had spoken, in a letter to Mme Bodichon, of the necessity of doing *"without opium" (Letters,* III, 366). It is Eliot's commitment to confronting reality, whatever its nature. For to rely on opium is, indeed, not to change reality in any way, but rather to put oneself even more at its mercy. Not only Bulstrode but Lydgate himself is a character who craves opium, metaphorically as well as literally. The depth of Lydgate's depression is marked by that short period of his life in which he experiments with the drug, feeling that it will relieve him of the external pressures he can no longer endure (p. 489). It is not that Lydgate believes the world will vanish if he ignores it. Lydgate is an intelligent man and a scientist, one who knows fact from fancy. But Eliot distinguishes here between levels and areas of man's knowing nature. Lydgate's intellect and his scientific convictions know the reali-

15

ty, but there is something primitive and uncontrollable which grasps at moments of oblivion as though in the full faith that these will annihilate the facts or remove him from their power.

Throughout her novels Eliot comments on this condition, using as a focal point those characters who commit their fortunes to chance, who ignore, that is, the factual world in which events occur only within the scope of cause and consequence. Although the god of chance takes many and varied forms, Eliot frequently roots her theme in the act of gambling itself. Not surprisingly, there are a very large number of gamblers in the novels, and among the most typical, and certainly the most obsessive, is the "spoiled child" (the title of book I) of *Daniel Deronda,* Gwendolen Harleth, whom, in fact, we meet, at the very opening of the novel, in a casino. Oblivious to causal law, Gwendolen confidently awaits the improbable. "Anything," the narrator soon tells us, "seemed more possible than that she could go on bearing miseries, great or small," for Gweldolen considered herself "fortunate" (p. 10). It is with some irony that Eliot takes us from the opening scene of chapter 1, where a self-assured Gwendolen strikes a "dynamic" pose at the roulette table, to the opening scene of chapter 2 in which a letter from Gwendolen's mother announces that Grapnell & Co. has lost the family income in speculation, another form of gambling. It is a fact that Gwendolen's consciousness cannot grasp; characteristically, the gambler cannot believe in the possibility of losing; that is something only others do. Convinced of holding a unique and favored place in the cosmic scheme, Gwendolen enacts the archetypal egotism of the gambler.

Fred Vincy, for example, always in need of money, which he squanders, trusts to his winning at the gaming tables what he will not take the trouble to earn. Like Gwendolen, he has a highly developed distaste for work, and like Gweldolen again, Fred believes that the high value he places on his own comfort must be shared not only by the world at large but by the very laws of the universe. Regardless of all other inclinations, the gambler inevitably reveals this same attitude. Whether the character has a potential for a clearer vision of reality, as Gwendolen and Fred do, or whether he is, like Dunstan Cass in *Silas Marner* or Mr. Christian in *Felix Holt,* hopelessly blind, the egotism is the same. Intelligence, too, has little influence on this primitive instinct. Lydgate, who as a scientist should, of all people, know how incompatible are the myths of luck with the laws of nature, turns, although not for long, to gambling in desperation as he had turned to opium in despair *(Middlemarch,* pp. 489 ff.).

Actual gambling is, however, only symptomatic of a far more general condition which appears frequently as a blind faith in some unspecified providence whose personal benevolence, the character believes, must interfere with the cosmic order on his behalf. When "Fred got into debt," the narrator of *Middlemarch* explains, "it always seemed to him highly probably that something or other—he did not necessarily conceive what—would come to pass enabling him to pay in due time" (p. 99). The most devastating fact that such characters must eventually confront is that, while their hopes usually remain unfulfilled, their refusal to recognize the real state of affairs has, in the natural course of things, brought about its own and far less desirable consequences. These most of the characters never deliberately intended, indeed, hardly ever suspected. In developing this theme, Eliot follows an almost formal rhetorical pattern. We see such characters first in their unbounded hopes; we see them later amid the consequences of their thoughtless actions; and we note in the relationship the disparity between expectation and fact. The steady irony of the narrator often compresses the time between the two revelations and anticipates from the first the inevitable end. Fred, the narrator remarks,

> had always felt confident that he would meet the bill himself, having ample funds at his disposal in his own hopefulness.

17

You will hardly demand that his confidence should have a basis in external facts; such confidence, we know, is something less coarse and materialistic; it is a comfortable disposition leading us to expect that the wisdom of providence or the folly of our friends, the mysteries of luck or the still greater mystery of our high individual value in the universe, will bring about agreeable issues, such as are consistent with our good taste in costume, and our general preference for the best style of thing. (p. 168)

Indefinite sources of fortune are not alone in fostering great expectations in such characters. Sometimes, in their eagerness, these characters mistake likelihood for certainty and start causal chains which end in inevitable disaster. So Lydgate, knowing his own funds inadequate for the establishment he would like to set up with Rosamond, does not "waste time in conjecturing how much his fahter-in-law would give in the form of dowry" (p. 260). But while Lydgate is planning his household, Mr. Vincy, as the reader has just learned, has decided not to give any dowry whatever (p. 259). Similarly, Fred, as do a long retinue of greedy relatives, expects to inherit Featherstone's fortune, and, while the cranky old gentleman is in the process of altering his will, proceeds to incur debts which he has no doubt his future wealth will be able to repay (p. 79). How difficult, and yet how necessary, it was for man to accept the very simple fact that a wish, as Feuerbach had said, can be attained only when it is made an end and the necessary action taken to bring it about as a consequence[17] Eliot saw not only in these various ways of gambling but in a gambling attitude to life in general, in any action, that is, taken without forethought of consequences.

Arthur Donnithorne, who greatly resembles Fred in his light, genial disposition and completely thoughtless selfishness, does not actually rely on gambling for money, but he acts, nevertheless, as though trusting to the same good fortune as Fred for the kindly arrangement of his life. As Eliot again contrasts reality to expectation, Arthur yet maintains the vision of happy endings because to recognize their unlikelihood would entail unpleasant duties on himself. He dreads what Hetty might do in the grief he has caused her but quickly manages to shake off the fear

> with the force of youth and *hope.* What was the ground for painting the future in that dark way? It was just as *likely* to be the reverse. Arthur told himself, he did not *deserve* that things should turn out badly—he had never *meant* beforehand to do anything his conscience disapproved—he had been led on by circumstances. There was a sort of implicit confidence in him that he was really such a good fellow at bottom, *Providence* would not treat him harshly. *(Adam Bede,* p. 322)

The key words which I have italicized above, words which appear over and over again in Eliot's analysis of such characters, is a virtual catalog of mistaken assumptions. The tone is not yet as bitter as it will become by the end of the novel, but the indictments could not be more serious. They itemize how far Arthur's thoughts have strayed from the reality in which hope is irrelevant, likelihood a poor substitute for that level of certainty which is within man's power to attain, in which neither desert nor intention are causal forces, and Providence, if it is something other than strict causation, does not exist. Hetty, unfortunately for them both, is in this respect just like Arthur. Even at the end, she envisions the interference of something that will not permit her to suffer, whatever she has done. "In young, childish, ignorant souls," the narrator comments, "there is constantly this blind trust in some unshapen chance" (p. 373).

In *Silas Marner,* Godfrey Cass is being prepared for a similar lesson in reality. When Godfrey refuses to accept the consequences of his marraige to Molly, lest his father disinherit him, he merely ensures other and, as it often happens, even less acceptable effects. But these he cannot foresee, for he is a gambler no less than his brother. After a particularly difficult moment, when he expects his father's discovery, although he had entered the conversation with the firm decision to confess everything—which, somehow, he never does—Godfrey flees "to his usual refuge, that of hoping for some unforeseen turn of fortune, some favorable chance which would save him from unpleasant consequences." [18] Since the novel makes its point allegorically, the consequences of his marriage are symbolized in his daughter, whom he denies even when his wife dies. Characteristically, Godfrey seeks to have what he wants without accepting disagreeable difficulties. He wants a child, but symbolically his second wife is barren. Moreover, Nancy refuses to adopt a child, and refuses as well, when Godfrey at last dares to urge it, to adopt Eppie until, many years later, Godfrey confesses his past. The confession is critical not because Eliot is concerned with Godfrey's spiritual purification but rather, ironically, because Godfrey is. For repentance Godfrey expects forgiveness of a special kind, a cancellation, as it were, of the debt to morality. But nothing could be further from the demands of reality in Eliot's view than Godfrey's moral equation. If he has learned too late to accept his guilt, he has not yet learned very much of the real world. In essence, he still persists in the unfounded faith of the gambler, expecting as he does that Eppie will be overjoyed to know her newly disclosed relationship to him, that Silas will gratefully relinquish the child he has cherished for sixteen years, as though these years of Godfrey's silence had had no consequences of their own. His enlightenment, insofar as it comes, is not the product of his guilt but of his recognition that consequences are irrevocable.

While it is generally ignorance and a distaste for the unpleasant that prompt Eliot's gamblers, occasionally we find characters whose actions seem an almost deliberate challenge to the causal law. Tito Melema and, even more, Gwendolen Harleth, seem at times as though in a deadly contest for supremacy with an unnamed, unspecified opponent. In the turnmoil of Florence, Tito pursues the game relentlessly, courting—one suspects sometimes almost with indifference as to the outcome—either fortune or death. As his spontaneous self-indulgence entangles him in one then another intrigue, life takes "more and more decidedly for him the aspect of a game in which there was an agreeable mingling of skill and chance." [19] There is some irony in the fact that this man, one of the most self-seeking, should so inevitably weave the net of his own destruction and with such passionate rebellion against less dangerous paths to prominence. But it is inherent in Tito's very egotism, in his certainty of superiority, that he will step, at some point, beyond the edge of retrievable safety. Gwendolen has even more of that same sense of personal power and an even greater recklessness in action. Her actual gambling in the casino had been, not surprisingly, merely a symptom of her general state of mind. It is, therefore, as a gambler, not as a prospective wife, that she approaches Grandcourt, the most important wager of her life. Reservations about marrying him are "surmounted and thrust down with a sort of exulting defiance" as she feels herself "standing at the game of life with many eyes upon her, daring everything to win much" *(Daniel Deronda,* p. 264).

In characters of this sort, as I will discuss later at greater length, Eliot seems to be exploring deeper than ever into the irrational roots of behavior and to touch at last on a perversity which almost knows the danger of defying cosmic laws and is thrilled by the possibility of success at such odds and thrilled even by the possibility of defeat. But in this latter alternative, anticipation is very different from actualization. There is no excitement in the experience of defeat for Gwendolen. Her "exulting defiance" is contrasted with a later passage in which Gwendolen, broken—she is often compared to a spirited horse—by her husband, confronts the world with "a sort of skill in which she was automatically practiced, to bear this last great gambling loss with an air of perfect self-possession" (p. 331). It is in this mechanical submission, as the language so precisely suggests, that Gwendolen learns of the painful reality of consequences.

The "gambling" theme constantly elaborates Eliot's secular and scientific concept of a destiny inherent in the natural laws of an indifferent universe. An even more acute comment may be found in those characters who put their faith not merely in unnamed gods of chance but in a specifically Christian God. Bulstrode takes this route of escape from recognizing a causal universe and provides Eliot with the subject of a bitter reflection. Like other egotists, he believes himself exempt from those laws of cause and effect which others may have to endure by virtue of his having been especially chosen by God. It is in this context, in a moment of extreme dread that his past actions will affect his present life, that Bulstrode hopes that "if he spontaneously did something right, God would save him from the consequences of wrong-doing" *(Middlemarch,* p. 454). But Bulstrode, the more objective narrator tells us, is "locked" in the "train of cause and effect" (p. 451). Neither God nor Eliot can save him.

In a letter to John Chapman, Eliot spoke of "hope unsustained by reason" *(Letters,* II, 48-49). Indeed, the two seldom coincide, for reason discerns a causal order which thwarts the unbounded egotism of human hope. Yet, we may argue, Bulstrode's case is not entirely convincing, for we are tempted to dismiss his disappointments as the result of his serious moral and religious misconceptions, especially as they concern his view of God and his own relationship to Him. The same, however, cannot be said of Dinah Morris, whose interpretation of Christianity is, as far as it goes, fairly accurate. Yet Eliot, no less persistently, demonstrates that Dinah, in her very Christianity, is in serious error in some vital respects. Trusting as thoughtlessly to Providence as others do to good luck, Dinah supposes a Divine Protection which frees man from the need of making plans. Although her authority for this text is Christ Himself, Dinah's is a very dangerous creed in Eliot's view, a fact we realize all the more when we recall that other characters are preparing their inevitable suffering precisely because they do not believe in the natural connection of past, present, and future. It is true that in contrast to these other characters Dinah seems harmless enough; but that is mainly because she does not often follow her own prescription. It is not what she does but what she says that Eliot quarrels with. For Dinah's advice to Seth—that it " 'isn't for you and me to lay plans; we've nothing to do but to obey and to trust' " *(Adam Bede,* p. 34)—is a virtual repudiation of reality. The common sense of Lisbeth Bede is a far more accurate guide to the truth. To Seth, who repeats Dinah's words to her, Lisbeth replies that if " 'Adam had been as aisy as thee, he'd niver ha' had no money to pay for thee. Take no thought for the morrow—take no thought—that's what thee't allays sayin'; an' what comes on't? Why, as Adam has to take thought for thee' " (p. 44).

What is interesting, moreover, about the contrast between Dinah's words and Lisbeth's is their epistemological bases. Not only does Dinah accept her views from a source which may be as wrong as any other, but, more seriously, she never thinks to test these against the empirical evidence that all around her would deny her conviction. And she does something else as well, equally characteristic of those who are led by rules which have no confirmation in empirical fact. On the Poyser farm, she observes the precise opposite of her injunction not to lay plans; she observes it in the agriculture, in the household husbandry, in the dairy, and she sees that it is only by laying plans that the Poysers prosper. It would not, and does not, occur to Dinah to preach her gospel to Mrs. Poyser in her household duties or to Mr. Poyser in his planting and harvesting, for here the evidence of the causal chain is so concrete that it is past discussion. It is only in human affairs, where complexity may obscure the clear outlines of causality, that Dinah applies untested dogma. It is not God that Eliot is anxious to show in error, but rather those rules which God is assumed to prescribe but which are in direct contrast to the demonstrable facts of reality. Lisbeth's text is Adam's text, and it is the common sense that long experience has confirmed. Although it retains God in the scheme, it is quite acceptable to Eliot, who clearly approves Lisbeth as she corrects Seth: " 'God helps them as helps theirsens!' " (p. 44).

The Laws of Consequence in Irreversible Time

That there is a causal relationship operating in the universe in all matters renders destiny inflexible, and so for Eliot it is, although the very fact of causality suggests possibilities for the improvement of man's lot which an arbitrary system, by making it impossible to guess what might come next, cannot permit. Yet there is one element in the causal relationship whose unalterable rigidity no compensatory potential can adjust us to, and that is the element of time. The temporal order is irreversible. Actor and action are locked, by every second of time, into the past of immutable memory. Obvious as the fact may seem, it is not one, in Eliot's view, of which we are easily convinced. Even more does human nature resist the fact that this is true not only of dramatic events—murder, suicide, and so on—of which we are usually willing to speak as irretrievable, but of the most ordinary and apparently insignificant actions. Yet, Eliot everywhere maintains, an intelligent adjustment to reality must not only concede but feel the full impact of the conviction that no action can be undone nor the consequences it has set in motion recalled. Nothing we can do will undo, alter, mitigate, redirect, or in any way rescind what at every moment becomes the past. This, says Felix Holt in his "Address to Working Men," is the " 'deepest curse of wrong doing' " *(Essays,* p. 418), a phrase repeated almost verbatim by Adam when he finally understands that to blame Arthur for Hetty's pain is, as far as effects are concerned, futile: " 'that's the deepest curse of all ... that's what makes the blackness of it ... *it can never be undone'* " *(Adam Bede,* p. 432).

So important to a mature vision of reality is this discovery that we find it over and over in the novels. It is one of Maggie Tulliver's most painful confrontations with herself to know that her yielding to the "feeling of a few short weeks" had brought about an "irrevocable wrong that must blot her life" and the lives of others *(The Mill on the Floss,* p. 413). Her moral anguish is not entirely in her awareness that she has done something "wrong"—error is inescapable—but in the knowledge that it is "irrevocable." For human nature, Eliot shows, tends to think that to do the opposite of what one has done before is equal to undoing the past. Alcharisi, in deciding to reveal her identity to Daniel after many years of silence, falls naturally into this supposition. Even Daniel begins with this assumption when he asks his mother why she has " 'undone' " the secrecy of so many years; but in this moment of self-discovery, Daniel quickly understands the error of his question; " 'no, not undone it,' " he corrects himself; " 'the effects will never be undone' " (*Daniel Deronda*, p. 477) " 'The effect of my education can never be done away with,' " he adds later. " 'The Christian sympathies in which my mind was reared can never die out of me' " (p. 497). The point is made by the narrator of *Romola,* long before the reader understands its full applicability to the events of the novel, that our deeds differ from our children in that a child may be strangled, but not a deed; deeds have an indestructible life (p. 170). Matter is begotten, born, and dies, but the intangible process by which matter is governed ironically persists.

Not only is the human mind reluctant to grasp this sometimes terrifying reality, but it also approaches it at times in terms of the wrong framework and makes, consequently, an innocent, though no less potentially deadly, error in interpretation. The course of cause and effect in time is an organic process, yet man continually thinks of it in purely mechanistic terms. His imagination stops short of conceiving the organic mutations which the combination of time and causality effects, altering every moment the identities of the objects involved. The more common assumption is that whatever has been placed in the container of time will remain static until it is removed. Eliot's view is graphically described by the narrator of *Felix Holt* in the heading to chapter 17:

> It is a good and soothfast saw;
> Half-roasted never will be raw;
> No dough is dried once more to meal;
> No crock new-shapen by the wheel;
> You can't turn curds to milk again,
> Nor Now, by wishing, back to Then;
> And having tasted stolen honey,
> You can't buy innocence for money.
>   (p. 190)

This organic process seems to become even more inflexible when we are made aware, as we constantly are in Eliot, that it is useless to "make amends." In this matter, Eliot distinguishes rather sharply between several factors. Often through her narrators, she is fully sympathetic to the character who wishes to make amends, for such a desire reveals a possibly promising state of mind. She shows too that the desire to make amends may usefully spend itself in helping the situation which past actions have brought about. But she allows neither character nor reader to confuse the desire with the ability to make amends. Arthur Donnithorne is a character who requires the length of the novel to make this distinction. All his life he has managed to convince himself that to do a kindness is equal to undoing an unkindness. It is an easy creed, especially for someone in his social and economic position. Once, as a boy, Arthur had kicked over an old gardener's pitcher of broth in a moment of energetic mischief. Not by nature malicious, Arthur had not paused to think that this was the old man's supper. Almost immediately, Arthur had regretted his action and produced his favorite pencil-case and silver-hafted knife as compensation; the gesture was well intentioned, but his offerings were hardly a suitable substitute for food, a point which Arthur had some difficulty grasping *(Adam Bede,* p. 318).

Later, older in years although in little else, Arthur repeats this prototypical pattern. Every moment of guilt—thoughtlessly incurred and easily rejected—is forgotten in light promises of good intentions, sincere enough while entertained. The habit is almost formulaic; it is impossible for Arthur to confess himself guilty unless he is prepared to explain to himself how he will make reparation for the cause of his guilt. If he admits that he has not been truly kind to Hetty in paying undue attention to her, he rapidly assures himself that "Hetty might have had trouble in some other way if not in this. And perhaps hereafter he might be able to do a great deal for her, and make up to her for all the tears she would shed about him. She would owe the advantage of his care for her in future years to the sorrow she had incurred now. *So* good comes out of evil. Such is the beautiful arrangement of things!" (p. 320). As the *"So"* implies, his argument seems to him to have an objective, and so unassailable, logic. In an identical way, much later, he still argues that he can salvage his image from that "ugly fault" in his life by ensuring that "the future should make amends." Encouraging himself to feel profoundly self-satisfied over his planned generosity to Hetty and Adam, he concludes on a note of self-congratulation: many "men would have retained a feeling of vindictiveness towards Adam; but *he* would not—he would resolutely overcome all littleness of that kind, for he had certainly been very much in the wrong; and though Adam had been harsh and violent, and had thrust on him a painful dilemma, the poor fellow was in love, and had real provocation. No; Arthur had not an evil feeling in his mind towards any human being; he was happy, and would make everyone else happy that came within his reach" (p. 451).

Arthur is not exactly repentant, although he is never happy to cause others pain, being merely too fond of his own pleasure to worry overmuch about possible suffering he might inflict. Yet even repentance would have no effect on the past. There is no place in Eliot's novels for Christian absolution; there are no fresh starts. This is the point of Silas Marner's answer to Godfrey Cass when the latter comes to acknowledge his daughter and take her with him; " 'repentance,' " Silas replies bitterly, " 'doesn't alter what's been going on for sixteen year' " (p. 231). The novel is far less Christian in content than its allegorical symbols would suggest; and, as I discussed earlier, it is Godfrey's, not Eliot's, Christian assumption of the efficacy of purification through confession that brings him to Silas and Eppie with such unquestioned hope of success. But, as is always the case in Eliot's novels, mere confession is not the point of the dramatic reversal. Especially since the welling of emotion brought on by a sense of newly discovered guilt tends to spend itself in self-congratulation, confession is considerably easier than reform. Indeed, it may preclude reform in the very ritual of the catharsis, misleading, as catharsis often does, a character into thinking himself absolved of his error. That is certainly what Godfrey thinks as he imagines himself ennobled by his confession, and it is always what Arthur Donnithorne thinks every one of the many times he pauses in his pursuit of Hetty to blame himself.

The climax of realization comes later, if at all, when one understands what Adam says to Arthur, namely that one " 'should make sacrifices to keep clear of doing wrong; sacrifices won't undo it when it's done' " *(Adam Bede,* p. 477). Although he does not always act on his own principles, Adam obviously states Eliot's view when he remarks that it is " 'well we should feel as life's a reckoning we can't make twice over; there's no real making amends in this world, any more nor you can mend a wrong subtraction by doing your addition right' " (p. 205). Godfrey comes at last to this knowledge when he sees, as he tells his wife, that " 'there's debts we can't pay like money debts, by paying extra for the years that have slipped by. While I've been putting off and putting off, the trees have been growing—it's too late now' " *(Silas Marner,* p. 236). The contrast in the imagery here highlights Eliot's point. Godfrey had always thought in terms of the banking metaphor—an ironic comment on the fact that it was through fear of losing his inheritance that he lost Eppie, his real inheritance—and sees, therefore, causal evolution in mechanical terms; what he comes in the end to recognize, in the natural metaphor, is the organic quality of time's effects.

To John Chapman, Eliot once wrote: "I have long wanted to fire away at the doctrine of Compensation, which I detest, considered as a theory of life" *(Letters,* II, 258). In another letter, she remarked that the "religion of the future must be one that enables us to do without consolation, instead of being what religion has been (I think pervertingly) held—chiefly precious as a source of consolation" *(Letters,* VI, 216). Whether in this world or the next, one fact cannot compensate for another; the good does not redeem the bad. If the doctrine of compensation does not exactly disregard suffering, it allows one not to be excessively discomforted by it. In that, Eliot saw, lay its powerful hold on man's egotism. But the notion of compensation obscured the essential empirical fact that each individual, at each moment of his life, is his own supreme and independent standard, that each moment of pain makes an inherent and absolute claim to sympathetic recognition. Bartle Massey calls on himself a passionate assault from Adam when he attempts to console him with the thought that some good may have come out of Hetty's sorrow, echoing, although for a different reason, Arthur's *"So* good comes out of evil." But Adam, with Eliot, finds such considerations meaningless. " 'Good come out of it!' " he cries. " 'That doesn't alter th' evil: *her* ruin can't be undone. I hate that talk o' people, as if there was a way o' making amends for everything.... When a man's spoiled his fellow-creature's life, he's no right to comfort himself with thinking good may come out of it; somebody else's good doesn't alter her shame and misery' " *(Adam Bede,* p. 469). Massey had referred to Adam's fortunate escape from a marriage that would have bound him for life to a woman like Hetty. But that, Eliot insists, is another fact, one that should never accommodate us to Hetty's suffering. Adam's point is a democratic rebellion against the implicit supposition that we are entitled to viewing some people as principals in the world's progress and some as instruments only whose fate can be made to serve those others. To believe fully, as Eliot does, that every man sees himself as the absolute criterion and others as relative to himself, and to allow, as Eliot does, the validity of such a view, is to know that no statistical preponderance to the contrary can mitigate the evil one person suffers.

It is the same with the punishment of the guilty. In deep frustration, Adam forgets himself and determines that Arthur must suffer for what he has done. It is then left to the wiser Irwine to remind him that no " 'amount of torture that you could inflict on *him* could benefit *her'* " (p. 432). Earlier, the narrator, observing Hetty and projecting a vision of her future, had hypothesized someone who would cry " 'Let that man bear the loss who loosed [the vessel] from its moorings!' " As a demand for justice of a certain sort, or even revenge, the feeling is understandable. Yet, the narrator goes on to say, "that will not save the vessel" (p. 347). To the degree that Eliot suspects human nature is inclined to defend itself against the full impact of the real consequences of action, to that degree is she determined to stress them by undercutting every argument that removes attention from the victim of the causal chain. The large, objective, view might favor the historical conclusion stated by the narrator of *The Mill on the Floss,* that "Nature repairs her ravages." But the narrator immediately rejects this compensatory doctrine for a more vivid recollection of the individual fact. Nature does not repair all her ravages. "The uptorn trees are not rooted again; the parted hills are left scarred; if there is a new growth, the trees are not the same as the old" (pp. 456-457).

Nature and Morality in Conflict

In "Some Metaphysical Problems Pragmatically Considered," William James wrote that a "world with a god in it to
say the last word, may indeed burn up or freeze, but we then
think of him as still mindful of the old ideals and sure to bring
them elsewhere to fruition; so that, where he is, tragedy is only
provisional and partial, and shipwreck and dissolution not the
absolutely final things."[20] Although James, concerned with es-
tablishing the beneficial consequences of belief, rejects the godless world because of what it logically entails, he describes here
why, beginning with a secular assumption, Eliot found the cosmic scheme governed only by causal laws a tragic one. For Eliot,
tragedy is neither provisional nor partial; shipwreck and dissolution *are* the absolutely final things. There is law, but there is no
moral order in Eliot's concept of the universe such as a God, even
a perverse God, would provide. With morality, Eliot's universe
has no commerce. In his essay "Nature," Mill wrote that "nearly
all the things which men are hanged or imprisoned for doing to
one another, are nature's every day performances." [21] To this
view Eliot also arrived and for very much the same secular and
empirical reasons as Mill.

We become painfully aware of this as Eliot, time and again,
stresses how distinct are the lines of morality and of consequence. John Holloway finds it disturbing that in Eliot
while righteousness "may be rewarded, or may have to be its own
reward," the "ultimate consequences of wickedness are never in
doubt. No one in George Eliot's novels ever sins and escapes." [22]
It would be for Eliot a far less complex world that man lives in if
this were the case. But the novels, in fact, show something rather
different. The list is long of characters who are not "punished" for
"wickedness." Rosamond Vincy, for one, does well enough with
both her first and second husbands. Most of the Dodsons survive
and flourish in all their petty oppressiveness; old Donnithorne

lives and dies a happy tyrant, as does old Featherstone. Nothing particularly unfortunate happens to most of the uncouth political opportunists and murderers of Florence in *Romola*. Moreover, the question of what Holloway calls "wickedness" is very far from Eliot's concern in this matter. It is true, certainly, that rewards are not necessarily supplied to the good, but equally true that punishment does not, by any means, invariably await the wicked. In fact, morally, consequences are not at all linearly descended from causes. Eliot's view is subtler and less prescriptive. In the indifferent cosmic order what men call rewards and punishments do not exist; there are only effects which, depending on human evaluation, men call good and evil, although of these terms too Eliot's universe knows nothing. It is precisely because man expects some inherent sense of moral rightness in the world that he sometimes errs so destructively. For Eliot, doing without opium is doing without the comforting thought, indulged in by so many characters, that sterling motives ensure equally sterling results and that suffering is the product of evil intentions. No writer concerned with moral ends can chart such a plot, Eliot claims in "The Morality of Wilhelm Meister," and she mocks those fictional resolutions in "which rewards and punishments are distributed according to those notions of justice on which the novel-writer would have recommended that the world should be governed if he had been consulted at the creation" *(Essays,* p. 145).

If nothing else, the fact that consequences are never confined to the agent that caused them must preclude such an equilibrium. Effects fall indiscriminately on all who happen to cross their paths. It is exactly because Arthur Donnithorne does not believe this that he is mistaken. " 'I'm a devil of a fellow for getting myself into a hobble,' " he confesses genially, adding " 'but I always take care the load shall fall on my own shoulders' " *(Adam Bede,* p. 125). Were the world patterned after Arthur's view, there would be little need for Eliot to advance her convictions. Each might choose for himself whether a pleasant action were worth the possible unpleasant consequences in a liberal Benthamite spirit. But in the world Eliot sees we do not choose for ourselves alone. "Unhappily," the narrator comments on Arthur's simple view, "there is no inherent poetical justice in hobbles, and they will sometimes refuse to inflict their worst consequences on the prime offender, in spite of his loudly-expressed wish" (p. 125).

" 'One soweth and another reapeth,' " as Rev. Lyon points out to Harold Transome *(Felix Holt,* p. 374). Harold is rather typical in resisting this conclusion; he is accustomed to self-reliance and has proved, indeed, how much control over one's life an energetic confidence in one's own power can effect. But perhaps this very confidence, his very success, has blinded him to that large portion of his life which is entirely out of his hands. It seems inconceivable to Harold that he should no longer have a valid claim to Transome Court. And the reality is a moral revelation. "It was the most serious moment in Harold Transome's life; for the first time the iron had entered into his soul, and he felt the hard pressure of our common lot, the yoke of that mighty resistless destiny laid upon us by the acts of other men as well as our own" (p. 470). Thus, "good" may lead to "evil" or "evil" to "good." Actions, not moral values, propagate themselves. Mr. Tulliver's lawsuit with Wakem demonstrates that so deeply "inherent is it in this life of ours that men have to suffer for each other's sins, so inevitably diffusive is human suffering . . . that we can conceive no retribution that does not spread itself beyond its mark in pulsations of unmerited pain." As a result, "even justice makes its victims" *(The Mill on the Floss,* p. 215).

Frequently in error as to the operation of action and consequence, man is even more often, Eliot believes, likely to suppose a relationship between unactualized intention and consequence. And here, the tragedy sinks deeper into the human condition. A moral order, one capable of making judgments, as God is, can evaluate intentions and make amends for whatever actions do not implement them, if not in this world, at least, as James says, elsewhere. And it is certainly, Eliot acknowledges, in a character's intentions that we see perhaps subtler, truer motives. Yet the events of the novels arise in actions, not in intentions, a fact which many readers find disagreeable in Eliot.[23]

This focus on action is not the result, as Prest and Harvey claim in defending Eliot,[24] of the fact that it is easier to ascertain actions than intentions, for Eliot is crucially concerned with the latter. It is rather because it is the very core of her convictions that intentions and motives, like hopes and wishes, do not, cannot, have consequences. In this respect, the narratives progress on two separate lines, one revealing the states of mind of the characters and the other revealing the causal sequence of events. These may merge but are not identical. It is this very distinction Eliot makes that forces on the reader the realization of human impotence and cosmic power, of cosmic indifference and human values. We are constantly aware of this double exposure. Rev. Irwine, for example, claims for Arthur that the " 'evil consequences that may lie folded in a single selfish indulgence, is a thought so awful that it ought surely to awaken some feeling less presumptuous than a rash desire to punish' " *(Adam Bede,* p. 433). Indeed, we cannot avoid knowing how terrible it is for Arthur to acknowledge himself the cause of such a painful situation as he has helped to bring about when all he meant to do was carry on a flirtation with a little dairymaid. Rev. Irwine's appeal is valid, as even Adam sees, for Arthur had not meant to do what he did. But he did it. No disparity between intention and action can alter the consequences. Arthur, not without some justification, believes that if any man had an excuse for wrongdoing, he was that man. "Pity," the narrator remarks bitterly, "that consequences are determined not be excuses but by actions" (p. 323).

It is the consequences of action also that, interlocked with the psychological past which always remains present in a character's evolution, make it impossible for anyone to leave what he may consider his "former life" behind him. "Could he not strip himself of the past," Tito wonders, "as of rehearsal clothing, and throw away the old bundle, to robe himself for the real scene?" *(Romola,* p. 492). What tempts Tito to think such a thing possible is the deceptive fact that in action he is an agent, in consequences he is passive. The former is therefore vivid to him but not the latter. And since the action whose consequences he wishes to avoid is in the past, he inclines to think it distinct from the present. But Tito cannot, for all his vivid involvement in new actions, escape what he has once instigated any more than he can escape Baldassarre, his personal embodied past.

In this mistaken belief in the possibility of new beginnings, Bulstrode, in *Middlemarch,* resembles Tito and, like Tito, must be reminded of his false hypothesis by a symbolic incarnation of the past. This is Raffles's primary function in the novel. He appears in Middlemarch like "an incorporate past which had not entered into" Bulstrode's "imagination of chastisement" (p. 384). Trusting to a God-ordered moral scheme with which he assumes himself in perfect harmony, Bulstrode rejects the actual order of events, ascribing, in revealing language, Raffles's sudden intrusion into his present life to "some hidden magic" (p. 384). But the physical presence of Raffles shakes Bulstrode into re-capturing his past with that immediacy it had not had for him when it was still present. "With memory set smarting," the narrator comments, "like a reopened wound, a man's past is not simply a dead history, an outworn preparation of the present: it is a still quivering part of himself" (p. 450). It might have been the case that Raffles could not have found Bulstrode—on a more literal level than his function suggests—that is, had other cir-cumstances conduced to that effect; but it is no surprise that Raffles does find him, just as it should be no surprise to Grand-court that he cannot dismiss Lydia Glasher merely because he has tired of her *(Daniel Deronda,* p. 259). The past as a totality is as irrevocable as any individual act, and forms a complete struc-ture in time.

Loose Threads in the Causal Web

That Raffles does appear to prod Bulstode's lagging conscience may raise a question which numerous other incidents in the novels suggest, and that is the apparent intrusion into the plots of events that seem not inevitably evolved from earlier ones. In lesser or greater degree, depending on the incident and the novel, such an intrusion bears some resemblance to a deus ex machina and seems, therefore, a striking contradiction to Eliot's fundamental principle of action. It is true that the possibility of such an incident is surprising only because Eliot is consistent in more cases than not; no one is startled by similar events in Dickens, for example, where old friends or enemies meet in unlikely places, inheritances are received from forgotten chance meetings with strangers, relatives appear and disappear without jarring the hypotheses Dickens has set up. But Eliot prepares the reader to anticipate something else. External explanations, informative as they are, will obviously not do as aesthetic justifications. Thus, however enlightening it is about the origins of the novel, Jerome Beaty's claim that most of the dramatic coincidences of *Middlemarch,* relating chiefly to the Bulstrode-Raffles-Featherstone-Ladislaw affair, are the result of the fusion of the two segments of the novel[25] fails to lay our aesthetic discomfort to rest.

Eliot herself seems to have been aware of the problem. In all the novels, and especially in *Felix Holt* and *Daniel Deronda,* where apparent coincidences abound in the plots, the narrators make frequently what seem to be embarrassed acknowledgments of the unlikelihood of some events. In *Deronda* especially, Eliot seems to go beyond the possible and the probable. Here, the reader is troubled by many questions. Why, for instance, is it Daniel who happens to find Mirah as she is about to commit suicide, an incident which leads him to the preparation of his own

long-delayed destiny? Why does it happen that Mordecai is
Mirah's brother? Why is it that Ezra Cohen, whom Daniel
believes to be Mirah's brother, is not but happens to employ the
man who is? As Daniel at last comes upon the right shop-window
bearing the name of Ezra Cohen, the narrator has to admit that
there "might be a hundred Ezra Cohens lettered above shop-
windows, but Deronda had not seen them" (p. 286). Perhaps
nothing demonstrates Eliot's discomfort as much as the quotation with which she opens book VI of the novel. The book is
entitled "Revelations," and the reader is often called on to
remember the opening words from Agathon, that it is a " 'part of
probability that many improbable things will happen' " (p. 382).
But in this half of the novel, although Daniel's life is somewhat
fantastic, Eliot is working with unusual assumptions. No doubt,
Daniel's racial consciouness must explain a good deal of what
happens to him, and indeed many events are foreshadowed, on
this basis, quite early. We learn from the beginning, for example,
that Daniel would like to be a "great leader, like Pericles or
Washington" (p. 128), and that he is waiting for something that
will make up his mind about his future (p. 137). Although the
modern reader is not likely to subscirbe to the explanatory
hypothesis, it is nevertheless inherent in Eliot's view of what is
possible, even probable. But in the Gwendolen half of the novel,
although the coincidences are far fewer, we have no such theory
to look to. Most of all, the reader wants to know why Grandcourt
drowns at so appropriate a moment. The practical Hans, and
perhaps the slightly embarrassed author through him, comments
that he had never known anyone to "'die conveniently before'"
(p. 547). Like many others, this incident had been foreshadowed
many times. Gwendolen believes her husband's death will be the
only means of relief for her (p. 456) and sees in the general
meteorological conditions a favorable sign (p. 509). When she
agrees to join Grandcourt on the boat it is in the vague hope that
they will both drown (p. 511). Yet foreshadowing is an aesthetic

device which can hardly expect to find realization in the real world which Eliot's fiction promises to mirror. The reader's doubt persists.

It is clear that such events must be divided into two major categories, one which can have no genuine internal explanation, and another which a variety of reasons may justify or indeed necessitate. The second category is far larger and leads to the conclusion that most of the incidents are thematically motivated.[26] Eliot makes a clear distinction between what is true and what is literal. In cases such as the drowning of Grandcourt, it seems fairly obvious that the literal recorder of facts must be in conflict with the analytic commentator on them. In a sense, Eliot looks on her characters as unknown entities whose natures are to be tested by the application of various stimuli. Like a scientist in the laboratory, the novelist mixes chemical elements, anticipating results but never entirely certain until the empirical evidence confirms the hypothesis. But a scientist has this advantage at least, that he may fill a number of test tubes with the same solution and by combining each with a different substance discover the behavior of his subject under a very large variety of circumstances. Eliot can have but one Gwendolen; yet the study of her character is not, especially for so scientific a writer, so very different from the study of the laboratory solution. Gwendolen's marriage to Grandcourt is one test of the character. But when the combination has been analyzed at length, we are interested to know in what way Gwendolen has evolved through these circumstances, and how she would behave in others. It is an interesting enough question to press the means of obtaining an answer. It is true that Grandcourt, on the purely literal level, would not be so accommodating as to drown to satisfy our curiosity, but it is the peculiar advantage of the novelist, as of the scientist, that he can do more than one may do in life.

Yet even such deflections from literal fact do not offer Eliot all the scope she sometimes requires. Very often we find Eliot compelled—or thinking she is compelled, which yields an identical consequence—to communicate not only on the literal level but on one or more symbolic levels. In *Silas Marner,* in fact, the balance is entirely even. The story's significance is conveyed on both the factually realistic and the mythically true level; and each demands a different set of rules. It is essential not to take the myth for the fact.[27] For, interestingly, one of the novel's major theses concerns the causal relationship itself, demonstrated on the literal level by the events which occur mainly in Godfrey Cass's life, but demonstrated on the mythical level in symbols which, if taken literally, deny the very hypotheses they are designed to enforce. When Dunstan, a gambler and therefore one who lives in illusion about the facts of the real world, falls into the Stone-pits, it is obviously false to ask whether it would be likely that someone of Dunstan's character would inevitably fall into oblivion in such a manner. What we are compelled to ask is whether illusion does not necessarily lead, through mistaken actions, to some sort of self-destruction.

Although less extreme, the other novels follow the same technique. The ending of *The Mill on the Floss,* which has been much debated, must seem on any literal level a rather weak conclusion to the events it follows. But, although Maggie and Tom drown literally, the ending is clearly a symbolic statement and concludes the elaborate water imagery of the novel. From the beginning, Mrs. Tulliver has feared her daughter's death by water, and the reader slowly sees a symbolic relationship developed between Maggie's passionate temperament and the turbulent waters of the Floss. It is this passionate nature, reflected in the water, that carries Maggie downstream with Stephen beyond her rational or willing control. But Maggie's yielding to the power of the river is also her desperate attempt to free herself from the torment of making decisions; always torn, as she is throughout the novel, by conflicting forces of one kind or another, Maggie concedes her human prerogative of foreseeing consequences and acting accordingly as she feels numbed by the pressure of her alternatives. If the incident is a baptism in sorrow, it is also a rehearsal of death in which no choice is required. The river becomes the restful haven for her emotional anguish. It is as an extension of this function that the river comes to reconcile brother and sister after years of emotional, intellectual, and spiritual separation.[28]

Another kind of thematic consideration helps to explain endings such as that of *The Mill on the Floss* as well as many apparently unlikely incidents in the novels yet differs from the strictly symbolic in its close connection with the literal level of the stories. Eliot's conviction that all human life is spatially and temporally interrelated must lead necessarily to the view that there can be no natural terminations to the webs of human activity. The "Finale" of *Middlemarch* begins with the tantalizing suggestion that every "limit is a beginning as well as an ending" (p. 607). Every attempt to extricate a segment from the whole is an absurd task, resulting often in absurd necessities. The heading to chapter I of *Daniel Deronda* expands on this: no "retrospect will take us to the true beginning," the narrator states; and "whether our prologue be in heaven or on earth, it is but a fraction of that all-presupposing fact with which our story set out" (p. 1). When confronted, as is any writer, by the formal and artificial confines of space and time, Eliot feels, more than most, that the whole story should have begun earlier, ended later, included more. Indeed, as the narrator of *Daniel Deronda* hints, short of a minute account of the world from Creation to Judgment, no story can claim completeness.

Forced, thus, to wrench out of the conceptual whole one describable portion, Eliot is at pains to indicate the false narrowness of such a world; among other devices, she introduces into each novel's scope the threads of the web that reach outside the novel's limits to their natural ties with all that has been excluded from the fictional sequence. Levine, I think, is right at least in most cases to point out that when "chance" events seem to occur, "Eliot is not suggesting" these lie "outside the normal laws of nature, but that the elaborate and complex system of causes has been working beyond the knowledge of her characters." [29] One might add that the reader's surprise is the result of these causes having worked outside his knowledge as well. The assumption here is that Eliot could trace, had she fictional world enough and time, a long chain of causes and effects which would make these events in question as naturally inevitable as others in the novels, a point the narrator of *Adam Bede* makes when he claims that "adequate knowledge will show" "every . . . anomaly . . . to be a natural sequence" (p. 16).

It is easy to understand why, more and more, Eliot turned to the refuge of symbolic endings, the only kind she could reasonably subscribe to. For nowhere are the problems of artificial fragmentation in fiction raised as acutely as in the endings, something Eliot always had difficulty with. Her views on the subject seem to have remained the same throughout her writing years. In 1857, for example, Blackwood had complained that the author of *Scenes of Clerical Life* "huddles up the conclusions . . . too much" *(Letters,* II, 323). Eliot had replied that conclusions "are the weak point of most authors, but some of the fault lies in the very nature of a conclusion, which is at best a negation" *(Letters,* II, 324). To John Blackwood again, in 1876, writing about the conclusion of *Daniel Deronda,* Eliot states that "endings are inevitably the least satisfactory part of any work in which there is any merit of development" *(Letters,* VI, 242). To end a plot, Eliot seems to imply in both letters, is easy enough, but to evolve a realistic world only to arrive at some point at which it is necessary to pretend that things "end" is self-contradictory, for at the end the writer, and Eliot especially, must negate the very things he has insisted on throughout, the consequences of actions evolving in time.

Perhaps for this reason, difficult as the task is, Eliot attempts to suggest at the end of every novel that the turning of the final page is a mere formality; the world continues, and does so, indeed, in pretty much the same way it had before. Eliot's endings are always a little disturbing to our sense of finality. There is, in fact, more irony in them than seems to be commonly supposed. One can hardly understand what Baker supposes to be the "concession of a happy ending" in *Romola*,[30] when we consider that Romola ends her life, much as Dorothea does, in resignation. After the bodies piled up are removed, the narrator comes to rest on the character for whom the author provides the dubious ecstasy of domestic cares—for her husband's other "wife." And Dorothea, who had once meant to live her life in the style of St. Theresa, has not even cottages to repair, only the company of a charming, if not exactly inspiring, husband. Even more is it difficult to think of a more cynical ending than that which Eliot grants Lydgate who spends the remainder of his life not in original and important research, as he had hoped and as his intellectual capacity had promised he might, but in the treatment of gout. Such endings conclude the works in fact, but they do so in a spirit of protest against the necessity of the form.

Not all intrusions, however, are thematic or necessary. Particularly in *Felix Holt, Daniel Deronda,* and even parts of *Romola,* an inventive reader would have exhausted his store of justifications before the plots had been fully accounted for. There are elements of melodrama which cannot be satisfactorily explained, although these are structural deviations rather than thematic retractions, especially in the matter of causality. Why Eliot devised these and thought them—as she must have—appropriate, or at least not inappropriate, must make a list of futile guesses. It was not that she conceded to what the public demanded. She suffers too much criticism from contemporary reviewers because she refused to write the novels the public was accustomed to for anyone to accuse her of even so minimal a charge of literary opportunism. But the form of the novel Eliot inherited does have some bearing on her plots. Formal considerations were never primary in Eliot's mind. She made few changes in this aspect of the novel, and then only when other necessities forced these on her. In plot, she never found a structure that suitably expressed her very unique vision in all points. Thus, the content of Eliot's novels is often revolutionary, modern, the form, not always. What Preyer says of *Daniel Deronda,* where it is more applicable, can to varying degrees be said of all the novels: Eliot was responding to "an order of experience which fitted uneasily (if at all) into the existing novelistic forms." [31]

Notes

1. Perhaps the vigorous protest against fiction in this letter to the rigid and religious Maria Lewis is partly prompted by Eliot's knowledge of what Miss Lewis would like to hear from a pupil she had instructed. But perhaps it is also an attempt on Eliot's part to suppress, in her still zealous evangelicalism, the attraction she confesses literature holds for her.

2. The word "new" is not quite accuate here. As Gordon Haight reports in the *Biography,* Eliot had "dreamed of writing stories" from early childhood and had made some early attempts at authorship (p. 206).

3. *Daniel Deronda,* ed. with an introduction by F. R. Leavis (New York, 1960), p. 137. (All references to this edition will hereafter be cited in the text.)

4. Eliot always felt the responsibility of her public role acutely, at times, no doubt, excessively, as when she denied Haim Guedalla's request to publish in the *Jewish Chronicle* a letter Eliot had written him. It was her function as an artist, she explained, "to act (if possible) for the good on the emotions and conceptions of my fellow-men." And to allow possible misinterpretation by the public of a casual private comment would be "stepping out of my proper function and acting for what I think is an evil result" *(Letters,* VI, 289).

5. Haight ascribes the remark to William Ernest Henley and adds that "it leaves us wondering which author he was more ignorant of" *(Letters,* I, ix). Henley himself, however, does not claim the insight as his own, introducing it and others as reports of what "has been said of her books" *(A Century of George Eliot Criticism,* ed. Gordon S. Haight [Boston, 1965], p. 162).

6. Among the many remarkable achievements of Bernard Paris's *Experiments in Life,* one of the chief must be the book's meticulous substantiation of Eliot's commitment to empiricism.

7. "Social Analysis in the Novels of George Eliot," *Victorian Literature: Modern Essays in Criticism,* ed. Austin Wright (New York, 1961), pp. 155-156.

8. Eliot's interests, as Haight's *Biography* and her letters prove, seem to have ranged over all areas of knowledge.

9. It is not my purpose in this book to argue for Eliot's Positivism. Gordon S. Haight believes her commitment to Comte has been "greatly exaggerated" *(Biography,* p. 301), but throughout *Experiments* Paris gives very convincing evidence that if she was not in the strictest sense a Positivist, Eliot did share with Comte some of her most basic convictions.

10. Eliot's criticism on this point has special bearing on her own novels which, although not "oracular" (not meant, that is, to "expound the writer's religious, philosophical or moral theories" [*Essays,* p. 310]), do undertake "the knottiest moral and speculative questions."

11. *Adam Bede,* ed. with an introduction by Gordon S. Haight (New York, 1957), p. 178. (All references to this edition will hereafter be cited in the text.)

12. These increase, significantly, from work to work, so much so that Samuel Butler's friend, Eliza Savage, remarked that she had had to buy a dictionary so as to be able to read *Daniel Deronda* " 'in the original' " (quoted by Gordon Haight in his Introduction to *A Century of George Eliot Criticism,* p. xi).

13. *Movement and Vision in George Eliot's Novels* (Seattle, 1959), p. 160.

14. Ed. with an introduction by Gordon S. Haight (New York, 1961), p. 400. (All references to this edition will hereafter be cited in the text.)

15. Edward Wagenknecht, *Cavalcade of the English Novel: From Elizabeth to George VI* (New York, 1954), p. 334. In this connection it is instructive to recall an anecdote related by Mathilde Blind. On one of their many walks together, Eliot and Tennyson had fallen into a discussion of evolution. As Tennyson left, he called after Eliot, " 'Well, good-by, you and your molecules.' " Unwilling to let pass even so humorous a slight to a favorite topic, Eliot called back, " 'I am quite

content with my molecules'" *(George Eliot* [Boston, 1883], p. 252).

16. "The Influence of Contemporary Criticism on George Eliot," *SP,* 30 (January 1933), 105.

17. Ludwig Feuerbach, *The Essence of Christianity,* trans. George Eliot (New York, 1957), p. 123. Bernard Paris, again, supplies an excellent discussion of Eliot's indebtedness to Feuerbach which may be gauged by her remark to Sara Hennell that with "the ideas of Feuerbach I everywhere agree" *(Letters,* II, 153).

18. Ed. with an introduction by Q. D. Leavis (Baltimore, 1967), p. 126. (All references to this edition will hereafter be cited in the text.)

19. *Romola,* with an introduction by Viola Meynell (New York, 1949), p. 324. (All references to this edition will hereafter be cited in the text.)

20. *Pragmatism and Four Essays from The Meaning of Truth* (New York, 1970), p. 77.

21. *The Philosophy of John Stuart Mill,* ed. Marshall Cohen (New York, 1961), p. 462.

22. *The Victorian Sage: Studies in Argument* (New York, 1965), p. 127.

23. See, for example, John S. Diekhoff, "The Happy Ending of *Adam Bede,*" *ELH,* 3 (September 1936), 224.

24. John Prest, *The Industrial Revolution in Coventry* (New York, 1960), pp. 8-9; W. J. Harvey, *The Art of George Eliot* (London, 1961), p. 117.

25. *Middlemarch from Notebook to Novel: A Study of George Eliot's Creative Method* (Urbana, 1960).

26. This is also the view of Barbara Hardy in *The Novels of George Eliot: A Study in Form* (London, 1959), pp. 115-134.

27. The caution is apparently necessary in view of such conclusions as Jerome Thale's that the coincidences of the novel are a proof or a justification for Silas's assumption of a providential and harmonious working in the universe *(The Novels of George Eliot* [New York, 1961], pp. 64-65).

28. The ending of *The Mill on the Floss* has disturbed and fascinated many. I list some of the more interesting discussions in the general bibliography.

29. "Determinism and Responsibility," p. 272.

30. Ernest Baker, *From the Brontës to Meredith: Romanticism in the English Novel: The History of the English Novel* (New York, 1960), VIII, 253.

31. Robert Preyer, "Beyond the Liberal Imagination: Visions and Unreality in *Daniel Deronda,*" *VS,* 4 (September 1960), 34.

CHAPTER II

Character in Action

In an explicatory note to *The Spanish Gypsy,* Eliot remarks that

> [if we] suppose for a moment that our conduct at great epochs was determined entirely by reflection, without the immediate intervention of feeling which supersedes reflection, our determination as to the right would consist in an adjustment of our individual needs to the dire necessity of our lot.... Tragedy consists in the terrible difficulty of this adjustment

If man's adjustment to the "dire necessity" of his lot—the destiny of facts which he is impotent to alter—is a matter of "terrible difficulty," it is because man is driven, without regard to his inevitable self-destruction, to act according to the causal laws of his own nature. For man, in Eliot's novels, is as thoroughly determined as the universe he inhabits. To some degree he is in relative harmony with his cosmic environment, else he could not survive at all. But in profoundly important ways, the laws which govern man's nature are blindly and fiercely antagonistic

to the limits of his power. In that collision Eliot finds the germ
of tragedy.

The Question of Determinism

Determinism in Eliot's novels has been much discussed.[2] Yet
her position seems clear—if complex—not only in her novels but
in her essays and letters where she frequently addressed herself
to the question. Long before she became a novelist, Eliot committed herself to what cannot be taken as anything but a deterministic view in her enthusiastic exposition of Mackay's thesis in
The Progress of the Intellect, where she speaks, among other
things, of the "invariability of sequence" that must be acknowledged as the operative law of human existence *(Essays,* p. 31). In a
letter to Charles Bray,[3] Eliot makes an even more direct statement of her belief in determinism, the major thesis of Bray's *The
Philosophy of Necessity: or Law in Mind as in Matter.*

> In the fundamental doctrine of your book—that mind presents
> itself under the same condition of invariableness of antecedent
> and consequent as all other phenomena (the only difference
> being that the true antecedent and consequent are propor-
> tionately difficult to discover as the phenomena are more
> complex)—I think you know that I agree. *(Letters,* II, 403)

More explicitly still, Eliot writes to John Chapman one of her
clearest and most precise assertions on the subject. Advising
him on a future choice for an editor, she writes:

> If you believe in Free Will . . . get one belonging to the Mar-
> tineau 'School of thought.' . . . If not—if you believe, as I do,
> that the thought which is to mould the Future has for its root
> a belief in necessity, that a nobler presentation of humanity
> has yet to be given in resignation to individual nothingness,

than could ever be shewn of a being who believes in the phantasmagoria of hope unsustained by reason—why then get a man of another calibre. *(Letters,* II, 48-49)

In the novels the reader is struck frequently by the persistent appearance of some form of the word "determined" in key moments of analysis.[4] Yet in every case we are tempted to argue that except for those limitations set on action by insurmountable external circumstances, the characters seem, far from being compelled, to be exercising a perfectly free choice in every action. Eliot takes more than normal care to show the psychological roots of action, the motives, reflections, and all other contributing conditions to each event. But, in a sense, this is precisely the nature of the determinism in question. In a characteristically scientific metaphor, Eliot defines, in the heading to chapter 16 of *Daniel Deronda,* both the subject and the method of the fictional biographer.

Men, like planets, have both a visible and an invisible history. The astronomer threads the darkness with strict deduction, accounting so for every visible arc in the wanderer's orbit; and the narrator of human actions, if he did his work with the same completeness, would have to thread the hidden pathways of feeling and thought which lead up to every moment of action. (p. 121)

In another scientific reference, in *The Mill on the Floss,* the narrator asks whether science does not

tell us that its highest striving is after the ascertainment of a unity which shall bind the smallest with the greatest? In natural science, I have understood, there is nothing petty to the mind that has a large vision of relations, and to which every single object suggests a vast sum of conditions. It is surely the same with the observation of human life. (p. 239)

Two points are of particular importance in these passages. First, the appeal to science—habitual in all of Eliot's writings[5]—is not merely an explanatory analogy. It is a substantive commitment through which Eliot places man (as she had done in the letter to Bray, above) in the natural order of the universe and so asserts the fundamentally material view of man she shared with such "scientific" thinkers as Mill, Comte, Marx, and others. Secondly, both passages accept scientific methodology in that they probe for a principle which will not only explicate the behavior revealed in empirical data but will enable the scientist (cosmic or human) to know and predict, by "strict deduction," that which must of necessity remain beyond observation. It is a view, clearly, which adheres most precisely to the evidence of matter and the concept of law.

But Eliot's determinism, especially as she reveals it in her novels, carries considerably more complex implications than are suggested by a position such as Bray's. It is, perhaps, one of the most radical aspects of her empiricism. An enlightening contrast can be found in two remarks Eliot made, one in 1840, the second in 1876. The first is a rather typical example of her early God-intoxicated letters in which she appears passionately committed to the immaterial. "May I unceasingly aspire," she writes to Martha Jackson, a girlhood friend, "to unclothe all around me of its conventional, human, temporary dress, to look at it in its essence and in its relation to eternity" *(Letters,* I, 70). Thirty-six years later she returns to the same metaphor but with the exact opposite commitment: "I become more and more timid —with less daring to adopt any formula which does not get itself clothed for me in some human figure and individual experience" *(Letters,* VI, 216-217). In the second passage—which states the view of her entire adult life—Eliot has discarded eternity and essences and substituted only the irreducibly concrete, the individual person, and, even more precisely, the individual experience. In 1840, it is very unlikely that Eliot knew what philosophic controversy she was entering in her letter to Martha

Jackson. She spoke, rather, in the terms provided for her by her religious reading and instruction. Yet the difference in diction between the two passages—a difference inherent in their philosophic commitments—marks the exact area within which Eliot's determinism can be understood. For in her delineation of character, Eliot transformed into a psychological conviction the empiricist contention that the notions of substance and essence are empty of content and that what Aristotle had called "accidents" alone can have ontological status.[6]

In terms of character analysis, the question revolves around what may validly be asserted to be the identity of the self. Common tradition had accepted the philosophic assumption that there was a core of identity which persisted through change but itself remained perennially the same. Such a categorical distinction between those qualities which may be predicated of a thing and the thing itself (of which the qualities are only predications) [7] insists, first, on the independent existence of identity entirely stripped of accidental predications and, second, on distinguishing that identity as eternal and necessary while, to a large degree, dismissing change and evolution as pertaining only to what is accidental. A grammatical distinction (as in most Indo-European languages it is), it held for many as an ontological one as well. Reenforced perhaps by the Christian dualism of body and soul, essentialism suggested an interpretation of man which credited him with a static, essential identity that remained, somehow, aloof from his mutable empirical existence.

Perhaps no writer this side of pure allegory has so systematically, if no doubt unwittingly, exploited the literary advantages that an exaggeration of this view can have as Dickens, especially in those characters who stand in complexity somewhere between the protagonist and the backdrop. Joe Gargery, for example, is who he is who he is, regardless of the circumstances of any particular situation, regardless of what point in time he is observed, for events can only, and minimally, alter Joe's attributive nature but can never affect his unchanging identity. From his first appearance to his last, he is the same man—good, sincere, generous, and so on—and we can speak in terms of "sameness" precisely because Dickens relies heavily on our capturing the "essence" of the character. Consequently, we can define Joe without reference to a particular moment in his existence.

By contrast, for Eliot there is no such static sanctuary of the self safe from continuous interaction with circumstances. Human identity is in a state of unending mutability, if, indeed, a term so suggestive of permanence as "identity" has any validity at all here. Eliot takes the empiricist, which is very much the modern, view: as Bertrand Russell puts it, when we take away the "accidents" and "try to imagine the substance by itself, we find that there is nothing left"; the substance, like the essence, has turned out to be only a "convenient way of collecting events into bundles," a "linguistic but not an ontological assertion." [8] The result is a far more chaotic and complex vision of man as a mass of interminably changing attributes. Individual man is in a constant state of evolution, and it is no longer reasonable to ask of any character, Who is he? as though there were a "he" who, although involved in interactions in time, place, and circumstance, yet retained a persistent identity; we ask, if anything, Who is he at this moment? Character becomes far more difficult to grasp because there is no longer a fixed center through which the mutable conditions of the self can be interpreted; these conditions are the self, and nothing else is. Character, in short, is fluid; it never is, it is always becoming.

When Farebrother and Dorothea discuss the issue briefly in *Middlemarch,* Dorothea takes an essentialist's view, justifying her a priori assumption of Lydgate's innocence by citing the " 'man's character,' " as though referring to a fixed entity. But character, Farebrother replies, is " 'not cut in marble—it is not something solid and unalterable. It is something living and changing' " (p. 538). The narrator of *Daniel Deronda* distinguishes between the tasks of the painter and those of the novelist in precisely these terms. Describing Gwendolen's beauty, he remarks that "Sir Joshua would have been glad to take her portrait; and he would have had an easier task than the historian at least in this, that he would not have had to represent the truth of change—only to give stability to one beautiful moment" (p. 84). The painter arrests time, but the novelist moves in it, through an infinite series of portraits. Consequently, his entire point of view differs radically. For, perhaps to the distress of the reader accustomed to other assumptions, Eliot's rejection of ontologically persistent entities compels her to explicate human nature in terms, rather, of another but more complex perennial principle, the laws of mutability; ontological unity, no longer a metaphysical reality, becomes the laws of temporal evolution.[9]

But, so redefined, character can no longer stand alone, or, more analytically, character cannot be thought about in that splendid isolation in which we see it from the essentialist point of view. It is one of the implicit claims of Eliot's fiction that destiny is indivisible. Character and event are only linguistically distinct. Indeed, looking at Eliot's notion of action from this angle of character, we see that the common terms of plot analysis apply very inaccurately. In obliterating the distinction between essential and attributive character, Eliot redefined the entire relationship between character and action.

A commitment to the existence of an essential center of character, a core which is the subject of change but which endures through it, which accounts for the continuity of personal identity and is therefore the real character, implies a commitment to two different types of action. Some things a character does must be seen to arise in his very essence, while others only in his attributive nature, and between these two types of action there is a qualitative difference. Actions of the first type are important, and those of the second are not, or, at the very least, the first are more important than the second; and they are, moreover, intrinsically so. For Eliot there can be no such distinction between events. Not only does every apparently minute detail of action acquire special meaning in Eliot, but, more significantly, it is impossible to tell, a priori, which event will be more important than another. For every event may be meaningful to the character who experiences it. The only criterion is the subjective one, and that is locked within the consciousness of the individual where each man's real drama is enacted, however apparently insignificant the external motive that impels it.

Standing outside, the observer is naturally enough biased toward certain kinds of events which seduce him to essentialist assumptions, especially since his task is thus considerably simplified. Knowing the essential nature of a character provides him with an instant key to differentiating between major and minor incidents. He is never surprised, for these are, correspondingly, the essential moments whose supreme intensity can move even one outside the action. But Eliot's novels do not provide the reader with such peaks and valleys. He finds himself rather on a plateau which may seem like a catalog of trivia but which he is expected to reinterpret with different assumptions. For every second of daily life is monumentally important. Heroic literature, Eliot thought, had ignored most of human existence in its concentration on essential events and had suggested, in consequence, a very incomplete relationship between character and circumstance. For in vital ways an essential character is quite distinct from his actions. Time and place may elicit one or another response from him, but his actions are only the things he does. They may move in a line parallel to that of his character, may reflect it as a mirror, but they are distinguishable from the entity that performs them, most especially because the character is conceived as removed from the links of his evolution which involve those apparently trivial circumstances. Faced with such a character and his actions, we never find ourselves at a loss to know which is which. In Eliot, we seldom find anything else. Plot becomes fused with character. It is, in fact, rather inaccurate to speak of character at all, for the term, evolved in a vocabulary based on different hypotheses, seems to bind us to the implication of some sort of essential quiddity, however elusive. Indeed, language is ill-equipped to name what character might be in such a vision of organic interrelationships as Eliot's. Character, says the narrator of *Middlemarch,* "is a process and an unfolding" (p. 111). "Process" is a very suggestive word, for, short of insisting on the physical as the unifying center—and even the physical identity is a process—we have lost all means of identifying character as a thing in itself.

It is tempting to rest part of the claim of Eliot's modernity on the argument that character rather than plot shapes her novels.[10] But the fact is, I think, that Eliot was more modern than that. If these intricate relationships between the world of what we call men and the world of what we distinguish as events can be defined at all, it would perhaps be better and more accurate—although more disturbing—to say that each novel consists of a web of events, interlocking in space and time, for which, at any given moment and only at a given moment, different characters may be physically but not conceptually extricated as centers of fictional gravity.

In such a framework, it makes little sense to ask whether a character has free will in his choices. Indeed, it may be argued that Eliot denies free will no more than she asserts it; rather, she restates the definition of "choice" in terms which render the notion of free will vacuous at exactly that point at which she makes the transition from essentialism to empiricism. It is a matter, once more, of deontologizing a semantic necessity. A sentence such as "Dorothea has free will" seems possible only in an essentialist context. It suggests an entity, Dorothea, and something else, distinct from Dorothea, which may be predicated of her—free will. It is analogous to a sentence such as "Dorothea has a passionate nature." But the latter, in Eliot's view, is a redundancy, grammatically necessary but ontologically confusing, for "a passionate nature" is not something predicated of Dorothea but rather one of a long list of characteristics the sum of which defines the totality of Dorothea. Once the concept of an essential identity is abandoned, when the total set of predications has been listed, it is absurd to ask whether there is yet one other thing, free will, in which the real source of action can be found. In these terms, "Dorothea has free will" is more or less meaningless; but "Dorothea is determined" says no more than "Dorothea is herself."

Thus, if in fact there is no "freedom," there is no inner sense of compulsion either. This point Eliot tried to make clear to Mrs. Ponsonby, who had anticipated a paralytic effect on her actions to follow an acceptance of the doctrine of determinism. As to "the necessary combinations through which life is manifested," Eliot writes, "and which seem to present themselves to you as a hideous fatalism, which ought logically to petrify your volition—have they, in *fact,* any such influence on your ordinary course of action?" *(Letters,* VI, 98). Here, Eliot is in complete agreement with John Stuart Mill. Like Mrs. Ponsonby, Mill had suffered from the fear that determinism would lead to paralysis. But, as he recognized in the *Autobiography,* this fear had arisen in his misinterpretation of determinism. "Philosophical Necessity weighed on my existence like an incubus," he explains, until he concluded that

> though our character is formed by circumstances, our desires can do much to shape those circumstances; and that what is really inspiriting and ennobling in the doctrine of free-will, is the conviction that we have real power over the formation of our own character; that our will, by influencing some of our circumstances, can modify our future habits or capabilities of willing.

In the end, Mill agrees that all "this was entirely consistent with the doctrine of circumstances, or rather, was that doctrine itself, properly understood." [11]

What Mill discovered, that determinism entails a process of self-creation, is a central theme in Eliot's analysis of the evolution of her characters. Man is not the victim but the agent of natural law. Arthur Donnithorne is a remarkable study of this principle, a man conspiring in his own moral corruption. From scene to scene we are presented with a series of portraits, no consecutive two so different that recognition is jarred, but together charting a succession of identities none precisely like the others. This the narrator is acutely aware of. "Are you inclined," he asks the reader at last,

> to ask whether this can be the same Arthur who, two months ago, had that freshness of feeling, that delicate honour which shrinks from wounding even a sentiment, and does not contemplate any more positive offence as possible for it?—who thought that his own self-respect was a higher tribunal than any external opinion? The same, I assure you, only under different conditions. Our deeds determine us, as much as we determine our deeds, and until we know what has been or will be the peculiar combination of outward with inward facts, which constitute a man's critical actions, it will be better not to think ourselves wise about his character. There is a terrible coercion in our deeds which may first turn the honest man into a deceiver, and then reconcile him to the change; for this reason—that the second wrong presents itself to him in the guise of the only practicable right. The action which before commission has been seen with that blended common-sense and fresh untarnished feeling which is the healthy eye of the soul, is looked at afterwards with the lens of apologetic ingenuity, through which all things that men call beautiful and ugly are seen to be made up of textures very much alike. *(Adam Bede,* p. 320)

It is the same Arthur, the narrator asserts, but obviously in a very qualified sense. His commitments, such as they are, are in principle the same; the laws of his nature are, at least in the potential world, the same. But, Eliot repeatedly instructs, it is in the concrete empirical fact and not in the realm of principle and potential that man lives his life. And it is the succession of empirical translations of his potentials that marks Arthur's moral degeneration. Ironically, this is made possible because Arthur does not recognize the distinction between potential and fact. Without knowing it, Arthur is, we see, an essentialist whose assumptions about his own identity permit him to stray so far from his image of his "true" self as to bring about the destruction of Hetty's life. Whatever he does, he knows "himself" to be the same generous, benevolent creature who, far from wishing or even having the capacity to harm anyone, is guided only by the noblest of motives. Like many other characters, he believes himself to act in his attributive aspect only, comforted in the knowledge that his essential nature is, somehow, a thing apart from his small mistranslations of the virtuous character he has once and forever defined in himself. He had, the narrator tells us early in the novel, an "agreeable confidence that his faults were all of a generous kind—impetuous, warm-blooded, leonine; never crawling, crafty, reptilian. *It was not possible* for Arthur Donnithorne to do anything mean, dastardly, or cruel" (pp. 124-125; my italics). Arthur does not believe in change. Thus, he lives on two planes of existence. On one, he is, and will always remain, impeccably scrupulous. On the other, he yields all the more easily to temptations which, he believes, can leave no permanent mark on either events or his own nature. Because of this distinction between "selves" in Arthur's mind he perceives no discrepancy in his conflicting potentials. Rather these potentials conspire together in the protection of his self-image to betray him into moral decline.

Arthur's progression from his first appearance to the seduction is an illuminating instance. We discover early that in principle some of the dominant laws of Arthur's nature are morally quite promising. As we are told and as we see—when he fills Totty's pockets with silver, for example (p. 86)—he is decidedly good-natured, prefers, indeed, to please and benefit where he can. Better still, he has a conscience, at least so much of one that his "own approbation was necessary to him, and it was not an approbation to be enjoyed quite gratuitously; it must be won by a fair amount of merit" (p. 124). Moreover, should he need reinforcement against temptation, he is susceptible to the good opinion of others. It is Irwine's warning, at the very beginning, that convinces Arthur he should not pay so much attention to Hetty (p. 128). On the other hand, he is weak, self-indulgent, and—a rather important fact in so shallow a young man—bored. Earlier, the narrator had asked whether "he would have self-mastery enough to be always as harmless and purely beneficial as his good nature led him to desire" (p. 125); at this point the question is still an open one. Yet the direction of the answer begins to be apparent when Arthur decides, after all, that it would do no harm to "amuse himself by seeing Hetty to-day, and get rid of the whole thing from his mind" (p. 130). The process of self-corruption has begun. For Arthur is incapable of confessing to what in fact he really wants—to flirt with Hetty just as he pleases—without an excusing condition.

The pattern, once established, repeats itself, but each time on a lower moral level. Thus, when he does see Hetty and finds himself "getting in love" with her, he vows, in italics, that he *"must not* see her alone again." The wish to see her, overwhelming as it is to his weak resistance, would not be enough for Arthur at this point to alter his decision; a subterfuge is necessary and because necessary readily found. "He would like to satisfy his soul for a day with looking" at her beautiful eyes; he *"must* see her again:—must see her, simply to remove any false impression from her mind about his manner to her just now" (pp. 134-135). With magnificent ingenuity, Arthur shifts from the prompting of his passion, which is unacceptable, to a moral imperative which, of course, his conscience compels him to obey. If the subterfuge is not altogether unconscious, it is not conscious either. It might not have been able to convince him once, but it can now. His newer self demands less stringent standards of explanation; self-indulgence is a habit to the degree that it generates not only more, but less critical, self-indulgence. This easier self-approval Arthur attempts to press Irwine to grant him. Having failed to make matters clear to Hetty, Arthur resolves to enlist Irwine's strength against his own weakness. To tell Irwine of the situation is to externalize, in an immovable judgment, the prohibitions of conscience. His argument is that on the premise that he must not see Hetty again, a confession to Irwine, whose approval is important to him, will act as a deterrent (p. 140).

But there is, we discover, an unacknowledged condition in Arthur's intention, a condition which even the rectitude of his self-image can begin to tolerate. He will confess, but only if he can be certain that Irwine will not judge him too harshly should he fail to keep his word. " 'It's a desperately vexatious thing,' " Arthur begins, " 'that after all one's reflections and quiet determination, we should be ruled by moods that one can't calculate on beforehand. I don't think a man ought to be blamed so much if he is betrayed into doing things in that way, in spite of his resolutions.' " But, against Irwine's firm moral stand, Arthur becomes more urgent and, inadvertently, more truthful: " 'surely you don't think a man who struggles against temptation into which he falls at last, as bad as the man who never struggles at all?" (pp. 174-175). Here, failure to resist temptation is no longer a possibility but a fact. And the first-person pronoun—Arthur's egotism disguised as moral generosity—shifts to the second person in a virtual demand for a priori absolution. It is no surprise that, unable to convince Irwine that the struggle is morally more significant than the action, Arthur decides not to make his confession after all. Ironically, the very reason he had first chosen to tell Irwine becomes the reason that prevents him from speaking. Conclusion and premise exchange places. The argument now begins with the assumption that he will see Hetty again. To have confessed, then, is to incur interference or at least criticism.

The scene reveals monumental alterations in Arthur's moral condition. Candor, one of Arthur's "favourite virtues," as the narrator had once ironically remarked (p. 124), has been fairly well sacrificed to convenience. Never again will Arthur attempt this level of sincerity, minimal though it was; for his intentions, whatever noble language he continues to articulate, have passed below the threshold of moral reluctance. Even his benevolent concern for Hetty's welfare has submitted to the egotism of his passion. And the weakness which he began by recognizing, on some level, as inimical to his better inclinations, has been accepted as a valid, if still uncomfortable, basis for action. Here, Eliot seems to mark the end of the first of two stages in Arthur's decline before the seduction, a decline whose confirmation we witness in the fact that the next time we see Hetty she is in possession of the earrings she had so fervently wished to have (p. 255).

The second stage is inaugurated and all but consummated at the celebration of Arthur's birthday. We are now no longer asking the same question, primarily because we are no longer dealing with the same man. The limits of possibility have been pushed considerably forward, and we no longer wonder whether Arthur can be so thoughtless and self-indulgent as to initiate a flirtation with Hetty which can end only in disappointment for her, but rather whether Arthur can end the affair before he commits Hetty to a lifetime of suffering. Such a question would have been absurd at the beginning; now, we do not even have much doubt of the story's end. Arthur himself is aware of no real change in his character. Mr. Poyser's toast, full of the tenants' good opinion of him, seems to Arthur generally accurate. A momentary "twinge of conscience" is now "too feeble to nullify the pleasure he felt in being praised." The good opinion of others, once at least in principle desired as a fair judgment of his actions, is now frankly sought by deception. "If there was something in his conduct that Poyser wouldn't have liked if he had known it," Arthur reasons, "Poyser was not likely to know it."

Not entirely at ease with falsehood (for the ideal self-image persists), Arthur intends, since a confession is no longer necessary for his conscience, to make his present reputation good by future actions. The "next time he was alone with Hetty, he would explain to her that she must not think seriously of him or of what had passed. It was necessary to Arthur, you perceive, to be satisfied with himself; uncomfortable thoughts must be got rid of by good intentions for the future, which can be formed so rapidly, that he had time to be uncomfortable and to become easy again before Mr. Poyser's slow speech was finished" (pp. 269-270). The narrator's tone, which had always been skeptical about Arthur, has now become cynical. We can no longer believe Arthur; or, rather, we cannot believe this Arthur, although we once, mistakenly it appears, believed another. We are, in fact, far less surprised that the next time Arthur sees Hetty he seduces her than we have been before at lesser trespasses.

Ultimately, what Arthur and many other characters in the novels do not believe in is the reality of time, as I discussed it in the last chapter. They live in an eternal moment in which time's effects can have no meaning. At most, time is a means of measuring the external world but never the internal one. The contrast between Arthur's self-image and the narrator's analysis of him is, in this sense, a temporal one. Arthur's story explicates time as a condition of man's identity, rooting him in the material world, subjecting him to the laws of organic change. For determined man is the product of time, potential, and circumstance, and his identity can be defined only as the locus of their intersections.

Heredity as Potential and Inclination

Before the individual enters on identity forming experience, his potential is already determined by his heredity, which impels

62

him in one or another of many hypothetically possible direc-
tions and ever thereafter continues to incline him to one or
another externally open alternative. For genetic laws are part of
the rigorous order of destiny and so form a segment of the
invisible thread the narrator, like the scientist, traces to understand the otherwise fragmented actions of a character's behavior. But, to change the analogy, heredity is a multi-layered
magnetic field in which the individual is seen to respond to a
large variety of predilections not merely as a complex aggregate
but as distinct levels of influence. For Eliot, each individual
stands, as it were, in the shadow of mankind's total identity,
absorbing at birth the inheritance of ever narrowing and in some
cases intensifying concentric circles of genetic affiliation. Human nature in general, the characteristics of his species, the
peculiarities of his race, familial predilections—in both the large
and the immediate sense—as well as something recognizably
embedded in these but still ineffably his own—all these structure
the binding framework of the individual's nature. Moreover,
these penetrate from what the essentialist might have considered the most external traits to the most internal, all of which
become for Eliot indistinguishably determining and interrelated molds of character.

In *The Mill on the Floss*, Eliot chooses as a major theme the
immediate, especially parental, genetic ties which define the
potentials of the two protagonists, Maggie and Tom. From the
very beginning of the novel, we are aware of the question of
heredity, emphasized, indeed, in the primitive terminology of
the beast fable in such characters as Mr. and Mrs. Pullet and in
such linguistic revelations as Mr. Tulliver's reference to the
" 'crossing o' breeds' " (p. 12). Also from the beginning, we learn
that the lines are drawn quite sharply; Tom resembles his
mother and the Dodsons, Maggie, her father and the other
Tullivers. In addition, these familial affiliations are pervasive.
Bessy Tulliver is a "blond comely woman" (p. 9); to her son she
has passed on her light complexion: "light-brown hair" and

"cheeks of cream and roses" (p. 30). Her daughter, on the other hand, she barely recognizes as her own. Maggie's dark hair, which refuses to curl even with the inducement of paper curlers, exasperates Mrs. Tulliver into exclaiming that her niece "'Lucy takes more after me nor my own child does' " (p. 13). But Lucy, of course, is a Dodson like Bessy herself. Here, the physical suggests both in metaphor and in fact far deeper associations. Tom is a Dodson in every way. Mrs. Tulliver, whose level of perception barely exceeds the obvious, recognizes this in the fact that Tom is " 'wonderful for liking a deal o' salt in his broth. That was my brother's way, and my father's, before him' " (p. 12). But Tom has also inherited this very shallowness of understanding that prompts so superficial an insight. " 'I picked the mother,' " Mr. Tulliver explains to Mr. Riley, " 'because she wasn't o'er 'cute.... But you see, when a man's got brains himself, there's no knowing where they'll run to; an' a pleasant sort o' soft woman may go on breeding you stupid lads and 'cute wenches' " (p. 18).

Not only physically and intellectually are the children genetic heirs of the two clans but temperamentally as well. The Dodsons are plodding, persistent, methodical. The Tullivers, the narrator pauses to explain in the middle of the novel, were of "richer blood, having elements of generous imprudence, warm affection, and hot-tempered rashness. Mr. Tulliver's grandfather had been heard to say that he was descended from one Ralph Tulliver, a wonderfully clever fellow, who had ruined himself. It is likely enough that the clever Ralph was a high liver, rode spirited horses, and was very decidedly of his own opinion. On the other hand, nobody ever heard of a Dodson who had ruined himself; it was not the way of that family" (p. 240).

Genetics provide the conflicts of the novel. Between Maggie and her environment, for example, Eliot develops a tension that persists to the end of the novel, that is, to the end of Maggie's life. For Tom, the narrow world of St. Ogg's is the seedfield of opportunity. No Dodson was ever ruined. The values of society set the terms of Tom's challenge. Success is difficult but both possible and desirable. The Dodson temperament is in complete harmony with these values; the two, indeed, are more or less one, for the Dodsons are the society not only of St. Ogg's but of the prevailing English temper, the "praiseworthy past of Pitt and high prices," as the narrator explains in alliterative mockery (p. 240). In Tom, genetic reproduction has minted another current coin. "He was," the narrator announces early, "one of thoes lads that grow everywhere in England, and, at twelve or thirteen years of age, look as much alike as goslings" (p. 30).

It is with Tom's inherited Dodsonness that Maggie clashes, just as, to take Tom's point of view for a moment, it is with Maggie's Tulliverness that Tom clashes. I will return later to the deep attachment Maggie feels for family and place, but it must be mentioned here that one of the particular tragedies of the tension Eliot describes in the relationship of the brother and sister is something which we would be tempted to assign not to the characters themselves but to the situation into which they are born, could the two be distinguished in Eliot. A Tulliver in her nature, Maggie's is an intense and "hungry" (p. 335) soul yearning for affection, which, in childhood, she builds, largely for lack of another object, for her brother. A Dodson, Tom feels only with that shallower affection that allows itself to be placed in the scheme of other affairs. This genetic inheritance prearranges the subsequent relationship, for Maggie, whose need is greater, will have to yield to Tom. Again, because their genetic heredities are so different, they cannot truly understand one another and so to the end of her life Maggie finds herself in a situation in which she is bound deeply to one from whom she is equally deeply separated. In *Adam Bede,* the narrator remarks on such irony of genetic affiliation as he describes Adam's likeness to his father whom he now despises.

Family likeness has often a deep sadness in it. Nature, the great tragic dramatist, knits us together by bone and muscle, and divides us by the subtler web of our brains; blends yearning and repulsion; and ties us by our heartstrings to the beings that jar us at every movement. We hear a voice with the very cadence of our own uttering the thoughts we despise; we see eyes—ah! so like our mother's—averted from us in cold alienation; and our last darling child startles us with the air and gestures of the sister we parted from in bitterness long years ago. (p. 37)

The relationship between Maggie and Tom in this respect is far from reciprocal, obviously. But it is not only because being a Tulliver is far more difficult; it is also because being a Tulliver is far more complex.

Ironically, the Tullivers too belong to that "praiseworthy past of Pitt and high prices," at least to the degree that they do not consciously question the values it cherishes, nor, consequently, escape the pressure to function in the same roles and to achieve the same ends. This is, in part, Mr. Tulliver's tragedy. Mr. Tulliver loves the old Mill and for this reason struggles to keep it. But this motive is complicated by another, from which the first is sometimes indistinguishable, and that is his competitively acquisitive instinct, a trait very near to the core of the Dodson nature. Mr. Tulliver can neither refute nor ignore the Dodson challenge to the competition for ownership because that wider influence which has helped to create the Dodsons has penetrated as well into the Tulliver spirit. The Tullivers, one must not fail to observe, have a bit of Dodsonness in them, although in the Tullivers the strain flows with "richer blood."

To return to Maggie with this insight is to understand, in genetic as well as in environmental terms, that Maggie, like Mr. Tulliver and their ancestor Ralph before them, is not involved in the simpler conflict of an alien spirit in a pettily inadequate context—although the shadow of this lurks archetypically over the situation—but rather in a conflict whose first and most important setting is Maggie's own divided nature. This is not to say that Maggie is a Dodson too. She is not, but she is a Tulliver in whom a vestigial Dodson chromosome can be unmistakably detected.

The subject raises some seldom-posed questions, especially some that concern Maggie's relationship to Stephen. The Dodsons are a very competitive clan, particularly in the public display of their success. Bessy Tulliver's sisters never tire of lamenting her degradation (to them, a social and economic term) with an all-too-obvious emphasis on the contrast of their own positions. Mrs. Tulliver concedes the disparity without question, indeed hints of it to her husband on all appropriate occasions. It would be a simplification of motives, certainly, to conclude from this Dodson trait that Maggie chooses Stephen in a spirit of competition with Lucy, for there are many passions at work in this situation, as I will discuss at a later time. Yet, there is an elementary, if partial, truth here.

The first time we see Maggie and Lucy together, we are aware of a resentment, faint but persistent, in Maggie toward her cousin. Maggie herself represses it completely, and Lucy, of course, never perceives it. The external focus of the scene is on Maggie's "mane," as the narrator early describes it (p. 13). Mrs. Tulliver suffers a "silent pang" as she watches Mrs. Deane adjusting Lucy's blond curls; Maggie always looked twice as dark as usual when she was by the side of Lucy" (p. 55). Maggie, all too aware of this contrast, is made even more self-conscious by Mrs. Pullet's open disapproval of her hair, by Mrs. Deane's "critical eye" (p. 56), and, finally, by Mrs. Tulliver who, no longer able to suffer her pang silently, orders Maggie to go get her hair brushed (p. 57). The instinct to self-destruction is strong in the Tullivers, as we observe not only in Maggie's father but in their archetypical ancestor Ralph. Instead of Martha, whose efforts had never met with much success, Maggie consults her scissors. This is the characteristic Tulliver rashness which defends itself with no calculation of effect but rather as though conceding the validity of the attack. Tom, in contrast, had a "wonderful instinctive discernment of what would turn to his advantage or disadvantage" (p. 58).

This early scene foreshadows, of course, what Maggie will be throughout her life. But there is another symbolic key here, one which touches on the Dodson kernel in the Tulliver nature. The narrator, describing the first meeting in the novel between Maggie and Lucy, remarks that "Maggie always looked at Lucy with delight. She was fond of fancying a world where the people never got any larger than children of their own age, and she made the queen of it just like Lucy . . . only the queen was Maggie herself in Lucy's form" (p. 55). Years later, the motif returns when Maggie remarks to Philip of Madame de Staël's *Corinne:* " 'I foresaw that the light-complexioned girl would win away all the love from Corinne and make her miserable. I'm determined to read no more books where the blond-haired women carry away all the happiness. I should begin to have a prejudice against them.' " " 'Well,' " Philip replies, " 'perhaps you will avenge the dark women in your own person, and carry away all the love from your cousin Lucy' " (pp. 290-291). Philip's prophetic words prove true primarily because when Maggie returns to visit Lucy from a two-year imprisonment in a "third-rate schoolroom, with its jarring sounds and petty round of tasks" (p. 335), she finds Lucy in a situation which seems to realize the very fantasies she had once entertained. Without distinctly appropriating Stephen, even in her thoughts, she feels "the half-remote presence of a world of love and beauty and delight, made up of vague, mingled images from all the poetry and romance she had ever read, or had ever woven in her dreamy reveries" (p. 335-336). She had come upon a "Duet in Paradise," ironically enough named by the narrator, and had confessed to Lucy, although not specifically about Lucy and Stephen: " 'I get angry sometimes at the sight of happy people. I think I get worse as I get older—more selfish' " (p. 396).

Maggie herself becomes aware of the connection between her present temptation and at least her earlier rebellion against the blond heroine. Answering Philip's renewed warning that she is again attempting to escape life in unnatural resignation—a notion to which Maggie now appeals, although unconsciously, only to avoid fulfilling her pledge of love to Philip—Maggie replies, of circumstances in general, that " 'many things have come true that you used to tell me.' " But Philip's eyes, "charged with a specific recollection," prompt Maggie's own memory, and she wonders, suddenly, whether his mind has "flown back to something that *she* now remembered?—something about a lover of Lucy's" (p. 362). But Maggie's memory does not go back to her envious childhood daydreams, nor can she grasp the ultimately genetic foundations of her present conflict.

In her relationship to both Stephen and Tom, Maggie also confronts something that is embedded in her Tulliver nature but which is also her own contribution to that hereditary strain. I suggested earlier that the Tullivers had, to a large degree, ruined themselves in consequence of their unquestioning acceptance of the goals set for them by natures quite different from their own. Maggie, however, seems to be the first of her line who questions the goals themselves, chiefly economic and social ones. She is ruined nonetheless, but she succumbs in a deeper awareness of the conflict in which she participates, and the burden of responsibility shifts, as a result, to a different cause. The tragedy of her Tulliver ancestors, distant and near, had been that they were Tullivers trying to be Dodsons, an impossible attempt. Maggie, confronting the same stifling reality, is different in that she probes, in a blundering enough way, for an identity that will refute the values of the Dodson world. To focus on the genetic meaning of such a search is to realize that Maggie is the first Tulliver who pursues, with increasing consciousness, the richer, more human life of the Tulliver instinct toward the fulfillment of the real impulses of that genetic heritage.

In retrospect, it is obvious that those vices which burden the

Tullivers are made vices only in a world governed by Dodson rules and values. The rashness and imprudence that persistently defeat the Tullivers, even Maggie herself, are expressions of passions embittered by the frustration of circumstances. This fact Eliot reveals very dramatically as Maggie is trapped between Philip and Tom. The freedom of mind, spirit, and understanding that Philip is capable of—the very qualities that attract Maggie to him—comes, through Maggie, in conflict with the rigid and shallow opposition set up by Tom. Unopposed, such virtues flourish; opposed, they are not only checked but become perverted. This is not to suggest that either Maggie or Philip can be analyzed in such simple terms; neither comes into adulthood unmodified by infinite complexities. Yet the generalization underlies the more concrete intricacy of fact. Stephen is, for Maggie, a perversion of the kind Philip had always anticipated when he warned her that self-repression would erupt in self-indulgence. In a freer world—one, that is, that would not have tried to force Maggie into a mold in which she could not possibly fit—Stephen would have been, in the strictest sense of psychological sequence, unnecessary. His inadequacy, on which critics have commented from Eliot's day to our own, is not Eliot's error, but her sharpest insight into the convolutions of her character's nature. Answering John Blackwood, who had sent her Sir Edward Bulwer-Lytton's criticism of the novel, Eliot writes of the relationship between Maggie and Stephen: if "I am wrong there—if I did not really know what my heroine would feel and do under the circumstances in which I deliberately placed her, I ought not to have written this book at all, but quite a different book, if any" *(Letters,* II, 317-318). In this last sense, genetics is an unrelenting impulse in the evolution of identity. To thwart it, as we see not only in Maggie's case but in some of the other Tullivers as well, is to transform the vital energy of life into a perverse death wish, a fact which helps us to understand far more precisely one of the symbolic meanings of the novel's ending.

In *Felix Holt,* Eliot develops this thesis from another point of view. In Harold Transome we find a young man to whom the knowledge of his genetic inheritance has been denied. Not only does Harold not know who his father is, but, in fact, he believes the wrong man to be his father; moreover, although he knows the physical identity of his mother, he is unaware of the deeper impulses which impel her. Again, Eliot develops the genetic chain on every level, from the physical to the most obscure psychological. Indeed, the connection between these levels is even more prominent here than in *The Mill on the Floss,* not because we are more aware of resemblances but because it is more importantly involved in Harold's discovery of self.

It is worthwhile to pause here to emphasize how deeply interlocked are "external" and "internal" characteristics in Eliot's nonessentialist view. Physiognomy is used not only as a clue to character (which it partly is in Eliot's novels, as it has been in many others), but as a filament in the organic inter-relationships within character. In *Middlemarch,* for instance, Eliot suggests an extensive analysis of the effect on character of physical appearance by presenting a striking contrast between Rosamond Vincy and Mary Garth. In Mary, moreover, Eliot shows at the same time the psychological falsity of the romantic myth which assures plain girls that they will, through some benevolent magic, grow in compensating virtues. Mary does not. Admirable in many respects, Mary is nevertheless remarkably susceptible to the way in which other people see her; context is very powerful, and one's self-image yields at last to the reflection we observe in the eyes of others. "Plainness," the narrator remarks, has its peculiar temptations and vices:

it is apt to either feign amiability, or, not feigning it, to show all the repulsiveness of discontent. . . . Mary had certainly not attained that perfect good sense and good principle which are usually recommended to the less fortunate girl, as if they were to be obtained in quantities ready mixed, with a flavor of resignation as required. Her shrewdness had a streak of satiric bitterness continually renewed and never carried utterly out of sight. (pp. 83-84)

The truth of this insight is immediately confirmed as Mary, not without envy, declares herself a " 'brown patch' " in comparison to Rosamond. The latter, who can afford to pronounce beauty " 'of very little consequence in reality' "—regarding herself with admiration in the mirror nevertheless—evokes from Mary a sardonic " 'You mean *my* beauty' " (p. 84). In consequence of the physical fact, Mary is defensive, less receptive to friendship, more suspicious of love. Similarly, Philip Waken, in *The Mill on the Floss,* has been taught by his deformity to expect less feeling for himself from others, although the knowledge has in no way lessened the pain. An indifferent glance appears to him a sign of "offensive pity" or "ill-repressed disgust." His "nervous irritation" is but half of the "peevish susceptibility" he is prone to, the other half being a persistent "heart-bitterness produced by the sense of his deformity" (p. 148). Thus, he offers himself more cautiously to others than the robust Tom who, like Rosamond, has never had reason to doubt his welcome.

But beauty, like plainness, is also attended by characteristic patterns of behavior. Critics sometimes propose psychological aberrations in Eliot's own mind as explanations of her tendency to make beautiful women especially selfish in the novels,[12] but it certainly requires no such extraneous insight to see that characters like Hetty, Gwendolen, Rosamond, and Esther, for example, are shown to persist in their infantile narcissism partly because their beauty inclines others to pamper them, to yield to them, to forgive them. If Philip and Mary have learned to discipline their expectations, it is only because they have had to. Not even Fred indulges Mary as Lydgate indulges the beautiful Rosamond. Ultimately, self-image is a determining condition of self, and it is to this question that Eliot turns in *Felix Holt.*

Early in the novel, Harold Transome's physical characteristics begin to foreshadow subsequent events. The first suspicion the reader has of Harold's real paternity—and of the fact that there is some question about it—is in Harold's surprise that he should tend to plumpness while Mr. Transome, whom Harold still supposes to be his father, had always been unusually thin. This "mystery" is paradigmatic, however, of considerably more important matters. Because inherited potential has so significant a part in the formation of character, self-knowledge depends, to a proportionate degree, on the recognition of ancestral continuity. So long as Harold continues to believe himself Transome's son, so long must he remain misinformed about the very seeds in himself which circumstances fertilize into character. Even without consciously reflecting on the matter, Harold senses the disruption in familial evolution; he becomes the "outsider" of the family, the more so since he appears to have, in the beginning, an unbounded faith in his own powers. But all this is an "illusion"; "trusting in his own skill to shape the success of his own morrows," Harold is ignorant "of what many yesterdays had determined for him beforehand" (p. 189).

The yesterdays are both circumstantial and genetic. The almost unconscious selfishness with which Harold attacks whatever he chooses to make a target—political office or Esther Lyon—is constantly explicated in the novel in the parallel exposition of Mr. Jermyn's ruthless ambition and Mrs. Transome's memory of her former self-indulgence. Until these two lines meet in Harold's consciousness, he can never hope to understand his own nature. Although Harold's "pride" rebels "against his sonship" to a man he despises (p. 468), the knowledge has immediate effects on his thoughts and actions. Diminished in both self-regard and property, Harold gains in the discovery a sense of connections. The bonds that thwart his ambition become, at the same time, a definition of place and proportion. Like Esther who, as Felix tells her, can be transformed only by a vision of the emptiness toward which her egotism drives her and who is transformed in her perception of Mrs. Transome, Harold acquires, suddenly, a vision of his own nature in the judgment he had passed on Jermyn. Mrs. Transome's confession, with all that it implies about her own nature as well as Harold's origins, provides him with the key to what had otherwise seemed to him meaningless and inexplicable.

How important is a character's knowledge of his heredity in Eliot's view can be surmised from the considerable list of orphaned, half-orphaned, and as-good-as orphaned young people: Hetty, Dinah, Philip, Eppie, Dorothea, Lydgate, Ladislaw, Gwendolen, Deronda, Tito (who is, as it were, twice orphaned), and Arthur, to name only the most conspicuous. One must conclude that, in addition to the literal, there is a symbolic condition of being orphaned—a blindness to hereditary continuity—from which each individual must mature into a knowledge of the self.

In *Daniel Deronda*, Eliot explores a crisis in identity very similar to Harold Transome's. But here we find in addition Eliot's most mature thought on the subject of national/racial heredity. Daniel is one of Eliot's many orphans, but he is an orphan on two levels, being separated not only from his immediate family but also from his racial heritage. Thus, Daniel is, in a rather special way, a split man. He has, indeed, been given some kind of conscious identity: an Englishman, a Christian, a man of some means and education. Inevitably, he defines, or attempts to define, his role in terms of this knowledge. Yet he is restless, almost lazy, unable to fasten on one or another specific purpose in life. He cannot know, being ignorant of his true heritage, that this is the reluctance of the conscious will to contradict the impulse of a primordial vocation. The circumstantial identity that Sir Hugo, at Alcharisi's request, had so exclusively invested him with is in a constant state of conflict with the irrepressible genetic identity which hovers over him like a puzzling and threatening shadow. The most important question man must answer to himself before he can evolve into a full and integrated existence—"Who am I?"—must remain, for Daniel, not only a question whose answer is unavailable to him but, worse, a question whose terms even are unknown. Daniel is in the agonizing grip of two identities which, significantly, are not in themselves incapable of being integrated but which remain distinct as long as he is ignorant of his parentage.

What is Daniel to think of himself when, knowing himself to have been given a specific position in life (for he suspects himself to be Sir Hugo's son), he feels, inexplicably, cut off from something, looking for something he does not even know the nature of? How is Daniel to explain to himself that he, a thorough Christian, is drawn to enter a synagogue and there feels an irresistible kinship with those around him, with the service itself? He is amazed at the "strength of his own feeling," thinking it "beyond the occasion" (p. 274). It is with exquisite relief that Daniel hears his mother, at last, disclose the truth to him. " 'I am glad of it,' " he answers Alcharisi's revelation that he is a Jew; " 'for months events have been preparing me to be glad that I am a Jew' " (p. 477), Daniel confesses of those events which had satisfied, much to Daniel's own surprise, the secret longings of his ancestry. Whatever we conclude about the "coincidences" that bring Daniel to Mordecai, we recognize that he commits himself to the apprenticeship in obedience to an irresistible compulsion. Genetics has been revenged on circumstance. " 'The effects prepared by generations are likely to triumph over a contrivance which would bend them all to the satisfaction of self,' " Daniel tells his mother. " 'Your will was strong, but my grandfather's trust which you accepted and did not fulfil—what you call his yoke—is the expression of something stronger, with deeper, farther-spreading roots, knit into the foundations of sacredness for all men.' " That " 'stronger Something has determined that I shall be all the more the grandson whom ... you willed to annihilate' " (p. 499).

Daniel's heritage, however, is far wider and deeper even than his first perception leads him to suspect. It synthesizes the threads, in ever widening circles of ancestral heredity, of a whole race. He is not mistaken that he resembles his grandfather. " 'You are a young copy of him in your face,' " his mother concedes (p. 473). But the grandfather was rigid, and Daniel has escaped that quality because within that circle of heredity there is also another; he is also the son of his father. Alcharisi remarks on the modification of her own genetic legacy to Daniel in recalling that her own husband, who had been " 'all lovingness and affection' " (p. 475), had made Daniel " 'milder' " than his grandfather (p. 476). All but Alcharisi had been passionate Zionists, but Daniel traces far more remote genetic precedents of the intense nationalism he discerns now in himself. Later, he tells Mordecai that the latter had " 'given shape to what, I believe, was an inherited yearning—the effect of brooding, passionate thoughts in my ancestors—thoughts that seem to have been intensely present in my grandfather' " (p. 565).

It is here that Daniel can at last integrate what had seemed earlier to him the disparate fragments of his identity. To the inherited characteristics of his nature Daniel has at last joined the knowledge that gives them a place in his conscious self-image. What had torn him apart and so brought him to a restless standstill now frees him to move forward in a predetermined direction. It is this insight that he explains, in a parable, to Mordecai when he asks him to imagine

"the stolen offspring of some mountain tribe brought up in a city of the plain, or one with an inherited genius for painting, and born blind—the ancestral life would lie within them as a dim longing for unknown objects and sensations, and the spell-bound habit of their inherited frames would be like a cunningly-wrought musical instrument, never played on, but quivering throughout in uneasy mysterious meanings of its intricate structure that, under the right touch, gives music. Something like that, I think, has been my experience. Since I began to read and know, I have always longed for some ideal task, in which I might feel myself the heart and brain of a multitude—some social captainship, which would come to me as a duty, and not to be striven for as a personal prize. You have raised the image of such a task for me—to bind our race together." (p. 565)

Circumstance as Identity and Limitation

Although more amorphous, potential is in one respect easier to describe than circumstanc, for the latter includes nothing less than every event of every kind which occurs in the circle at the center of which the individual stands. And ultimately, the circumference of that circle proves to be forever beyond the visible horizon. As for Aristotle, so for Eliot, man is an animal that lives in a polis;[13] or, perhaps more accurately, in Eliot's terms of human identity, man is an animal who evolves in the context of the polis. Individually discernible as is a single cell in an organism, man is nevertheless as inextricably inherent in his environment and as incapable of being analyzed independently.

"It is the habit of my imagination," Eliot wrote to R. H. Hutton in connection with his review of *Romola,* "to strive after as full a vision of the medium in which a character moves as of the character itself. The psychological causes which prompted me to give such details of Florentine life and history as I have given, are precisely the same as those which determined me in giving the details of English village life in 'Silas Marner,' or the 'Dodson' life, out of which were developed the destinies of poor Tom and Maggie." Hutton had been aesthetically unhappy with Eliot's handling of the historical background in the novel, and Eliot herself concedes in the letter that "it is likely enough that my mental constitution would always render the issue of my labour something excessive—wanting due proportion" *(Letters,* IV, 97). Both are right. The political, religious, and sociological analysis, which Eliot had painstakingly researched, is poorly integrated into the structure of the novel and seems to carry less conviction than does her contextual analysis in the other two novels she mentions. In part, we must blame the fact that in *Romola* Eliot is forced to rely too much on historical data rather than on memory and observation. The scholar dangerously begins to supersede the writer. Many times the novel seems to split into two: one, a political retrospection of fifteenth-century Florence, the other, a study of the daily lives of characters. It is difficult to avoid the conclusion that Eliot did not have the skill to so fully integrate the larger and the smaller focus that the reader could in fact experience their interrelationships in the novel's progress. She achieves far better results when the context does not exceed the limits of the immediate community, as in *The Mill on the Floss* or *Middlemarch*. In these two novels, while larger events are suggested in the background—the full context is still present to the reader—the exposition generally remains within the smaller unit. Yet the fact that, knowing her tendency to miss due proportion, Eliot is still willing to risk partial failure in novels like *Romola* is a convincing argument in itself that a decontextualized character cannot exist for her.

As her letter to Hutton only partially suggests, circumstances are important in the life of her characters in two intimately related but at least hypothetically distinct ways. They are important psychologically, as persistent forces in the continuously evolving character of the individual, and they are important socially, as limits to possibilities and so reminders of the highly dependent nature of individual existence.

"You have seized," Eliot writes in the same letter to Hutton, "with a fulness which I had hardly hoped that my book could suggest ... the relation of the Florentine political life to the development of Tito's nature." Here, the focus is psychological, although, obviously, Florentine political life is also the definitive arena of Tito's actions. We do not have a full study of Tito's earlier life, as we do of the Tulliver children, and must accept him, as it were, ready-made with only enough information about his background to make intelligible the inclinations he reveals at the opening of the novel. The emphasis will be on his evolution. And the terms of this Hutton has captured completely.[14] He is not, Hutton writes, "originally false," but rather "naturally pleasure-loving," "swerving aside before every unpleasant obstacle in the straight path, at the instance of a quick intelligence and a keen dislike both to personal collision and to personal sacrifices." This is true of Tito throughout the novel, but it is true only descriptively, for the events which are the concrete instantiations of this generalization become progressively more sinister, and with them Tito's motives and character. For this, circumstances are half responsible. In another time, in another place, a character who could be described in the same terms (but not Tito, for Tito's identity, like that of every individual, is irrevocably locked in the concrete fact) might have evolved quite differently. But in fifteenth-century Florence, a time and place of "political passion," as Hutton calls it,[15] this description is realized in the Tito of the novel.

It is not precisely because here Tito has opportunities he might not have had, for example, in Middlemarch. Opportunity, although a necessary condition, can only explain what Tito does, whereas Eliot is far more interested in what Tito becomes. Florentine political life is not the stage of Tito's performance; it is an organically active determinant in his moral degeneration. In fact, the language here confuses the issue, for we speak of Tito and of Florence as two entities and are tempted to think of them as touching but still distinct. Actually, neither is. As Tito's presence changes the political life of Florence, so Florence becomes an ingredient in Tito's nature, neither static, neither independent of the other.

In *Middlemarch,* Eliot elaborates very strikingly on the nature of such a relationship. The "Prelude" and the novel it introduces define a perfect antithesis with circumstances as the argument. We are presented with one general category and two very different realizations of it. For it is circumstances that determine, to a very large degree, whether the description "a young girl of noble aspirations, religious fervor, and intense dedication" is actualized in St. Theresa or Dorothea Brooke. The specific context determines this because it provides or withholds values in terms of which certain goals can be nurtured, the "coherent social faith" of which the narrator speaks (p. 3). It does so again because it allows or denies, through that same presence or absence of coherent social faith, outlets for human pursuits. But it does so mostly because it functions, from the birth of the individual, in the formation of character. The fact that Dorothea's world is not St. Theresa's does not limit Dorothea's heroism; it limits, in fact, no one, however frustrated Dorothea may sometimes feel, for such a world has not created a St. Theresa but only someone who wishes she had been. Were it possible, for a single moment of trial, to somehow magically transport the nineteenth-century character to another age, however suited for heroic action, Dorothea would not suddenly take on the stature of the saint; for that it would have been necessary to re-create the entire environment as well as internal potential of St. Theresa; and, of course, in that case we would have St. Theresa herself and not Dorothea. It is one of the burdens of the novel to expound, in distressing detail, the exact reasons why the later age did not create the martyr described in the "Prelude," and it is the function of the "Prelude" to stipulate the touchstones against which we evaluate Dorothea's world. "For there is no creature," the narrator concludes at the end of the novel, "whose inward being is so strong that it is not greatly determined by what lies outside it" (p. 612).

As each character is in the process of being psychologically in part created by circumstances, he also lives within those circumstances; and one of Eliot's most persistent themes is the deep interdependence of all things, especially of all human beings. In some novels Eliot explores the inward thrust of more and more remote events and still finds none, however distant, that does not in some fashion press against individual existence. In *Felix Holt,* a novel which, like *Romola* and *Daniel Deronda,* attempts, not always successfully, to follow the widening spiral of influences on the central characters, the narrator feels compelled to explain his reasons:

> social changes in Treby parish are comparatively public matters, and this history is chiefly concerned with the private lot of a few men and women; but there is no private life which has not been determined by a wider public life, from the time when the primeval milkmaid had to wander with the wandering of her clan, because the cow she milked was one of a herd which had made the pastures bare. Even in that conservatory existence where the fair Camellia is sighed for by the noble Pine-apple, neither of them needing to care about the frost, or rain outside, there is a nether apparatus of hot water pipes liable to cool down on a strike of the gardeners or a scarcity of coal. (p. 51)

Frequently, Eliot speaks of the larger unit in terms of a "web,"[16] but I think the analogy she turns to in the "Address to Working Men by Felix Holt" conveys her meaning better. " 'Society,' " Felix states, " 'stands before us like that wonderful piece of life, the human body, with all its various parts depending on one another, and with a terrible liability to get wrong because of that delicate dependence' " *(Essay,* p. 420). The focus of the analogy is on life, that property of the entire organism which cannot exist independently in any single part; out of the totality emerges something different from what each of its constituent segments contributes, although it is the mass of individual parts which collectively creates it.

On this point, as on many others, Eliot attacks the reader as though in formal debate. We are offered any number of positive proofs in the interweaving lives of the characters, and we are challenged to refute, if still unconvinced, the constrasting attempts at negative proofs. In these latter cases, we find characters who, mistaking the true state of affairs, strive, for one reason or another, to disengage themselves from everything, to lead entirely independent lives. Before the end of the novels, Eliot shows the effort futile, but in the beginning she always provides generous scope for the experiment whose subsequent failure proves her view all the more conclusively.

When Lydgate, for example, arrives in Middlemarch, he does so with an articulated intention to remain isolated. A stranger, he has, he thinks, the perfect opportunity to dictate the terms of all his relationships. Nothing ties him to anything. As a physician, he calculates, he need contact no more than the physical. And it is only as a physician that he proposes to exist. But his story is an ironic comment on the naïve concept Lydgate has of human interaction. Neither professionally nor personally can Lydgate resist the seductive forces of interrelationships, nor, indeed, can these two parts of his life be kept so strictly apart. Lydgate had not reckoned with Bulstrode's ambition, with Rosamond's schemes, with the suspicious bias of provincial society, and never with those vulnerable points in his own nature that these and other external pressures would touch. His mind fragments and categorizes, dissecting an irrational living organism into its rationally mechanical parts. Rapidly entangled in the affairs of those around him, creating, to his surprise, entanglements of his own, Lydgate discovers suddenly that he has become dependent on other people, on their prejudices and good wills. He had not meant to yield the strength of his freedom, and he resents his new weakness, but there was no alternative.

In different terms, Silas Marner resembles Lydgate, for he, too, chooses to move to a strange community with the conscious intention of remaining entirely independent. Like Lydgate, too, Marner had been deeply wounded by a relationship he had willingly formed and has come to the conclusion that strength, or at least safety, lies in isolation. Eliot develops Marner's story more symbolically but to the same end. And here it is inescapably clear that in neither case is the social involvement entirely a matter of external necessity. For Marner, much more than Lydgate, can practice his trade virtually alone. As much as more external considerations, psychological need of human contact impels the individual into social exchange, even, paradoxically, against his will. Marner could have, for example, given Eppie up as soon as he found her had he not been lonely for the very relationships he had rejected, just as Lydgate could have arranged, hypothetically, to see less of Rosamond Vincy. This, in fact, Lydgate determines to do, and succeeds very admirably for a time. But, again, interactions are inevitable. Fred's illness forces him into calling on the Vincys, and the combination of Rosamond's shrewdness and his own inclinations finds him leaving the house an engaged man. For it is obvious that when Lydgate permits himself what he considers merely a mild flirtation, he is deceiving himself. When the two first meet, as Lydgate reviews in his mind the reasons he cannot marry, the ironic narrator remarks that "when a man has seen the woman whom he would have chosen if he had intended to marry speedily, his remaining a bachelor will usually depend on her resolution rather than on his" (p. 70). It is certainly so in Lydgate's case. Lydgate may not be, any more than Marner, willing to confess the spiritually debilitating effects of his self-imposed social exile, but he acts according to the nature of the species nonetheless.

For a long time there is in Lydgate a painful tension between rational choice and human instinct. The more pressing the latter becomes, the harder does he try to assert the former. It is almost as though Lydgate were placating his intellectual decision to remain independent when he rejects other possible relationships with rigid determination. But, ironically, it becomes clear that one may not choose dependencies any more than one may choose to have none. When Lydgate first meets Dorothea, he dismisses her as not at all suiting his conception of ideal womanhood. "Certainly nothing at present could seem much less important to Lydgate than the turn of Miss Brooke's mind," the narrator comments. Yet, much later, Lydgate is to discover that it is only on the generous turn of Dorothea's mind that his future in

Middlemarch depends. The narrator foreshadows the end in reflecting that "anyone watching keenly the stealthy convergance of human lots, sees a slow preparation of effects from one life on another, which tells like a calculated irony on the indifference or the frozen stare with which we look at our unintroduced neighbor. Destiny stands by sarcastic with our *dramatis personae* folded in her hand" (p. 70).

Both Lydgate and Marner are only exaggerations, in Eliot's view, of the natural human inclination of each individual to consider himself free in relation to the world around him. It is, of course, the position of maximum personal power, and this sense of power in the self is the inheritance of every member of the species. Seen from the special angle of perception of any character who begins in the illusion of personal independence, Eliot's novels unfold like unrelenting lessons in the reality of circumstantial determination.

In her last novel, Eliot creates a character who lives more intensely, more deliberately, more consciously in this illusion than any she had created before. Gwendolen's sense of mastery is so complete that it conceives of no exceptions. What we know of her life before the beginning of the novel and what we see of it at the beginning help us to understand that this humanly natural delusion has been more encouraged than thwarted by a comparatively weak-willed family. Gwendolen, indeed, is forceful, competent, beautiful—three advantages with which nature tempts her to self-destruction. Even the reader is inclined to excuse her. But the opening scene of the novel, on which I have commented before, defines, by contrasting the fortune Gwendolen expects to win to her actual losses, the very strict limits to personal freedom that even so superior a young woman as Gwendolen must come to recognize. From that scene on, the circumstances of the novel relentlessly drive Gwendolen to acknowledge her weakness. The contrast, in fact, between the first and last time we see Gwendolen is startling. In the first paragraph of the novel the narrator asks the questions being raised in Daniel's mind by his first glimpse of Gwendolen at the roulette table.

> Was she beautiful or not beautiful? and what was the secret of form or expression which gave the dynamic quality to her glance? Was the good or the evil genius dominant in those beams? Probably the evil; else why was the effect that of unrest rather than of undisturbed charm? Why was the wish to look again felt as coercion and not as a longing in which the whole being consents? *(Daniel Deronda,* p. 1)

Everything here denotes and connotes power. But the last time we see Gwendolen, in her farewell scene with Daniel and immediately after, everything is uncertain, tentative. In contrast to the supreme confidence expressed in the "dynamic quality" of her "glance," we find Gwendolen at the end confessing that she has " 'deserved nothing,' " and, moreover, so "tremulous" that she is unable to finish a sentence of broken phrases. Replacing the extreme alternatives of "the good or the evil genius" Daniel had speculated about is Gwendolen's far more moderate hope that she will " 'be better.' " In the first scene, the "effect" is of "unrest"; in the last Gwendolen's mother finds her "sitting motionless," almost, it would seem, numbed. At the beginning, it is Gwendolen who exercises a coercive force; at the end, it is Daniel who controls the relationship while Gwendolen has so far lost even self-control that "her frame tottered under" the burden of "difficult rectitude" Daniel imposes on her, that she bursts "out hysterically" when her mother speaks to her, and that she falls into "fits of shrieking" (p. 609).

This complete transformation is the inevitable end of Gwendolen's finding herself at the center of a series of concentric circles which mark the converging influences on her life. As Eliot's comment on the cosmic reality to which all men and all nature must submit, Gwendolen's gambling, in life as well as in the casino, is the largest of these circles; it is the final arrogance in which Gwendolen cannot acknowledge herself subject even to the indifferent laws of consequence. In this respect, her actions are no different from Hetty's. But Hetty, although she gambles, is too ignorant and too stupid to know that she is gambling, or, in fact, to know anything about the obscure impulses that defeat her. In Gwendolen, on the other hand, the natural faith each individual has that he and no other is an exception to all laws is completely conscious. That she is wrong, and therefore ignorant and stupid in this sense, is true; but the psychological distinction is very important because with Gwendolen we enter the problem of choice. Gwendolen sees herself as one who controls but is not controlled. The choices are always hers to make. This, in effect, is the vision of total freedom. From this cosmic level to the most personally immediate, Eliot tightens one after another circle of interdependence. At the next level, Gwendolen challenges history itself. Toward the end of the novel, the narrator remarks that

> there comes a terrible moment to many souls when the great movements of the world, the larger destinies of mankind, which have lain aloof in newspapers and other neglected reading, enter like an earthquake into their own lives. . . . That was the sort of crisis which was at this moment beginning in Gwendolen's small life; she was for the first time feeling the pressure of a vast mysterious movement, for the first time being dislodged from her supremacy in her own world, and getting a sense that her horizon was but a dipping onward of an existence with which her own was revolving. (pp. 606-607)

In the person of Daniel, Gwendolen's freedom is being questioned not only by one exception among so many admiring suitors but by the forces of five thousand years of history which have produced, in her lifetime, the Zionist movement. It is certainly not Eliot's point that had she never met Daniel Gwendolen could have escaped the vast pressures of that history; the past sweeps her along toward the future whether she knows it or not, regardless of whatever other ways she and her life might have been different without Daniel. In this respect, Daniel is for Gwendolen only the concrete embodiment that forces on her consciousness the reality of historical determination.

This as well as other realities Gwendolen avoids as long as possible. With characteristic egocentricity, Gwendolen attempts, throughout the novel, to draw everyone and everything within the smallest possible circle of which she is the center—the circle, in fact, over which she can retain control as long as she can protect it against the intrusions of remoter influences. Even when she comes to question Mirah about Daniel, for example, although her earlier confidence in herself has already been radically shaken, she can still not allow into her calculations the information so obviously before her. It was, the narrator comments, "characteristic of her that apart from the impression gained concerning Deronda in that visit, her imagination was little occupied with Mirah or the eulogised brother." Mirah had volunteered to tell Gwendolen that Daniel was " 'reading Hebrew' " with Mordecai, but the phrase "had fleeted unimpressively across her sense of hearing" (p. 447). Yet the information she ignored was far more important than the information she had come to inquire about. In this scene, Gwendolen has been exposed not only to one rival, the ancestral vocation to which she must ultimately lose Daniel, but to the more traditional one, the other woman. Neither boundary to her freedom can Gwendolen recognize.

But of the fact that Gwendolen is blind even to the curtailment of personal choice imposed by the existence of specific individuals we already have abundant evidence. It is not only on the moral level that Gwendolen errs in this respect. When she chooses to ignore Lydia Glasher's claim on Grandcourt, it is her selfishness that chooses to place her own wishes above the rights of others; but that selfishness is also a blindness that refuses to acknowledge the sinister prophecy implicit in Grandcourt's behavior to Lydia. Before she marries him, Gwendolen believes, at least on a conscious level, as I will discuss later, that she can control Grandcourt as easily as she had controlled her cousin Rex. The fact, however, is that Gwendolen is being hedged in between two parallel situations; Grandcourt and Daniel, who have little enough in common otherwise, share the structural task of eluding her and so fixing ever more finally the context of Gwendolen's circumstances; behind them, Lydia and Mirah, also dissimilar in other ways, extend Gwendolen's circumstantial contingency both spatially and, more interestingly, temporally; a remote past, from Gwendolen's point of view, in Grandcourt's life foreshadows the limits of her present condition; a remote future, in a distant part of the globe, reaches into Gwendolen's present through Mordecai and Mirah to thwart her expectations.

Daniel, who is as we see pivotal on almost every level of Gwendolen's enlightenment, has two other functions as well. In one function, Daniel acts as a teacher, lecturing Gwendolen incessantly on the subject of interdependence, articulating, at the same time, one of Eliot's own themes in the novel. More or less concurrently, this formal lesson is being supported empirically by Gwendolen's actual relationship with Daniel and, in a surprisingly parallel way, by her relationship with Grandcourt.

At the other extreme of cosmic laws, the farthest reaches of Gwendolen's claim to power, are the unique impulses of her own nature which are, not paradoxically, as indifferent to her freedom as is universal causality; indeed, they are the same thing, in two different manifestations. What she learns, or should learn, at the roulette table is what she will be taught by her own irrepressible needs. The latter are as much circumstantial restrictions on her life as the former, notwithstanding the fact that they are physically contained in her, for they compel her to become involved with others and are no less antagonistic to that part of her that demands free choices than the statistical laws of gambling or Grandcourt's superior mastery of will. These needs, from which she first thinks herself exempt, render her vulnerable to Daniel entirely against her will.

It is true that at first Gwendolen sees Daniel as a potential conquest, much as she sees Grandcourt. But there is never any genuine question of choice in her submission to Daniel's influence as there is, on some level, in her decision to marry Grandcourt. Simply, Daniel answers the needs of her deepest insecurities. Here we see the full correspondence between Daniel's and Grandcourt's roles as well as the important psychological difference between them. To Grandcourt, Gwendolen is tied only in an external sense. She would leave him if she had the courage to endure the "scenes" Grandcourt would make, the distress she would cause her family, the social scandal that would ensue, and, above all, Daniel's judgment of her actions (pp. 453-454). Thus, Grandcourt becomes for her an objective fact illustrating concretely in her life the pressures of human dependence. Valuable as it is, this knowledge is not, however, internalized precisely because Grandcourt is so completely excluded from her inner existence. In relation to him, Gwendolen comes to see only where her power over external objects fails. But in relation to Daniel, she begins to discern that, whereas the external constrictions are real enough—and Daniel himself shares in enforcing this conviction—total human interdependence is not always played out in the contest between self and other but often between self and self; in the end, the battleground is Gwendolen's own consciousness, and she herself acquiesces, if sometimes bitterly, in her own contingency.

The events of the novel confirm this fact by removing first Grandcourt, then Daniel, from Gwendolen's life. She is once more alone, as she had been in the beginning. The external opportunity to declare herself free is once more available to her. But, far from rejoicing, Gwendolen can only promise Daniel that she " 'will try—try to live' " (p. 609). The proud independence with which she began has turned, in an awareness of limitations which no longer needs any external object to confirm it, into loneliness and self-doubt. There is no question now of conquest, only of survival. The sense of self standing statuesquely apart from an indistinct and insignificant background has yielded to a struggle in which a stoical resignation is necessary to sustain one's identity even in low relief.

Egoism: Patterns of Will

All that heredity and circumstance conspire to create at any given moment is what we distinguish at that moment as the "self" of a particular individual. And this self has a unique and compelling characteristic which does not grow out of either heredity—unless it is the common heredity of the species—or environment, but is, rather, an irreducible empirical property or organic matter. This property is egotism, that inclination of the self to be and remain entirely and fully what it is. In asserting its existence, the self demands absolute freedom and responds to any constraint with instant rebellion. Eliot agreed with Spencer, Darwin, Lewes, and Comte (as well as others) that natural selection had, randomly, propagated those in whom some degree of social sympathy existed, since these were the best able to survive in social conditions which, in turn, were necessary for the survival of the individuals in the species. Thus, we have characters in the novels who seem more open to others than those around them: Bob Jakin, Caleb Garth, Rev. Lyon, and occasionally one or two others. But these impulses to social sympathy are, compared with the very complex vision Eliot had of the nature of egotism, partial and weak.

"We are all of us born in moral stupidity," the narrator of *Middlemarch* remarks, "taking the world as an udder to feed our supreme selves." [17] What inspires this scathing remark on human nature is not one of the obvious egotists of the novel—not Rosamond or Featherstone, or even Fred Vincy—but, in fact, the apparently least egotistical character in the novel, Dorothea. "Dorothea had early begun to emerge from that stupidity," the narrator adds (p. 156), leaving the reader to conclude that, first, even Dorothea had not escaped the burden of this inheritance and, second, Dorothea, having only "begun to emerge," has yet a long struggle before her.

It is clear throughout *Middlemarch* that, tempted as we may be by conventional categories to exempt Dorothea from the self-seeking motives so obviously governing Rosamond, we must look in Eliot for a far more comprehensive definition of egotism than the common use of the term implies. The patterns of behavior which reveal the display of the will may seem, on more traditional lines, neutral or even altruistic, but there is no character in the novels who is not some kind of egotist, and every novel could well have been subtitled "Patterns of Will."

On the simplest level, there is the egotism of self-gratification. In this category, characters are largely impelled by their inclination to pleasure. Tessa is a typical example, for with her we come very close to the animal level of existence. She eats, she sleeps, she breeds. Her emotions, too, are entirely primitive. She is capable of fear and of a purring affection when she is secure and cared for. Something of this nature Eliot had already suggested in Hetty Sorrel. But Tessa is more a reduction than a duplication of Hetty, for Hetty has been brought to the point of having social as well as animal desires. Finery and position are for Hetty as important as food and shelter. Yet Hetty has no more consciousness of self than Tessa, and it is this that ultimately distinguishes these two characters as acting on the most fundamental and least complex level of egotism.

How powerful is the impulse to the primitive self-indulgence Tessa and Hetty practice is more clearly apparent in more complicated characters, where a rather basic egotism finds itself in conflict with contrasting inclinations. Esther Lyon, for example, is not only more intelligent but has as well an embryonic sensibility and some potential for sympathy. Her genuine tenderness for her adopted father makes it possible for us to believe, even in her worst moments, that there is a better side in her nature. Her vanity seems, in consequence, more superficial than Hetty's, whose whole internal existence it appears to consume. But Esther's vanity is quite as real as Hetty's and, in fact, more dangerous. In essence, both women want the same things: admiration, flattery, luxury, and position. But in Hetty these cravings take comparatively petty forms. New earrings, white stockings, and a carpeted parlor will be enough to make her happy. Esther, because she is more intelligent, better educated, in a higher social class, and, ultimately, endowed with a wider imagination, can satisfy her vanity only by a far deeper commitment to the worldly life.

Significantly, Eliot places Esther in a situation remarkably similar to Hetty's. Both are given a choice between two men, one of whom offers pleasure and the other the "honest" life, although half of Hetty's choice, of course, is entirely illusory. The similarity helps to focus very sharply on one vital difference. Hetty does not care for Adam and thinks, at least, that she does care for Arthur. If the opportunity were available, she could choose Arthur without conflict. Esther, on the other hand, does care for Felix, even before she herself is aware of it. Moreover, her feelings for Harold are not unlike Hetty's for Arthur, centered in the man but more genuinely aroused by his position. In Esther's case, then, it is much easier to distinguish the strength of ego which resists Felix, who threatens to humble her, and draws her to Harold. Even more, the primitive level of the ego is such that it is blind to the subtler humiliation to which Harold subjects her, particularly at the beginning of their relationship, the time at which Esther is most attracted to him. Felix at least takes Esther seriously enough to scold her, whereas Harold offers more readily the indifferent gallantries that flatter Esther's moral complacency because for him women are largely an adornment. When he comes to know Esther well enough to revise his first and harshest judgment of her, Felix recognizes the intensity of her conflict. " 'I do believe in you,' " Felix tells her, " 'but I want you to have such a vision of the future that you may never lose your best self' "; and " 'nothing but a good strong terrible vision will save you' " *(Felix Holt, p. 269)*.

In a scene whose theme and language realize Felix's prophecy, Esther finds her salvation. "The dimly-suggested tragedy" of Mrs. Transome's life, the narrator explains, "the dreary waste of years empty of sweet trust and affection, afflicted her even to horror. It seemed to have come as a last vision to urge her toward the life where the draughts of joy sprang from the unchanging fountains of reverence and devout love" (p. 479). But this cathartic moment does not come to Esther until the very end of the novel, long after she has begun to care deeply for Felix, long after she has ceased to find conscious satisfaction in Harold and the life he promises; the cravings of the ego linger irrationally beyond moral discovery and yield but slowly and with difficulty to the promptings of the better self.

Although Esther is considerably more intelligent than Hetty, her egotism, as I have suggested, is still the same unconscious egotism as Hetty's. While her intelligence modifies the ends toward which her ego drives her, it does not serve her egotism; quite the contrary, in fact, for it is Esther's intelligence that helps her to understand the different values Felix reveals to her. But it is on a more sophisticated level of egotism that we find characters like Harold Transome—a case structurally parallel in the novel —and Tito Melema. They too are given to a very basic self-gratification, but they are capable as well of self-interest, a new element which introduces the conscious will that enlists mental faculties in the fulfillment of the ego's demands.

The difference between these two levels becomes apparent if we contrast Harold and Tito to three men they partially resemble but who act more on impulse than on deliberation: Arthur Donnithorne, Fred Vincy, and Stephen Guest. On the whole,

Arthur is largely free of self-interest, despite the fact that for a long time he allows nothing to interfere with his pleasures. But Arthur resists intrusions on his gratifications without actual calculation; very much like Hetty, Arthur falls into action. He does what he likes, as does Fred Vincy. Both are equally incapable of malice, indeed the very opposite, for both are generally amiable creatures. So, in fact, is Stephen Guest. All three seem morally transitional figures between Hetty and Esther, with Stephen perhaps slightly ahead. In none is the potential for growth as rich as in Esther, but, unlike Hetty, each can at least formulate a generous attitude toward others; if they fail, as they do often, in acting as well as they intend it is because, as I will discuss later, they have not yet understood the nature of the real world or felt for others with the intensity that can conquer temptation. In contrast, Harold and Tito are not only capable of conscious calculation but so much so that they can, at times, deny themselves immediate enjoyment for the sake of subsequent advantage. Seldom do they act on the impulse of the moment, as Arthur and Fred—and even Stephen—do. Nor is intelligence in conflict with instinct, as it is in Esther, through most of Harold's and Tito's well-planned designs for success.

Harold and Tito do differ from one another, of course, in one vital point; in the moment of crisis, Harold shows himself a less hardened egotist than Tito and, in the end, accessible to human needs of a more social order. Even his return to Treby Magna, which we suspect at first of being merely another means of self-service—and is so to some degree, in any case—becomes partially understandable as a deeper desire for a return to the human world in which his emotional roots had been nurtured. Tito, on the other hand, can never be touched that deeply. If we compare Harold's love for Esther with Tito's for Romola, we see that Tito's ultimately dissolves in self-interest; his love is no less real for being shallow, but the very fact that it is real reveals how profoundly Tito's whole nature has been absorbed into the center of self.

This egotism, in introducing consciousness of will, adds a characteristic, merely latent in the most basic level, which transforms markedly the human relationships of the egotist. Paradoxically, it renders the intelligence, in which the consciousness arises, a source of special stupidity. The conscious egotist is an emotional solipsist, using others as objects to the degree that he is aware of his own deliberate purposes. There is virtually a categorical distinction in the minds of characters like Harold and Tito between themselves and others; the world outside the self becomes unreal in the psychological sense that other people are thought of not as creatures who have their own centers of self but as instruments to be used to one's own advantage.

It is in this consciousness that Eliot begins to find the possibility of a kind of evil which ultimately evolves in a character like Grandcourt. Grandcourt is, of course, a rather special case in Eliot, and I will return to him shortly. In the earlier novels, Eliot seems less convinced of the human capacity for such Dantesque deprivation. We have, consequently, less allegorical cases like Jermyn who can, at least, yield to more human passions than Grandcourt. Yet Jermyn is only a little less indifferent to others and no less capable of using others, including Mrs. Transome and their son, to fulfill his ambitions. Harold, who naturally resembles Jermyn to some degree, has happily inherited from his mother a capacity for guilt entirely lacking in his father. The contrast between Mrs. Transome and Jermyn is most marked in the remorse which the former is never able to escape from, even after so many years. Such guilt is always salutary, for it is a symptom of a suppressed conflict with a better self.

We see this very sharply in the contrast between the brothers Cass. Godfrey is no less an egotist than Dunstan, nor less inclined to regarding others as the tools of his own interest. But unlike Dunstan, Godfrey can feel guilt, and in developing Godfrey's story Eliot shows that even in the very using of other

people such guilt forms a progression in the making of a conscience. At first, Godfrey's actions arise in the simplest egotism:
his father is the instrument of his expected wealth, and his first
wife is, apparently, the object of a brief and aberrated lust. But
here, self-judgment is born in Godfrey. Nancy becomes a means
through which Godfrey hopes to undo the past and so relieve his
guilt; Eppie, in the end, he seeks to adopt as a way of assuaging
the still smarting conscience. But Godfrey, as Dunstan illustrates, is by no means the necessary case. The capacity for guilt
is not, it would seem, inborn in the species.

The distinction between Godfrey and Dunstan would suggest,
at first, that remorse is not altogether an advantage from the
purely egotistic point of view, for Godfrey comes to be tor-
mented by it. But such categorical distinctions between self and
not self as egotists like Jermyn and Dunstan make inevitably
isolate them in a way that seems to render even gratification
empty of joy. Characters like Rosamond Vincy—a supreme
egotist—remain, fundamentally, unsatisfied, whatever degree of
external success they achieve.

Rosamond is a rather typical character among those dedicated to self-interest, a fact which distinguishes her from Hetty
whom she otherwise resembles in many ways. Perhaps deliberately, Eliot constructs two points of similarity in their lives in
which their actions most sharply differentiate the levels of their
egotism. First, both Hetty and Rosamond set their marital
hopes on men who, at least at the time at which they make their
choices, are not accessible to them. Yet Rosamond succeeds and
Hetty fails. She fails, certainly, because her choice was less
realistic; but she fails as well because she lacks precisely what
Rosamond has, a clear vision of where her self-interest lies; the
very fact that Hetty's choice is less possible than Rosamond's is
part of this difference between them. Yet if Rosamond is
shrewder—and so better able to survive—she is also colder. Hetty
goes about her affairs stupidly but not without feelings all too
real. If her love for Arthur depends to a great degree on his

wealth and position, Hetty does not really know it; in her muddled mind the two are indistinct, and she yields to him the whole of her selfish little heart. Rosamond too is concerned with position, but she is able to distinguish it from the man quite clearheadedly. Although she likes Lydgate well enough, she has long before made her decision to marry a prominent stranger. We can be certain that Rosamond would never so far confuse the man with what she expects him to confer on her that she would, like Hetty, risk her own security.

The same distinction obtains in the manner in which the two manage their unwanted pregnancies. Hetty can think of no alternative to having her baby and, wanting it no more than Rosamond wants hers, feels forced to abandon it to die. Rosamond, on the other hand, precipitates a miscarriage, escaping consequences far less serious than those Hetty faced. Moreover, although the claims of the embryo may seem less pressing than those of the born child, she appears more deliberately capable of murder than Hetty, for Hetty is responsible for her baby's death somewhat inadvertently, leaving it in the woods in the hope that it would be found. Rosamond, one suspects, would never consider suicide at such a moment, as Hetty does, nor be drawn back, as Hetty is, by the crying in the woods. Yet, although in the end Rosamond always wins—even to the point of destroying Lydgate—she appears incapable of experiencing genuine pleasure. For Rosamond, nothing seems to be quite enough. The claims of the ego are endless and self-propagating; to the thoroughly undisciplined ego, fulfillment is, ultimately, impossible.

This characteristic in the nature of egotism has not yet reached in Rosamond the peak of frenzy. But in *Daniel Deronda* Eliot probes this darkest recess of the irrationality of will: in Gwendolen and, more deeply, in Grandcourt. Rosamond had once declared her uncompromising platform: " 'I never give up anything I choose to do' " *(Middlemarch,* p. 257). This, unfortunately, Lydgate had taken as a sign of her courage against her father's objections to their engagement but not as a hint of her subsequent behavior toward himself. Gwendolen, we learn, had the same "key to life," which was "doing as she liked" *(Daniel Deronda,* p. 99). Watching her, we cannot doubt it. But the assertion does not seem to mean quite the same thing in both cases. The very diction suggests this, Rosamond quite rightly using "choose"—a signal of deliberation—and the narrator of *Daniel Deronda* significantly omitting such a word. For Gwendolen, although she sometimes enjoys gratifying her craving for certain pleasures, is too unhappy on the whole to convince us that she seeks pure self-gratification; moreover, she seems often free even of self-interest, for she almost always fails, and we can attribute this, considering her intelligence, to miscalculation only up to a certain point. It is true she believes she can rule Grandcourt, not realizing, as the reader does, that Grandcourt too insists on the "gratification" of his "will" (p. 110). But perhaps it is true on one level only. On another, it seems as though Gwendolen always knew Grandcourt would debase and oppress her and married him because of it.

The hints of Gwendolen's pathology prepare us for such a conclusion. Her fierce virginity—she prefers to sleep in her mother's bed, does not like to be touched, and is invariably compared to Artemis—seems to lead her, through dark perversions, to undertake a bloodless contest of wills with Grandcourt. In Gwendolen we have, apparently, a diagram of the "sick will," the will so furiously intent on asserting itself that it happily concedes self-gratification, self-interest, even craves humiliation, as long as it senses itself alive. It is an aberration, no doubt, of the more moderate purpose of egotism, but at the same time a natural end of will taken to the extreme of self-expression.

This condition Eliot seems to have faintly foreshadowed in earlier characters. Mrs. Transome, for example, is early described by the narrator as a woman of "imperious will." In this sense, will is in no way identical with self-indulgence, which Mrs. Transome is also prone to, or with self-interest, something rather alien to her. It is, rather, a coercive force whose only end appears to be self-assertion. Thwarted in more meaningful ways, Mrs. Transome's will exerts itself "about smaller things. She was not cruel, and could not enjoy thoroughly what she called the old woman's pleasure of tormenting; but she liked every little sign of power her lot had left her" *(Felix Holt,* p. 31). This power, inevitably, can be tested and exerted only in relation to other wills. The ultimate criterion of power is one's ability to crush others, for the contest takes place on the primitive level of the irrational. Mrs. Transome controls her husband and Denner easily enough, for the one is weak and the other in her service. But for this very reason neither conquest is altogether satisfactory. It is Harold, her independent equal, whom she wishes to rule. "Mrs. Transome," the narrator remarks at their first meeting after Harold's return, "had not the feminine tendency to seek influence through pathos; she had been used to rule in virtue of acknowledged superiority"; "she cared especially that her son . . . should feel that he was come home to a mother who was to be consulted on all things" (p. 17). To this egotism, her son's love—which she courts less than his submission—can assume only a secondary importance.

We see the same tendency, to some degree caricatured, in Featherstone. All his life he has yielded the pleasure of company and amiable relationships for the sake of exercising a dominating will. In the climactic scene, enacted on his deathbed, Featherstone demands that his will—a pun undoubtedly, as it is when Casaubon binds Dorothea by his "will"—be altered according to his latest whim. The scene is not only typical but symbolic. Featherstone is a crotchety old man whose financial independence gives him greater freedom to do as he likes than most; but as he exercises this freedom, even he seems to suspect how volatile and mutable will is. Indeed, we begin to understand that it is the very essence of will that it be entirely inconsistent with itself in time, that at every moment it contradict its former and future identities; for, as Dostoevski's Underground Man explains at great length, we feel that we have this kind of freedom of the will only in the moment in which we use it, and we suspect it of being planned judgment or determined action unless its aim and result are irrational and explicitly deny consistency and reason. Thus, Featherstone must seek to enact, even in this last moment of his life, the impulse of will which asserts his free egotistic choice. At this moment of his imminent death, he can no longer be concerned with consequences to himself of his present actions; the act is purely self-assertive, an act of control over those who await the results of his decision. Irrationally, Featherstone feels thwarted when, to Mary Garth's objections that she places herself in jeopardy to tamper with legal matters, he cries with dying strength, " 'I shall do as I like' " *(Middlemarch, p. 234)*.

In a more complex way, the same pattern is true of Bulstrode. But here the ego finds fulfillment through a diabolic subtlety. Bulstrode's Christian name—an irony in definition—as well as its familiar form, "Nick," are hardly necessary as reminders of the Satanic sin through which he challenges his God by magnifying his own ego into the divine will. So converted, Bulstrode's will exercises itself on all who are vulnerable to it. But Bulstrode stops short of the complete extreme precisely because he finds the digression through God essential to his conscience. His religious feeling, however aberrated, is real; the final step to complete self-assertion is therefore impossible for him.

This is not the case with Grandcourt, who appears to be Eliot's darkest study of the implications of the nature of will. For Grandcourt, power to subject other wills is the highest gratification. But in its ultimate perversion, will craves not only such complete power but the opposition which makes the subsequent victory all the more exhilarating. As Gwendolen thrills at the risks of the gaming tables, then at the living wager that Grandcourt's proposal offers her, so Grandcourt gravitates to his most willful opponent. It is obvious that Grandcourt chooses Gwendolen neither for her beauty or virtues nor for his love of her. When Lush asks, sneeringly, " 'Have you fallen in love?' " Grandcourt can only answer " 'I am going to marry her' " *(Daniel Deronda,* p. 93), a statement which neither answers the question nor explains his decision but merely reasserts the impulse of his will. And, of equal significance, he is here acting clearly against his own self-interest. Lush recommends Miss Arrowpoint as a fitter object of pursuit, for she will come with a large dowry as Gwendolen will not; "'after your experience,'" Lush remonstrates, "'will you let a whim interfere with your comfortable settlement in life?' " (p. 92). But Lush is not very perceptive about such matters, especially since he is himself very thoroughly a man of self-interest. He cannot see that the very irrationality of Grandcourt's choice—the very fact that it is a "whim"—is, for Grandcourt, its ultimate justification.

In Gwendolen, Grandcourt senses the promise, implicit in her attitude, that she will be a difficult antagonist whose conquest will confirm the invulnerability of his own will. When Gwendolen flees his first proposal, Grandcourt is not displeased. "To have brought her so near a tender admission, and then to have walked headlong away from further opportunities of *winning the contest which he had made her understand him to be asking for,* was enough to provoke a girl of spirit; and *to be worth his mastering it was proper that she should have some spirit*" (p. 115; my italics). Of mere power, Grandcourt has enough. But characters like Lydia, already submissive, and Lush—on whom Grandcourt exercises his "peremptory will" (p. 92)—who cannot or would not oppose him are inadequate tests of his power. They do not offer the challenge without which the will cannot be entirely certain that it still has the strength to dominate. That is why Grandcourt's and Gwendolen's marriage progresses through a series of confrontations. The scene in which Grandcourt commands Gwendolen to wear the "poisoned diamonds" is, as the narrator says, "typical." Gwendolen's reluctance only spurs Grandcourt to further insistence. The fact that he rightly suspects Gwendolen's conscience as the cause of her refusal merely spices the contest. The more she objects, the firmer

Grandcourt's will becomes until even Gwendolen perceives that "his eyes showed a delight in torturing her." " 'He delights in making the dogs and horses quail,' " Gwendolen reflects; " 'that is half his pleasure in calling them his.' " " 'It will come to be so with me; and I shall quail' " (pp. 318-320).

Indeed, there is little difference between Grandcourt's attitude toward his animals and his attitude toward his wife. Quite clearly, Grandcourt confronts the whole animate world (as well as the inanimate, for he drowns in waters he knew to be dangerous and which he challenged precisely because they were) with the same passion to control. Early in the novel we had observed Grandcourt with his dogs. Although reputed to be an animal lover, Grandcourt seems to enjoy them only as objects of his control. Noticing that his water-spaniel, Fetch, is jealous that he has accidentally petted his Maltese dog, Fluff, Grandcourt raises Fluff deliberately to his chin and gives it caressing pats, all the while watching Fetch tortured by her master's neglect (pp. 90-91). With Gwendolen, too, he yields only to entice her to the next confrontation in which he can again exercise his control. In their relationship, Grandcourt also reminds one of the Underground Man, who, in the final section of *Notes*, must perennially search for new forms of attack on Lisa each time he manages to render her submissive. The consequences are, on the domestic level, no more desirable to Grandcourt than to Gwendolen; but for him, as in their courtship for her too, it is a matter of psychological priorities which, in the matter of will, must at this extreme always place the power of conquest first.

Self in Isolation: The Empirical Boundaries of Imagination

There is yet another form of egotism different in many ways from even the most extreme expression of the first and in one way at least more terrifying to contemplate. In a fundamental sense, Eliot maintains, every individual is born in complete isolation and in vital respects remains insular throughout his life. Irrevocably bound to the limits of his own consciousness —again, Eliot accepts the empiricist view—each man finds himself unable to participate directly in the equally isolated consciousness of another or to understand, even indirectly, its true nature. Each man sees, as a result, only from his own point of view, and can never know either the point of view of another or the objective fact as it really is. Perhaps in deliberate reply to Donne, Eliot writes to Mrs. Charles Bray that when

> I spoke of myself as an island, I did not mean that I was so exceptionally. We are all islands—
> "Each in his hidden sphere of joy or woe,
> Our hermit spirits dwell and roam apart"—
> ... When we are young we think ourselves a mighty business—that the world is spread out expressly as a stage for the particular drama of our lives and that we have a right to rant and foam at the mouth if we are crossed. ... But we begin at last to understand that these things are important only to one's own consciousness. *(Letters,* II, 156)

Partially remediable although this form of egotism is in certain cases, as Eliot suggests in her letter, so tenacious is the conviction of personal centricity, so clear the belief in personal truth of vision, that, unlike the earlier form of egotism, this kind is the more dangerous for feeling itself entirely accurate, even, at times, inspired. Locked in its own angle of interpretation, it actually sees its views confirmed in reality.

Hetty, for example, is obviously foolish to wish for Arthur. But she does more than wish. She imagines—that is, it is her interpretation of reality—that Arthur "couldn't like her to go on doing work; he would like to see her in nice clothes, and thin shoes and white stockings, perhaps with a silk clock to them; for he must love her very much—no one else had ever put his arm round her and kissed her in that way. He would want to marry

her, and make a lady of her" *(Adam Bede,* pp. 152-153). It would
not be accurate to say that Hetty is lying to herself, although
she is entirely mistaken. It would be of no use to ask Hetty to
look at the evidence; for she is looking at the evidence: had he
not put his arm round her and kissed her? It is, indeed, the very
sincerity of such egotism that makes it so potentially destructive. As the narrator of *Middlemarch* points out about Bulstrode, "the egoism which enters into our theories does not
affect their sincerity; rather, the more our egoism is satisfied,
the more robust is our belief" (p. 382). In explaining the harsh
decision of the judge before whom Felix is brought to trial, the
narrator stresses a subtle distinction. It "was not that the judge
had severe intentions; it was only that he saw with severity"
(Felix Holt, p. 459). The gentleman is no less worthy than most
of his profession, and had he come with "severe intentions" he
might have suspected himself of bias. But the condition Eliot
describes is beyond self-criticism; with the strictest honesty,
which has no relation to objective truth or fairness, he can find
Felix guilty and never reflect that his judgment is severe.

As Eliot conceives him, man is, in his natural state, imprisoned in a chamber of mirrors in which wherever he turns he
sees only himself. In the novels, in fact, we frequently assume
the egotist's point of view by standing with him before his own
reflection. And the egotists of the novels are habitually attracted to mirrors. Arthur, for example, cannot resist the
temptation of glancing at himself, briefly, as he passes a mirror
(Adam Bede, p. 124); Gwendolen often kisses "her fortunate
image in the glass" *(Daniel Deronda,* p. 317); and one of our first
impressions of Rosamond finds her arranging her beautiful hair
before a mirror *(Middlemarch,* p. 83). More than any other
character, Hetty seeks and finds her reflection everywhere. Not
only does she indulge in long hours before he own looking glass
in her room *(Adam Bede,* pp. 150 ff.), but, characteristically, she
converts into mirrors objects which were meant to serve other
functions, such as Mrs. Poyser's furniture, where she constantly

searches for her image in the highly polished surfaces (p. 72, for example).

That characters like Hetty or Rosamond are so imprisoned in their own visions is not surprising. But in Eliot's view there are no exceptions to this kind of isolation. Even those characters who have passed or bypassed those first stages of egotism in which they insisted on pleasure or self-interest, even those born with a higher degree of social sympathy, must still contend with this second kind of egotism, which tends to close to every consciousness the reality outside the self. The specific nature of the individual has, in this matter, nothing to do with this inescapable law of human nature, the "superior" having as little natural capacity as the "inferior" to find a point of pivot outside their own selves.

It is enlightening to compare Eliot's view on this question with John Stuart Mill's assumption of a wider comprehension in "superior" people. Attempting to modify Bentham's purely quantitative scale of pleasure, Mill declares that choices should be made on a qualitative distinction between kinds of pleasure. Confronted with the obvious difficulty of proving that such a qualitative scale exists, Mill adduces the testimony of the "superior" man who, supposedly, has experienced both kinds. "It is better," Mill concludes, "to be a human being dissatisfied than a pig satisfied; better to be a Socrates dissatisfied, than a fool satisfied. And if the fool or the pig are of a different opinion, it is because they only know their own side of the question. The other party to the comparison knows both sides." [18] In a passage in *Adam Bede* Eliot refutes such a hypothesis and argues that an assumption such as Mill's, that Socrates can know the pleasure of the fool as well as of the wise man and can therefore judge between them, confuses external and internal facts. Socrates can indeed participate in the activities of the fool, while the fool can obviously not participate in the activities of Socrates, namely, philosophy, but the degree and kind of pleasure an experience yields are purely subjective matters, Socrates being in no better a position than others to judge for anyone but himself. In connection with Dinah, the narrator remarks that it "is our habit to say that while the lower nature can never understand the higher, the higher nature commands a complete view of the lower. But I think the higher nature has to learn this comprehension . . . by a good deal of hard experience" (p. 163). We are, as Eliot suggests, easily convinced that Hetty cannot understand Dinah, but ready to believe that Dinah can understand Hetty. Confused perhaps by the traditional metaphors of "higher" and "lower," we often fail to focus on the real distinction, which is not the nature of the people but the fact that they are two separate and therefore isolated individuals.

The novels offer a series of contrasts such as is typified by Hetty and Dinah, contrasts between egotistic visions at various stages of evolution, with the inevitable suggestion that purely selfish motives are no more insulating than self-referenced interpretations of reality, however "noble" the intentions. A passage whose beginning I quoted earlier in connection with the first kind of egotism develops this very point about Dorothea, a figure who would not, traditionally, be subject to such a charge. "We are all of us born in moral stupidity, taking the world as an udder to feed our supreme selves; Dorothea had early begun to emerge from that stupidity, but," the narrator continues significantly, "it had been easier to her to imagine how she would devote herself to Mr. Casaubon, and become wise and strong in his strength and wisdom, than to conceive . . . that he had an equivalent centre of self, whence the lights and shadows must always fall with a certain difference" *(Middlemarch,* pp. 156-157).

The key here is the recognition that each has a different "centre of self," an otherness in relation to everything else in the world. In such close relationships as those between Dorothea and Casaubon, Maggie and Tom, Romola and Tito, Adam and Hetty, Dinah and Hetty, Felix and Esther, Lydgate and Rosamond, we see, certainly, the corrosive effect of the less imaginative, less comprehensive, characters. Tom and Casaubon—and one must add Nancy Cass, who rather resembles them—are paradigmatic cases in Eliot of characters who, if implacably honest to their own most rigid standards, are fortressed inside the narrow testimony of their identities, not because they are intolerant of other possibilities, but because they can no more imagine such possibilities than Mill's "fool" could grasp Platonic Forms, even with the help of the plainest dialectic. Yet just as the second of each pair cannot enter the internal reality of the first, so the first too cannot fully enter the internal reality of the second. Identities are mutually exclusive. The difficulties in each relationship are mostly the responsibility of both characters rather than of one.

There is a difference, of course, between such characters as Lydgate and Rosamond, Dorothea and Casaubon, Romola and Tito; it is a difference in the imaginative capacity which can profit from the experience to which the narrator of *Adam Bede* referred in Dinah's case (see p. 106, above). But it is, obviously, a skill to be learned—and a difficult one—not a natural gift. By nature, it is inherent in every individual to assume himself not only the center of the universe but the characteristic sample of the species. So Mrs. Davilow believes Gwendolen overstates her misfortune when she faces the necessity of working as a governess, and asks her not to " 'exaggerate evils.' " In reply, Gwendolen wonders how anyone " 'can know I exaggerate, when I am speaking of my feelings'" (*Daniel Deronda,* p. 205). Evaluating the situation from her own point of view, Mrs. Davilow meant, but did not know it, that such a prospect would not be as terrible to her as to be suitably described in Gwendolen's strong language. She missed, thus, Eliot's crucial point, namely, that if the objective world is the same for all, it impresses itself differently on each individual. Feeling and its cause do not have an invariable relationship. Only Gwendolen, as she says, can know whether or not something is a catastrophe to her.

Because each is born in this natural isolation, even imagination can project itself only to subjective degrees. So closely are the limits of understanding confined to the contents of our own internal lives that even that pseudo-knowledge that may be gained of others must be gained through comparison to the self. To "shift one's point of view beyond certain limits is impossible to the most liberal and expansive mind," the narrator of *Adam Bede* comments. "We are none of us aware of the impression we produce on Brazilian monkeys of feeble understanding—it is possible they see hardly anything in us" (p. 208). Ventures into conjecture of what the not self might be must remain, in the end, subjective. Ultimately, only one's own pain is real.

Notes

1. Cross, III, 33.

2. The subject has been a matter of debate among critics for some time. Some, like Hyde, Cecil, Preyer, Wagenknecht, Haight, see no determinism in Eliot's novels. Others, like George Levine and Bernard Paris, argue that Eliot was a determinist.

3. It seems likely that Bray's view had some influence on Eliot's thought if only as a catalyst at a period in her life, in their earliest acquaintance, when Eliot's convictions were undergoing their most radical transformation. Gordon S. Haight gives a full account of their friendship in the *Biography* and Bernard Paris, in *Experiments,* studies more closely the philosophic impact on Eliot of Bray's ideas.

4. It will appear, for example, in significant places in passages that will be quoted in this chapter on pp. 57, 73, 75, 80, and 81.

5. For example, the conviction as well as the model of the analogy in this passage from *Daniel Deronda* had appeared before in the passage in which Eliot described, as a binding center to a major theme in the novel, Lydgate's (and her own) concept of imagination (see p. 00 above).

6. Eliot's familiarity with the literature on this controversial point is difficult to estimate. She was undoubtedly well acquainted with Aristotle, for even before she helped Lewes through his long study of Aristotle, she refers—with the unconscious ease that suggests complete absorption—to Aristotle's terminology (as in her discussion of *Antigone* [*Essays,* p. 262]). She had studied Kant, on whom she wrote an

article for the *Leader* in October 1855. She was probably familiar with Berkeley, if only through Lewes's interest in him (see *Letters,* IV, 501), although if this is her first acquaintance it comes rather late, in 1868. How much of Hobbes, Locke, Hume, Leibniz, and Descartes she had read is impossible to say; we do know, from the fact that she translated his work, that her knowledge of Spinoza was extensive.

7. That Aristotle's meaning is not always clear does not affect the basic distinction with which I am concerned here. Nor does the elaborate philosophic literature on the ramifications of the controversy between essentialism and nonessentialism have much bearing on what seems to be Eliot's main focus. Eliot was, I am suggesting, not attempting—at least not in the novels—to solve a philosophic debate but rather to clarify for herself principles of human nature and so of fictional characterization. And in this attempt she was, I think, following by conviction the main lines of British empiricism and directing them into previously little explored applications.

8. *A History of Western Philosophy* (New York, 1945), pp. 9-10. The echo of Hume's "bundle of perceptions," obvious in Russell's statement, seems also to have inspired Eliot's language in a letter written in July 1870 in which she refers to "the small bundle of facts that make our own personality" *(Letters,* V, 107).

9. It is of course impossible to develop every character of every novel to quite the extent necessary to this conviction. But those characters on whom the novels focus are so developed and suggest, I think, an analogical statement about the others.

10. This is commonly the argument of recent criticism. W. J. Hyde believes that Eliot's realism is contingent on the fact that "character, not events, lies at the center of George Eliot's novels" ("George Eliot and the Climate of Realism," *PMLA,* 72 [March 1957], 164). Richard Stang, in "The Literary Criticism of George Eliot" *(PMLA,* 72 [December 1957], 955), points to this as one of Eliot's touchstones of literary criticism.

11. *Essential Works of John Stuart Mill* (New York, 1961), p. 103. The similarity of Eliot's view to Mill's on this point was brought to my attention by Prof. William E. Buckler.

12. V. S. Pritchett, for example, suggests that Eliot was "punishing" herself and that Hetty "had to suffer" for the " 'sins' " her author had committed and "for which, to her perhaps unconscious dismay, she

herself was never punished" *(The Living Novel* [New York, 1947], p. 91). Such interpretations seem to me biographically rash and aesthetically both inadequate and unnecessary.

13. In this respect, Eliot is a true heir—although with a tremendous difference—of the Godwinian novel.

14. The review itself was unsigned. In *George Eliot and Her Readers,* Lerner and Holmstrom suggest Hutton (p. 6). The facts that the review appeared on July 18, 1863, and that its content corresponds with issues Eliot raised in her letter to Hutton (August 8, 1863) about his review of *Romola* tend to confirm this conclusion. Although Eliot remarks in her letter that had she been "called on to expound my own book, there are things that I should want to say, or things that I should say somewhat otherwise," she acknowledges that she "can point to nothing in your exposition of which my consciousness tells me that it is erroneous, in the sense of saying something which I neither thought nor felt" *(Letters,* IV, 96-97).

15. *George Eliot and Her Readers,* p. 61.

16. See, for example, *Middlemarch,* pp. 105 and 607, and *The Mill on the Floss,* p. 313.

17. In his note to this passage, Gordon Haight argues with Kettle's supposition that the statement commits Eliot to determinism, seeing rather that the concept of free will is implicit in it. To the degree that the passage suggests that man is determined, by the nature of the species, to be born an egotist, Haight is, I believe, mistaken. (See *Middlemarch,* p. 156 n.1.)

18. "Utilitarianism," *The Philosophy of John Stuart Mill,* p. 333.

CHAPTER III

Knowledge and Morality

Will and Destiny:
A Collision of Forces

Impelled by his ego, man challenges, consciously or not, the destiny of natural laws. It is in this contest that Eliot finds the "collision of forces" which is the "germ of tragedy" ("Liszt, Wagner, and Weimar," *Essays,* p. 104). The tragedy begins, significantly, in neither one power nor the other; both are neutral forces, and even the fact that they collide is but another neutral law in the workings of the universe. Man is, in a sense, the unfortunate battlefield of the contest.

In her early Christian zeal, especially in her letters to Maria Lewis, Eliot speaks often and with passion of the intrinsic evil of egotism, of the intrinsic good of self-abasement, and of the benevolent deity who fixed the former as a moral maxim and provided man with many opportunities of benefiting from the latter. "I set so high a value on 'the sweet uses of adversity' that I am in danger of failing in sympathy for those who are experiencing it," Eliot writes in one letter; "and yet the word of God is not more express on any point than on the inevitable endurance of suffering to the Christian more peculiarly than to the worldling and on the special blessings derived from that endurance" *(Letters,* I, 15-16). But, as she relinquished Christianity and at last religion altogether, Eliot rejected, as fully as she did the likelihood of God's existence, her belief in the inherent evil of egotism.[1] By the time she came to write fiction, and indeed long before, Eliot had neutralized egotism in precisely the same way in which she had neutralized cosmic forces; in fact, the two constitute a correlative logic. For when God—so might the argument run—is seen as the moral center of the cosmic order, it is obvious that any action man takes against the laws He has enjoined must be in itself evil. But in an indifferent universe, such as Eliot's novels reveal, there can be no sin, although there is much error. The criterion has shifted from obedience to God's laws to the promotion of human welfare. As Feuerbach urged, man becomes his own god, owing allegiance to himself partly because there is nothing else for him to owe allegiance to. In a letter to Francois D'Albert-Durade in which Eliot explains her evolution from her early militant atheism to a more sympathetic understanding of the human ideals of Christianity, she remarks that, nevertheless, the "immediate object and the proper sphere of all our highest emotions are our struggling fellow-men and this earthly existence" *(Letters,* III, 230-231). With Bentham, Mill, Comte, and others, and for very much the same reasons, Eliot lifts the conventional restraints on egotism.

No longer unacceptable in the conventional sense, egotism falls, however, under the far stricter jurisdiction of cosmic necessity. It is not evil, but it is impossible as a rule of life. The "facts of existence compel obedience at our peril," Eliot writes.[2] The contest between will and destiny is highly unequal. Our sympathy, as I will discuss in the next chapter, is entirely with the struggling individual, but power is in the immutable laws that govern man's life.[3] Generally, to act in egotism is to live in illusion. In what is likely a reference to a scientific illustration called to her attention by Herbert Spencer, Eliot defines the problem through the narrator of *Middlemarch.*

> An eminent philosopher among my friends . . . has shown me this pregnant little fact. Your pier-glass or extensive surface of polished steel ... will be minutely and multitudinously scratched in all directions; but place now against it a lighted candle as a centre of illumination, and lo! the scratches will be seen to arrange themselves in a fine series of concentric circles round that little sun. It is demonstrable that the scratches are going everywhere impartially, and it is only your candle which produces the flattering illusion of concentric arrangement, its light falling with an exclusive optical selection. (pp. 194-195)

Whatever "flattering" concentric arrangement of facts egotism is inclined to see, reality is independent of man's will and, moreover, inescapable. For the same reasons that Homer found the euphoric life among the lotos eaters undesirable, Eliot declares that "it is better to suffer with real suffering than to be happy in the imagination of an unreal good" *(Letters,* IV, 13).

Eliot's view in this matter is, in fact, very Greek, as she recognizes.[4] As a test and a clarification of her own convictions, Eliot looks to Greek tragedy and finds there her own definition entirely confirmed. The Greeks, she adds, "were not taking an artificial, entirely erroneous standpoint which disappeared altogether with their religion and their art. They had the same essential elements of life presented to them as we have, and their art symbolised these in grand schematic forms." [5] In fixing as the center of tragedy the collision of will and destiny, Eliot, indeed, is reasserting what the Greeks had expressed in the relation between hybris and nemesis, terms so completely parallel to Eliot's that hers seem more than likely to be a translation of the Greek.[6] In "schematic form," the Hellenic gods personify those forces which Eliot's demythologized universe defines in more scientific terms; and Eliot's concept of human will is prefigured, in that condition of egotism in which man attempts what is beyond his power, in hybris. Like will, hybris is an inherently neutral term, and like destiny, the nemesis of the gods is amoral.

Eliot defines her concept of nemesis implicitly in a review of Harriet Beecher Stowe's *Dred: A Tale of the Great Dismal Swamp.*[7] The error that Eliot finds perverts even Mrs. Stowe's best intentions is the "absence of any proportionate exhibition of the negro character in its less amiable phase." Mrs. Stowe's novel, Eliot continues, "loses by it the most terribly tragic element in the relation of the two races—the Nemesis lurking in the vices of the oppressed" ("Three Novels," *Essays,* pp. 327-328). *Dred* is a prescriptive novel and lacks, therefore, an accurate description of the reality of the causal connection in human psychology. The nemesis, as Eliot writes, that the novel avoids dealing with is not an event in some projected future about which various speculations may have equal degrees of probability. It is already in existence, *in* the vices of the oppressed; although still "lurking," and so not evident to all, it is nevertheless inevitable, a potential energy in the hybris of the oppressors waiting to be released by the impact of time.

Knowledge as Virtue

It is in the context of this fairly rigidly fixed contest between will and destiny that Eliot looks for her moral criteria. What she finds is two different but related standards of action, both of which she suggests in her notes to *The Spanish Gypsy* while analyzing a hypothetical case in answer to the question "what is the fact about our individual lots?" She imagines a woman with some "inherited misfortunes" and remarks that the "utmost approach to well-being that can be made in such a case is through large resignation and acceptance of the inevitable, with as much effort to overcome any disadvantage as good sense will show to be attended with a likelihood of success." [8]

The first principle of Eliot's morality is that whatever cannot be changed must be accepted. This is an empirical truism, and it is, in fact, as such that it recommends itself to Eliot. It is one, however, which Eliot felt had been generally rejected as a premise in conventional morality which had prescribed actions (not necessarily undesirable in Eliot's view either) with a reckless indifference to the possible. In one of his political speeches, Felix Holt remarks that a "fool or idiot is one who expects things to happen that never can happen" (p. 261). In this Felix speaks for Eliot. In her notes to *The Spanish Gypsy,* Eliot had defined morality ("our determination as to the right") as consisting in an "adjustment of our individual needs to the dire necessity of our lot." [9] Destiny does not demand morality, but what destiny demands becomes, for Eliot, a moral requirement. For this reason, in her review of *The Progress of the Intellect,* Eliot had enthusiastically supported Mackay's conclusion that "the seal of prohibition and of sanction, are effectually impressed on human deeds and aspirations ... by that inexorable law of consequence; ... and human duty is comprised in the earnest study of this law and patient obedience to its teaching" *(Essays,* p. 31). Against the opposite view of human duty she energetically argues in her notes to *The Spanish Gypsy.* "That favourite view, expressed so often in Clough's poems," she writes, "of doing duty in blindness as to the result, is likely to deepen the substitution of egoistic yearnings for really moral impulses. We cannot be utterly blind to the results of duty, since that cannot be duty which is not already judged to be for human good. To say the contrary is to say that mankind have reached no inductions as to what is for their good or evil." [10] Especially interesting in this passage is that the alternative to "really moral impulses" is "egoistic yearnings"; again, as we drift away from the compulsion of fact, we are drawn into the illusion of self-reference through which we lose the opportunity of achieving genuine "human good."

The laws of destiny are all rigidly inflexible. But those in which human beings participate may be, through that very participation, redirected in humanly more desirable ways. As she wrote in a letter to Sara Hennell, Eliot believed that while man was "in subjection to the external world," he also "to a certain extent controls it" *(Letters,* IV, 204). And Eliot's morality stresses, as much as the necessary concession to inexorable power, the equally necessary effort to do whatever "good sense will show to be attended with a likelihood of success." This aspect of morality becomes an attempt to mitigate what little it is possible to mitigate of the tragic confrontation which defines human existence. This, in effect, Eliot had explained as her position to John Morley when she wrote that a "growing moral force" would have to "lighten the pressure of hard non-moral outward conditions" *(Letters,* IV, 364-365). Eliot's moral criterion of human welfare makes this second moral end a logical complement, in antithesis, of the first.

To both these moral requirements man is born hostile. The natural egotism which subjectifies his perception of the external world keeps man in ignorance of the laws which he is compelled to obey, of the opportunities through which he may improve his lot, and of the difference between the two. Nothing is for Eliot as antagonistic to human welfare as this ignorance, although the opposite usually appears true to the egotist, who is impatient of restraints, and it is for this reason that Eliot arrived at the basically Hellenic stipulation that knowledge is virtue.[11] The indifferent universe responds to nothing else. Where will and destiny merge, instinctual conduct is enough. But where they do not, even that limited power man has can be perverted for lack of the knowledge which makes the difference between failure and survival.

But knowledge for Eliot has a far more comprehensive meaning than the merely intellectual which it commonly suggests. Just as there is a knowledge which teaches man how to objectify the world so that he may know the difference between self and that which has an existence independent of the self, so there is a knowledge in a sense opposite to the first through which man subjectifies that which is not self and so learns to know it truly, from the center of its own identity. One is intellectual; for the other no English word is quite adequate. In her essay on Young, Eliot remarked that on "its theoretic and perceptive side, morality touches science"; but morality had as well an emotional side *(Essays,* p. 379). Although the two must in the end be synthesized, they have very different existences in human psychology and must be cultivated, if not independently, at least not on the assumption that one will invariably evoke the other.

Intellectual Knowledge: The Distinction Between Self and Other

Essentially, Eliot's diagnosis of one of the most destructive of human errors concerns the fact that man reacts when he should act. Impelled blindly by the will (and all that that involves), human conduct has its roots in the past; yet the creation of a better life, of success to some degree, depends on man's looking forward, on his evaluating actions for the sake of shaping the consequences of the future. Such a moral requirement is an implicit demand for man to escape his determinants, the passions of his will, for as long as he is driven by these, he is a victim, not an agent, of the future. Yet among the facts of which Eliot was reasonably certain was that the irrational was inescapable. Here, the tragic collision is enacted again and again. As a willing animal, as the product of his past, man is almost trapped into an inevitable march to defeat.

Almost, but not entirely. If will cannot be rooted out, it can be subdued, transformed; if the deterministic chain cannot be broken,[12] it can be interrupted. The preponderance of what constitutes human nature for Eliot can look only backward, can do nothing more than fulfill the laws of its evolving nature. But

117

thought, alone among human faculties, can escape and intervene between impulse or determinant and action; it can become, in fact, another determinant (but of a different kind), although it can do so only when it has itself been freed from its own habits of the past and its dependence on will. The point is succinctly illustrated—significantly in an allusion to Greek mythology—in an illuminating passage in *Daniel Deronda*. Like Phaethon, Gwendolen had "wished to mount the chariot and drive the plunging horses herself" (p. 99). The narrator need not add that Phaethon, willful and ignorant of his limitations, crashed to the ground in a fiery holocaust, destroying himself and many others, even threatening the end of the world. It was not that the horses could not be driven; it was just that Phaethon did not know how.

Genuine thought, however, is extremely difficult. Even where the capacity for thought exists, man turns, far more naturally, to the daydreaming and fantasy more satisfying to the ego. Nowhere is the need for, or the difficulty of, thought so well defined as in those characters who, having in some form benevolent intentions and adequate or even superior understanding, lack, nevertheless, the kind of thought necessary to implement their best purposes.

Characters of this kind divide themselves, roughly, into two groups. In one are some of those who are also rather primitively selfish: Arthur Donnithorne, Godfrey Cass, Fred Vincy, even Esther Lyon. These characters tend to be vain and weak. Yet the unhappy consequences they often effect are not always the result of egotism, for they are amiable and generally well-intentioned individuals. Unlike characters like Grandcourt, Lush, Dunstan Cass, Rosamond, and others, they exhibit a certain sensitivity, low-level but real. What perverts, rather, their best purposes is their helplessness in the face of a reality which they interpret in purely subjective terms. Their judgments, that is, are not in conflict with their egotism but dependent on it; the distinction between hope and thought is so obliterated that, even while indulging themselves in the former, they genuinely believe they are engaging in the latter.

Fred Vincy, who reminds one a great deal of Arthur Donnithorne, is a prototypical character in this group. A thoroughly appealing young man, he has managed to win the affections of the sensible Mary Garth even against her better judgment. As Caleb Garth knows, there is a considerable potential for good in Fred, although none of it has been realized at the opening of the novel. Yet even the reader is hopeful about Fred, as he is not about Fred's sister, for Fred is not only incapable of malice but has not even Rosamond's indifference to the claims of others. Quite the contrary; his egotism is entirely unconscious. He wishes others well and would be ashamed to take advantage of them. But what he does do—which comes to the same thing—is assume in all his calculations that the function of the universe is to make him happy. From that premise all his actions follow with faultless logic. Illusion and reality are confronted in the novel, characteristically for Eliot, in the contrast between Fred's projection of the future and the evolving consequences in his story. In the second half of the novel, Fred's growing maturity is measured by the increasing convergence of these two lines.

From his egocentric interpretation of his place in the scheme of things emerge the two chief problems in Fred's life: money and love. In both, Fred believes himself thwarted by the arbitrary stubbornness of old Featherstone and Mary Garth, for he sincerely, even humbly, considers himself the proper object of the former's will and the latter's affection. From the first, Fred is in debt. This situation has developed because, ironically, from Fred's point of view it is not he who is in debt, his financial deficit being a mysterious contradiction to the fact that it is the world which is in debt to him. Thus, again in Fred's view, he does not borrow irresponsibly. The inheritance he expects from Featherstone is not to him a possibility or a probability but a fact, in the potential world to be sure, but to be inevitably actualized in time.

Moreover, his promissory notes do not draw, exactly, on these expectations, although he had spoken "with some confidence (perhaps with more than he exactly remembered) about his prospect of getting Featherstone's land as a future means of paying present debts" *(Middlemarch,* p. 81). In Fred's mind that, certainly, is a more than necessary concession to caution.

Of the objectivity required to learn from negative evidence Fred has as yet very little . Thus, when Featherstone threatens that he can still alter his will (p. 81), Fred assumes that the old man wants only to "exercise his power by tormenting him a little." The insight is a dramatic demonstration of the defense illusion raises against knowledge. Perceptive enough to probe, thus, to the very core of Featherstone's motive, Fred cannot, on the other hand, imagine the implied possibility that Featherstone may continue to exercise his power and torment him more than "a little" by fulfilling his threat. Half of what Fred saw in his uncle's actions was, the narrator remarks, "the reflex of his own inclinations. The difficult task of knowing another soul is not for young gentlemen whose consciousness is chiefly made up of their own wishes" (p. 89). Eliot's language here leaves little doubt as to her meaning; Fred's "reflex" assumption is prompted by the sincere belief that others share his own self-concern.

In miniature, the problem is reenacted when Fred brings Featherstone the letter in which Bulstrode attests to Fred's good character. Although he denies it, Fred expects not only to receive the present Featherstone had mentioned at their earlier meeting but, indeed, that it will be large enough to deliver him from his debts. "Fred was of a hopeful disposition," the narrator adds; when he "got into debt, it always seemed to him highly probable that something or other—he did not necessarily conceive what—would come to pass enabling him to pay in due time." At this moment, Fred believes, the "providential occurence" is at hand (p. 99). Here we are very much aware that, unlikely as the comparison at first appears, Fred has become a structural parallel to Bulstrode. The two are presented in entirely different modalities, but like Bulstrode, although unconsciously, Fred assumes himself the special concern of a cosmic power. It is to this attitude that the narrator ironically refers when, a moment later, Fred discovers that the banknotes Featherstone gives him "actually presented the absurdity of being less than his hopefulness had decided that they must be. What can the fitness of things mean, if not their fitness to a man's expectations? Failing this, absurdity and atheism gape behind him" (p. 100).

In Fred's mind there is a very strict connection between the two chief difficulties in his life. For Eliot too the connection is very strict, although it is entirely different from the one Fred conceives. When Fred discovers that Featherstone's will, like his earlier gift, falls far short of his expectations, he is "utterly depressed." "'Twenty-four hours ago he had thought that instead of needing to know what he should do, he should by this time know that he needed to do nothing: that he should hunt in pink, have a first-rate hunter, ride to cover on a fine hack, and be generally respected for doing so; moreover, that he should be able at once to pay Mr. Garth, and that Mary could no longer have any reason for not marrying him. And all this was to have come without study or other inconvenience, purely by the favour of providence in the shape of an old gentleman's caprice" (p. 250). At this moment, Fred's life has reached its climactic crisis. No more prospects such as Featherstone's estate are before him; somehow, events have behaved unreasonably. But in preparation for this scene Eliot has given us another, foreshadowing the climax, in which we see not only the collision of Fred's illusion and the reality of facts but the utter helplessness of Fred's good intentions inherent in his miscalculation of effects.

The creditor to whom Fred owed a hundred and sixty pounds, we had learned earlier, held in security a bill for that amount signed by Caleb Garth. In this fact Eliot connects, in their external aspects, Fred's financial and romantic problems, placing Fred—who, in any case, would not have wished to defraud anyone—under the double pressure of repaying his debt and not failing Mary by disappointing her father. So determined is Fred, in fact, to act honorably that he even thinks of the precaution of depositing eighty of the hundred pounds Featherstone had given him with his mother, out of temptation's way. But the very form of Fred's precaution is, ironically, a psychological subterfuge against precaution, for, as the narrator suggests, he might better have given the money directly to Mr. Garth (p. 172). It is not that Fred means to cheat Caleb nor, at this point, that he would consider indulging his taste for small luxuries. Indeed, we have never known Fred more in earnest, and it is, as far as motive is concerned, his very sincerity that will thwart him now.

Featherstone's gift had fallen sixty pounds short of Fred's debt, and this amount Fred is resolved to raise before his note comes due. It is true that at this time in his life Fred has no apparent means of earning money. But this is part of Eliot's central statement about Fred. Of time and opportunity Fred has had enough to find a driection for his life. Yet the comfort of an upper-middle-class household, the expectation of an inheritance, and his own general hopefulness about the future had made preparation for a career seem an unnecessary "inconvenience." Mary's refusal to accept him until he proves better than he appears seems to him an unreasonable demand. " 'I should not have made a bad fellow if I had been rich,' " Fred justifies himself. For Mary's sake, he suggests, he might undertake something concrete, but only if he could be sure of her love. " 'Might, could, would,' " Mary replies, " 'are contemptible auxiliaries' " (pp. 102-103). Here, of course, Eliot implies the real connection between the two poles of Fred's dilemma. Inexplicably, he has suffered setbacks in both, but these are to him still exceptions to the cosmic law which guarantees his welfare. In this frame of mind he continues to believe that his persistence will overcome Mary's reluctance and that the next turn of fate will provide what he needs to pay his debts.

It was on this assumption that Fred had kept twenty of Featherstone's hundred pounds in his pocket, as a "sort of seed-corn, which, planted by judgment, and watered by luck, might yield more than threefold—a very poor rate of multiplication when the field is a young gentleman's infinite soul, with all the numerals at command" (p. 172).[13] In this preclimactic scene, as Fred begins a series of actions prompted by his excellent intention of making good his own debts, but based on assumptions conceived in egotistic hopefulness rather than on objective reasoning on empirical evidence, Eliot alludes repeatedly to the contrast between what Fred sincerely imagines to be the nature of things and the actual state of affairs. Fred, the narrator assures us, is not that kind of gambler who feverishly risks ruin; on the contrary, he does nothing but what his "judgment" promises success in. In fact, from his own point of view, he is not a gambler at all, for what may look like a risk to others Fred enters with a "joyous imaginative activity which fashions events according to desire." "Hopefulness," the narrator continues, "has a pleasure in making a throw of any kind, because the prospect of success is certain."

Although again and again, the consequences prove his expectations wrong, Fred is never disappointed. As dogmatic in his faith as is Bulstrode, Fred continues to interpret events in terms of theory—in his case an unconscious assumption—rather than to formulate theory in terms of events. The twenty pounds is quickly lost, but, Fred concludes, it had been planted in a "seductive green plot." The burden of guilt, once more, is on the universe. Fred's successive resolutions, such as they are, digress every so often into reality. Close to the term of payment but with no money beyond the eighty pounds which he had deposited with his mother, Fred decides to raise whatever additional money he can by selling his horse. The transition from this decision to the plan Fred quickly substitutes for it is a superb illustration of egotism reshuffling possibilities until it can conclude, in all sencerity, that its own wishes are also the ends toward which all creation moves.

The sale of his horse Fred contemplates with "a sense of

heroism," for it is a "sacrifice"; without the horse "life would certainly be worth little." But the "dread of breaking his word to Mr. Garth," his "love for Mary and awe of her opinion" allow him no alternative. "He would start for Houndsley horse-fair which was to be held next morning, and—simply sell his horse, bringing back the money by coach?—Well, the horse would hardly fetch more than thirty pounds, and there was no knowing what might happen; it would be folly to balk himself of luck beforehand. It was a hundred to one that some good chance would fall in his way." Reentering his fantasy world between two dashes, Fred elaborates an argument far more acceptable to his egotism until he believes that the most responsible action he can take is to reclaim the eighty pounds from his mother and await his imminent good fortune (pp. 172-173).

Not surprisingly, Fred's regeneration begins in the moment in which the total subjectivity within which he had been trapped is dramatically shaken by a concrete consequence. This, of course, Fred has encountered before, but until this moment he had himself been the victim of his miscalculations, and so strong had been his conviction of ultimate success that failure had seemed a small cosmic error in his progress. But now Fred has at last collided with an irremediable fact. The money Caleb Garth will have to supply toward Fred's debt must come not only from his own Christmas funds but from Mary's savings and, worst of all, from what Mrs. Garth had carefully laid aside for Alfred's education. No hopeful visions of good luck can alter this necessity. For the first time, Fred feels "something like the tooth of remorse." Characteristically, Fred had approached this event egotistically: "his pain in the affair beforehand had consisted almost entirely in the sense that he must seem dishonourable, and sink in the opinion of the Garths; he had not occupied himself with the inconvenience and possible injury that his breach might occasion them, for this exercise of the imagination on other people's needs is not common with hopeful young gentlemen." "But at this moment he suddenly saw himself as a pitiful rascal who was robbing two women of their savings" (p. 183).

That this fact is a matter of concern to Fred is the germ of his salvation. But this quality in Fred we are not surprised at, for it has been Eliot's point up to this very event that at least in motive Fred is a genuinely decent man. The narrative focus has been on his helplessness and on the consequent necessity for knowledge of the objective facts. The terrifying area of human impotence to which cases like Fred's point constitutes a far more scathing evaluation of reality than even as sadistic a character as Grand-court whose actions show us that one can cause evil by wishing evil; whatever the consequences, a fulfilled intention at least brings the world within human control. But Eliot is far less interested in evil of this stark form, for the larger share of suffering in the world she sees is the result not of malice but of Fred's special kind of ignorance.

Even more obvious is this in the second group, where the implications of human impotence are explored in deeper tones. Here we find characters who are so far above being merely amiable that they are, or think they are, actually inspired, often passionately, by lofty and noble intentions. Visionaries of sorts, their failures in the world of concrete effects are no less inevitable than those of characters like Fred or Hetty, although the dispar-ity between what they hoped for and what they caused is, pain-fully, much greater. Romola, Dorothea, Maggie, and Daniel, who stand out as examples in this category, are all sympathetic and sensitive, at times even self-sacrificing. Yet they find themselves, at least at first, incapable of contributing, as they often fervently wish, to the growing good of the world.

Dorothea is not only characteristic of the group but meta-phorically its prototype and, in a sense, the main theme on which Fred's story is a variation. Dorothea lives as though a disembod-ied spirit in an immaterial world. Her mind works, it would seem, constantly, but its contents are, rather than the plainly visible world around her, something largely spun out of illusory suppositions. Like all characters who have steadfastly refused to accept the empirical world, Dorothea shows a vagueness of thought which Eliot early characterizes. In a vision of the world more conventional than Eliot's this passage would introduce a heroic figure; but it is with characteristic irony that the narrator informs us that Dorothea's "mind was theoretic and yearned by its nature after some lofty conception of the world which might frankly include the parish of Tipton and her own rule of conduct there; she was enamoured of intensity and greatness" *(Middlemarch,* p. 6).

A first impression of this early description suggests something of an intellectual approach to life, but closer analysis assures us that this is not at all the case. "Enamoured of intensity and greatness," Dorothea confronts life emotionally rather than thoughtfully, in the grips, that is, of the determinants of her character—as "by its nature" implies—but not in reflection on external evidence which might distinguish for her between the world and self. Prodded by this same emotionalism, Dorothea encourages in herself a passion for martyrdom in a sincere but mistaken concept of humility. Her notion of "service," somewhat like Dinah's, is dangerously close to a desire for self-mortification, to Eliot a sure sign, as it is in Maggie, of a nature prone to self-indulgence. Thus, we are not surprised that Dorothea's mind is "theoretic," a term which describes for Eliot, in rather strict philosophic language, a general disregard of factual evidence. Dorothea is a metaphysician rather than an empiricist. She is guided, that is, by her "yearning" after a "lofty conception," evolving, in consequence, theories that satisfy the root of that yearning, the heroic mirror in which her ego reflects itself, but do not satisfy empirical data.

That Eliot is sympathetic to Dorothea's metaphysical inclinations cannot be doubted; indeed, Eliot never denied their appeal, only their validity. Significantly, Dorothea is impatient of details; understandably, she is attracted by Casaubon's fuzzy plans for a Key to All Mythologies. Moreover, Dorothea has a "love of extremes" to which the narrator often refers (see, for example, pp. 6-7 and 13-14). Inspired by the militant zeal of her emotions, Dorothea's mind rampages through the obstructive nubbles of fact, leveling the complexities of the real world and formulating concepts of stark simplicity. The patterns of her mind are large and flat. And in characteristic subjectivity, she quite literally—she is, we know, short-sighted—cannot come to terms with what is there. She always sees, Celia tells her, " 'what nobody else sees,' " but never " 'what is quite plain' " (p. 27). Even the first half, in Eliot's view, is far from flattering. When we learn as well, then, that Dorothea has a "rash" temperament (p. 6)—does not, that is, consider the consequences of action—we understand that the cycle of ignorance is complete, from passion, to thought, to action.

Dorothea's enlightenment comes, like Fred's, in a collision with the concrete fact, in this case Casaubon, the choice of her theoretic yearnings whose glory fades in the translation into experience. It is the daily dissatisfaction with her marriage, in all its aspects, that brings Dorothea to understand the egotism through which she had interpreted the world. " 'Two years ago,' " she confesses to Will, " 'I had no notion . . . of the unexpected way in which trouble comes, and ties our hands, and makes us silent when we long to speak. I used to despise women a little for not shaping their lives more, and doing better things. I was very fond of doing as I liked' " (p. 397).

The novel, at this point, is little more than half over, and Dorothea has barely begun to grasp the distinction between subject and object. Consequences still seem "unexpected," although the reader, like Celia, has predicted them from the beginning, at least in outline. Dorothea is only at the middle of the pattern which generally dominates the evolution of such characters in Eliot's novels, namely, illusion, failure, and either defeat or realization. Yet, although just entering the last stage here, Dorothea shows that she has learned the most valuable premise on which choices must rest in Eliot's view, for she had learned to distinguish between doing as one likes and necessity. It is the antidote to her philosophic disease, the knowledge that curbs and redirects her passion, structures her thought, and dictates her actions. Quixotic she will remain, but not in the same sense.

As we find her at the beginning of the novel, Dorothea does not know what risks she takes; she walks casually over the edge of the precipice. This is not heroism but stupidity. Only later can one say that Dorothea makes genuine choices. When she marries Casaubon, she envisions ideal happiness for herself; when, disillusioned, she chooses to remain with him, it is in the full knowledge of the terms she accepts. When she undertakes to reform the world, beginning with her cottages, social utopia seems imminent to her; when she chooses to help Lydgate, she is conscious of a risk. And, when she marries Will, both private and public expectations are scaled to the limits of possibility. To recognize the futility of fantasy, whether it shows itself in self-gratification or reckless idealism, is a strict exercise in discipline, but knowledge of this kind is, for Eliot, a necessary concession to the inevitable.

Will Ladislaw and Adolf Naumann: Subjective and Objective Points of View

In a letter written in 1873, Eliot remarks (in a tone that seems impatient of disagreement) that much "superfluous stuff is written on all sides about purpose in art. A nasty mind makes nasty art. And a meagre mind will bring forth what is meagre" *(Letters, V, 391).* If one accepts this as Eliot's genuine view—and there seems to be no reason not to—one must conclude that her definitions of "nasty" and "meagre" show only a vestigial trace of their common usages. For the critical center of analysis in the many artists and would-be artists of the novels concerns the nature of the knowledge to which they have arrived. The most obvious generalization that can be made is that the real artist is one who has achieved at least the ability to press, sometimes ruthlessly, toward the last possible recess of objectified knowledge. This is a quality that many would-be artists lack. They may, and in many cases do, lack sufficient talent as well, but this is another and quite different distinction.

In *Middlemarch,* for example, Eliot contrats Will Ladislaw and his friend—and sometimes teacher—Adolf Naumann. Will, of course, does not have the genius Naumann has, as he himself knows and confesses to Dorothea (p. 153). He could not be a great artist; but he could be a real one. That he is not is due to his " 'dilettantish and amateurish' " attitude, as Naumann tells him. The subject of their conversation is Dorothea, and in the very different ways the two men see her we become aware of Eliot's distinction. When Naumann first sees Dorothea it is, in his mind, as a painting: " 'here stands beauty in its breathing life, with the consciousness of Christian centuries in its bosom.' " So much does Dorothea capture Naumann's artistic imagination that he presses Will for an introduction so that he might offer to paint her as the Madonna. But in this, as in subsequent discussions with Naumann about Dorothea, Will is unconsciously angry and impatient. " 'If you were an artist,' " Naumann tells him, " 'you would think of Mistress Second-Cousin as antique form animated by Christian sentiment—a sort of Christian Antigone—sensuous force controlled by spiritual passion' " (pp. 140-141). With the characteristic intuitive insight of the real artist, Naumann has pierced the solid fact in a moment, grasped something about Dorothea which those who have known her long have not yet understood. Will, it is true, is on the threshold of falling in love with Dorothea, and one can hardly expect him to be capable of the same objectivity. But it is not only Dorothea that Will has difficulty objectifying; he lives in many aspects in a very subjective world and, indeed, resists the concrete as though instinctively aware of its threat to his egotism.

Will, in fact, is a structural transition in the novel from Fred to Dorothea, sharing the best and worst of their characteristics.

Like Fred, Will refuses to be prepared for a specific career or for anything that will put an end to that state of dreamy leisure he calls freedom. Casaubon reports that Will has no " 'desire for a more accurate knowledge of the earth's surface' " and would " 'prefer not to know the source of the Nile.' " Will's argument is that " 'there should be some unknown regions preserved as hunting grounds for the poetic imagination' " (p. 60). His dislike of detail and precision is a peculiar creed for a would-be painter, and Will, in fact, declares his preference for a questionable form of poetry because, as he explains, the vagueness possible in language is far more desirable (p. 142). Characteristically, when Will travels to the Continent, he declines "to fix on any more precise destination than the entire area of Europe." For Will is waiting to be inspired. Genius, the ironic narrator informs us, Will believes to be "necessarily intolerant of fetters; on the one hand it must have the utmost play for its spontaneity; on the other, it may confidently await those messages from the universe which summon it to its peculiar work, only placing itself in an attitude of receptivity towards all sublime chances. The attitudes of receptivity are various, and Will had sincerely tried many of them" (p. 61).

In short, Will, like all egotists, is very fond of doing as he likes, as his names suggests and as he finally recognizes halfway through the novel (p. 397). Nowhere, in fact, is he captured as synthetically as in the description of his habit of "shaking his head backward somewhat after the manner of a spirited horse" (p. 267). Like the Trojan Paris—Eliot's simile seems to be directly derived from the one which ends Book VI of the *Iliad*—Will does not seem to mind starting a war by abducting Helen, for he intrudes, like Paris, into the domestic equilibrium, in this case of both the Casaubons and the Lydgates; but, like Paris, too, Will prefers the bedchamber, or at least the drawing room—Rosamond's, since Dorothea's is not available—to the battlefield. His personal and artistic lives reflect one another. For him, the world is still an udder feeding his supreme self.

But if the artist must objectify the world and distinguish it from self, he must do so without falling victim to another form of egotism that lies at the extreme of this very process. Naumann has already come dangerously close to this condition. Charged with not objectifying Dorothea, Will answers that Naumann objectifies her too much, that he depersonalizes her, making his painting her " 'the chief outcome of her existence.' " " 'I am amateurish if you like,' " Will remarks; " 'I do *not* think that all the universe is straining towards the obscure significance of your pictures' " (p. 141). The knowledge that penetrates with analytic eye may become so detached that its perception becomes thoroughly externalized; all things acquire real existence for it only as objects of the analysis. Thus, to objectify completely or exclusively is, paradoxically, to subjectify to the solipsistic degree that no object is perceived from its own center of self. This, for Eliot, is to miss one half of what knowledge consists of, a half which can be acquired not intellectually but empirically, and only by rendering objectivity itself subjective.

Empirical Knowledge: The Mystery of Imagination

In "Looking Inward," from *Impressions of Theophrastus Such,* Theophrastus remarks that no "man can know his brother simply as a spectator." If "I laugh at you, O fellowmen!" he explains,

> if I trace with curious interest your labyrinthine self-delusions, note the inconsistencies in your zealous adhesions, and smile at your helpless endeavours in a rashly chosen part, it is not that I feel myself aloof from you; the more intimately I seem to discern your weakness, the stronger to me is the proof that I share them. How otherwise could I get the discernment?—for even what we are averse to, what we vow not to

entertain, must have shaped or shadowed itself within us as a possibility, before we can think of exorcising it.[14]

Despite the intellectually inclined language ("trace," "note," "discern," "proof"), which indeed seems necessary in English by default, Theophrastus's (and one must assume Eliot's under so thin a disguise) exposition here probes toward a definition of a knowledge quite distinct from what the intellect can acquire. But it is knowledge nonetheless. Emily Davies, reporting a conversation during a visit at the Leweses, remarks that Eliot had agreed that "stupidity prevails more than anything," but had added that it was a mistake to suppose "that stupidity is only intellectual" *(Letters,* VI, 287). Adam Bede makes a similar point to Dinah whom he, now transformed by his experiences, tries to persuade to marry him. It " 'seems to me it's the same with love and happiness as with sorrow,' " Adam says; " 'the more we know of it the better we can feel what other people's lives are or might be, and so we shall only be more tender to 'em, and wishful to help 'em. The more knowledge a man has, the better he'll do's work; and *feeling's a sort o' knowledge'* " (p. 521; my italics).

In a radical concession to empiricist psychology, Eliot stresses the independent existences of two quite separate areas of man's apprehension of reality. The reality itself, indeed, is one, essentially the same whether it is understood by thought or by feeling. Or at least it seems to be so hypothetically, for no evidence can refute that insofar as man perceives that reality, he does so on one level only through his intellect but on another must turn to that which is uniquely available to the central nervous system, to the awareness, that is, which only experience can acquire. The conclusions gathered by this knowledge are capable, certainly, of being generalized in the same kind of descriptive language as some intellectual conclusions, but here language fails to the degree that it tends to intellectualize the purely empirical fact. In *Daniel Deronda* Eliot illustrates the distinction very concisely in Gwendolen's attitude to Rex. Early in the novel, Gwendolen deals rather harshly with her cousin. She was, the narrator explains, "perfectly aware that her cousin was in love with her; but she had no idea that the matter was of any consequence, having never had the lightest visitation of painful love herself" (p. 49). It is certainly not the case that Gwendolen is intellectually ignorant of the denotative meaning of the word *love,* and it is accurate to say, therefore, that Gwendolen "knows" what "love" is; but it is true on one level only; another knowledge is as yet closed to her and must remain closed until she experiences "love" in her own person.

To some degree, each is a "spectator," as Theophrastus puts it, in the life of another. But degree is very important here. One may be a spectator like Hetty Sorrel, or one may be a spectator like Dorothea Brooke, as we find her at the end of the novel. Clearly, this knowledge gained through the individual's own experiences is not inevitably or easily transformed into a knowledge that others share the same experiences and feelings. And even where the potential for such understanding is high, as in Dorothea, it is a slowly evolving process, for this knowledge is concurrent with the range of an individual's experiences and accumulates, if at all, in the indifferent progress of time.

Yet, that man is at all able to transform the knowledge of his own experiences into a knowledge, of some sort, of the experiences of others is, for Eliot, in a sense miraculous. Partially, this transformation is possible through an intellectual detour. Man is able to recognize self in others; he is conscious, that is, of himself as a species, is, indeed, the only animal that has such consciousness, as Feuerback argues at great length. But to say this is to describe more than to explain. For Eliot, man's capacity, even as limited and selective as it is, to make an imaginative leap in which he substitutes self for others is a mystery in the strictly Hellenic meaning of the term. It is as a mystery that Eliot contrasts this emotional knowledge to the intellectual in *Romola* where the subject is not only explored at some length, as it is in every novel, but schematized as well with a symbolic thoroughnees and clarity not repeated—or attempted —in the other novels.

The symbols of the antithesis between intellectual and empirical knowledge are, characteristically, drawn from Hellenic and Hebraic sources respectively. For in this second kind of knowledge, Eliot recognizes a certain limited affiliation with Hebraism. In *Daniel Deronda,* where Eliot probes the meaning of the Judeo-Christian tradition through Daniel (a Jew brought up as a Christian), Israel is defined as the "heart of mankind" (p. 399). Yet—it seems necessary to clarify since it is easy to mistake Eliot's meaning on this point—this does not constitute for her a return either to Christianity or to Judeo-Christian morality. It appears absurd now to read that J. C. Brown believed Eliot "laboured to set before us the Christian and therefore the only exhaustively true ideal of life." [15] But very recently, Cox—and he is not alone among contemporary critics—takes virtually the same position when he argues—unlike Brown, with regret—that in the end Eliot "had nothing practical to offer except simple Christian truisms." [16] But the fact is, I think, that Eliot found in the Judeo-Christian tradition an approach to life which, stripped of its dogma, responded validly, if partially, to human experience just as in the Hellenic tradition she found the other and equally necessary center of man's accumulated insights into his condition.

In late fifteenth-century Florence, where Eliot chooses to set the symbolic drama, we are shown a city in which Hellenism and Hebraism are active and colliding forces. The issues are, as William James would say, still live options, for Renaissance scholars, like Bardo, commit not only their studies but their lives to the Hellenic ideal. At the same time, the Dominican revival grips its converts with the passion of discovery. Through the circle of the central characters, for whom the rest provide variations and elaborations, Eliot probes the best and worst of both traditions.

Romola's brother Dino is entirely Hebraic. Ravished by the spiritual life, he is lost to the concrete world. Ironically, the fellowship of man toward which the Hebraic ideal directs us has been perverted by Dino's extremism and by his misunderstanding of the function of religion, a function, for Eliot, whose goal is ultimately a secular one. This fact Eliot concentrates in the last meeting between brother and sister. Dying, Dino summons Romola to deliver an urgent message to her. Confident of divine inspiration, he feels he has been sent to her " 'not to renew the bonds of earthly affection, but to deliver the heavenly warning conveyed in a vision' " (p. 164). The vision, in fact, is entirely prophetic; he sees her marrying a man who is " 'the Great Tempter,' " in a ceremony performed by a priest who has " 'the face of death.' " " 'I believe,' " he concludes, " 'it is a revelation meant for thee: to warn thee against marriage as a temptation of the enemy; it calls upon thee to dedicate thyself...' " (pp. 166-167). Although he cannot finish the sentence, it is clear both to the reader and to Romola that Dino's warning is prompted by the same spiritual zeal that called him to the monastic life and is in no way related to the specific events of Romola's earth-bound existence.

Yet, although he is not aware of it, Dino has knowledge of the very facts which assure the reader that the prophecy will be fulfilled. It is Dino, as Fra Luca, who happens to carry to Florence the letter in which Baldassarre announces that he has been sold into slavery and asks to be ransomed, a letter which Dino delivers to Tito and whose contents he very accurately conjectures (pp. 118-119). Only one link is missing for Dino to understand Romola's place in these events, and that is for Dino to learn that this is the man Romola intends to marry. Tito, in fact, cannot conceive Dino's failing to make this last connection. "He foresaw the impulse that would prompt Romola to dwell" on the prospect of their marriage and "what would follow on the mention of the future husband's name. Fra Luca would tell all he knew and conjectured, and Tito saw no possible falsity by which he could now ward off the worst consequences of his former dissimulation. It was all over with his prospects in Florence" (p. 144).

The meeting between brother and sister should, indeed, have been as Tito imagined it, but Dino has so far rejected the concerns of this life that he addresses himself exclusively to Romola's "soul." "The prevision that Fra Luca's words had imparted to Romola," the narrator concludes the chapter, "had been such as comes from the shadowy region where human souls seek wisdom apart from the human sympathies which are the very life and substance of our wisdom; the revelation that might have come from the simple questions of filial and brotherly affection had been carried into irrevocable silence" (p. 169). In Dino, Hebraism has cultivated isolation and inadvertent indifference rather than the generous human impulses through which it was meant to ease the inescapable difficulties of man's existence.

Yet into this extremism Dino was driven by the failings of the Hellenic ideal to which his father tried to bind him. This ideal, Romola claims, was a life to be " 'lived according to the purest maxims of philosophy.' " Reason and light it had, but what it refused to acknowledge was the reality of weakness and suffering. " 'What were the maxims of philosophy to me?' " Dino replies. " 'They told me to be strong, when I felt myself weak.' " " 'My father,' " he tells her, " 'has lived amidst human sin and misery without believing in them: he has been like one busy picking shining stones in a mine, while there was a world dying of plague above him' " (pp. 162-163).

In Bardo, Eliot defines the limitations of the Hellenic tradition even at its best. But it is impossible to understand fully the vacuum this tradition conceals at its center until we turn to Tito Melema in whom Eliot concentrates, in contrast to Bardo, the same shortcomings in Hellenism, but in Tito revealed in their worst forms. Like Dino, Tito is at the extreme, but he is Dino's opposite. Although Dino dies quite early in the novel, it is between these two, at least symbolically, that Romola is torn throughout the novel.

Tito is entirely Hellenic. He is, in fact, a Greek, and of the very few biblical allusions which involve him, it is interesting that two are made by Tessa, who is hardly aware of the Hellenic world, and that both have reference only to his beauty, a superficial and amoral quality.[17] Endowed with a Hellenic intelligence—he is quick, alert, shrewd, learned—Tito's emotional nature is, nevertheless, thoroughly primitive. The painter Piero discerns in the softness of his face the self-indulgence of a morally weak man and asks him to sit for a portrait of Sinon deceiving Priam, another prophetic vision which Tito will actualize in his betrayal of both Baldassarre and Bardo. Piero's insight is particularly significant as a rejection of biblical imagery, for Nello the barber—a man of more limited moral perception than the artist—had just offered to introduce Tito to Brado as a kind of St. Stephen (p. 43). Yet earlier even Nello had seen something in the curl of Tito's lips when his Florentine pride had been injured by Tito's apparent contempt for the great Duomo, as though, Nello thought, he " 'were the Angel Gabriel come straight from Paradise' " (p. 33). And Nello had remarked of the Greeks in general that it was said of them " 'that their honesty begins at what is the hanging-point with us, and that since the old Furies went to sleep, your Christian Greek is of so easy a conscience that he would make a stepping-stone of his father's corpse' " (p. 39)—again a prophetic remark.

The suggestion of treachery implied in the image of Sinon is amplified in references to Orpheus (p. 138), to Paris (p.100), and leads to a repeated allusion to Odysseus. At the beginning of the novel, Tito refers to the Augustinian monk from whom he accepted advice as a " 'fallacious Minerva' " (p. 31), identifying himself with the wandering Odysseus. He sees Tessa as a " 'siren' " (p. 113), luring him to ruin, an image unconsciously picked up by Nello, who speaks of Tito's ears as " 'double-waxed against all siren invitations' " (p. 139). And his political co-conspirators trust his talent for deception as though he were " 'Ulysses himself' " (p. 358).

Not only is Tito Hellenic but he is explicitly anti-Hebraic, a fact he implies early when he expresses his contempt for the cathedrals and churches of Florence because they " 'smack too much of Christian barbarism' " (p. 34). Inevitably, he takes on diabolic overtones. In Christian terms, he is the " 'Great Tempter,' " as Dino calls him, and in Hellenic terms he becomes one of the " 'demoni' " with minds too nimble " 'to be weighted with all the stuff we men carry about in our hearts' " (p. 220). Here we come very close to identifying the hiatus in Tito's nature. Tito himself, without the slightest awareness of what he implied, had defined himself by associating his self-image, in the triptych he designed for Romola, with Bacchus who saved Ariadne from the island of Naxos where Theseus had abandoned her (p. 194). But Bacchus has a far deeper significance and is, ultimately, not a savior. Rather, he is the god of "beauty and joy" (p. 341) who, in the absence of the convictions of the heart, becomes the lust for pleasure and self-gratification. It is as a follower of Bacchus that Tito rejects the offer Romola implicitly makes to him to probe with her the mystery of human suffering symbolized in the cross Dino had given her.

Romola herself comes very slowly to the awareness of that suffering, and it is in her that Eliot symbolizes, in two striking metaphors, the transition from the intellectual to the empirical knowledge of pain. As an obedient pupil of her father, Romola begins as a Hellene. At the beginning, we see her reading to her father quite ably from classical texts (p. 51). Tito, thinking of her in his own idiom, calls her his " 'goddess' " (pp. 185 and 189, for example), or a " 'Pleiad' " that may " 'grow dim by marrying any mortal' " (p. 139), the latter foreshadowing his own later reference to light when he calls her his " 'golden-tressed Aurora' " (p. 188). Casually, Tito refers to her as his Alcestis (p. 139), the faithful wife of the faithless husband, while the painter Piero sees her as Antigone leading the blind Oedipus (p. 196), an image of fidelity that is a precise contrast to his vision of Tito as Sinon. Clearly, the Hellenic imagery Eliot uses for Romola is quite different from that she uses for Tito. Like Bardo, Romola embodies the highest ethical as well as intellectual commitments of

Hellenism. And, once again, even at this moral level, the tradition is inadequate.

Unlike her father, Romola senses its weaknesses as the reality
of a world represented by Dino's cross presses on her own existence. At first, the symbol puzzles her; ironically, as she studies
the cross, Tito, with typical blindness to her inner life, asks her to
dismiss the thoughts he sees reflected on her face as being more
suitable to a nun (p. 188), foreshadowing the fact that it is in
nun's habit that Romola chooses to flee from him later in her
transition to another life. The cross and the triptych become
intimately connected. As she leaves Florence in nun's habit, she
is referred to as Ariadne uncrowning herself of the golden wreath
Tito had insisted on in the painting (p. 194), and we recognize the
change in dress from Bacchic crown to Christian habit as a
transformation in Romola's vision of life. The experience is
synthesized in the narrator's suggestion that the "crowned"
Ariadne of the painting had felt "more and more the presence of
unexpected thorns" (p. 251). Thus, in this central image, Romola
moves from the Bacchic life of joy to the Christian discipline of
pain.

But the actual baptism in sorrow is yet to come, in her dream-
like descent into the plague-stricken village. The scene, Eliot
reports, belonged to her "earliest vision of the story" *(Letters,* IV,
104); and the novel gives metaphoric evidence that this is true.
Dino's cross had introduced Romola to the fact of suffering but
had not yet taught her the human fellowship of pain. It had, in
fact, threatened to alienate her from the world even as it had
alienated him; in her nun's habit she seems to accept Dino's
dying injunction to repudiate marriage and, one assumes he
would have said had he concluded his sentence, " 'dedicate' "
herself to a life of ascetic contemplation. As a nun, her life would
parallel his as a monk, and it seems to be the life, at this point,
toward which Romola is moving, for her flight from Florence
reenacts Dino's retreat from human involvement. But in the
village, Romola learns that neither her father nor her brother

had known how to deal with suffering. There, confronted literally by the plague of Dino's metaphor, she neither refuses to acknowledge pain as her father had nor attempts to withdraw from it as Dino had. There, the meaning of the cross is presented to her in its incarnate reality: suffering is inescapable; neither philosophy nor religion can transcend this empirical fact.

It is part of Eliot's structural irony that in this least realistic, most symbolic and fantasylike scene in the novel, she brings Romola at last into full collision with the raw facts of existence. It is not that Romola's earlier life had been unreal; it is merely that it had not been all of reality. Ironically, too, it is Tito who elucidates the relationship between Hellenic and Hebraic symbols when, attempting to refuse pain into his own life, he opens the triptych, places Dino's cross inside, and closes it again. Romola is troubled, but does not, at this time, wish to prevent him; "on the contrary, she herself wished to subdue certain importunate memories and questionings which still flitted like unexplained shadows across her happier thought" (209). But in his symbolic action, Tito has unwittingly stated the fact. " 'It is a little shrine,' " Tito had said of the triptych, " 'which is to hide away from you for ever that remembrance of sadness' " (pp. 208-209). Yet, within the shrine dedicated to joy is locked the secret of pain.

Here, Eliot's symbolic statement reminds one very closely of Thomas Mann's vision in the chapter "Snow" in *The Magic Mountain*. In a dream, Hans Castorp envisions a Hellenic temple erected by the children of the sun; but on closer inspection, he discovers within the mystery of the human blood sacrifice. Like Hans, Romola is being tested and enlightened. That she would accept her full humanity Romola had already promised earlier when she had rehearsed, as it were, her subsequent role in the village in her protective relationship with Tessa for whom Romola had become the image of the Virgin. Timid and ignorant, Tessa had appealed for help and Romola, halfway through her evolution, had understood the cry of despair. Symbolically, she had assumed Hebraic roles, passing from the Unseen Madonna (p. 389), to the Visible Madonna (p. 396), to the Holy Madonna (p. 445), the "heavenly lady" (p. 447) with the "heavenly face" (p. 445). Similarly, the villagers come to see her as the Virgin protectress (see, for example, pp. 571, 572, 575, 578, and 579), and Romola, now in complete submission to the common destiny, accepts the burden. The imagery through which Eliot has defined Romola has moved from Hellenic to Hebraic, but the latter is not a substitution for the former. Rather, we see that Romola had added a second kind of knowledge to the first and has found, in the synthesis, an approach to life in which each contributes its own best perceptions and guards against the extreme of the other.

As the symbolic structure of *Romola* suggests the paradigmatic evolution into complete knowledge, so in her first novel Eliot created a character in whom this pattern is concretely represented. Adam Bede is a character whose intellect has reached a fair level of sophistication, not, as in Romola, in the scholarly sense, but in the more practical matters which concern daily human activities and realtionships. But in the knowledge of the heart he is grossly deficient. His emotional ignorance is a contrasting parallel to the intellectual ignorance of characters like Dorothea.

The novel takes Adam through three stages of emotional evolution. The first, a state of personal subjectivity in which the self is the only center of perception, is the characteristic egotism which interprets entirely within the terms of its own consciousness. In the second stage, Adam learns to objectify, to recognize, that is, the independent existence of what is not the self; yet he remains a "spectator" in that he acknowledges but does not participate in the internal lives of others. This stage is necessary but incomplete except as a transition to the third in which he becomes subjective once more, but this time not on his own behalf but rather on behalf of others. In a synthetic identification, he assumes, at last, a larger identity of self than his own physical being; he becomes capable of feeling for others as though for himself. Significantly, the intellectual "morality" to which Adam held at the beginning of the novel has become transformed at the end by his emotional enlightenment; the relationship between the two is not mechanical but organic; heart and head are so interdependent in mutually modifying the content of knowledge each acquires that the absence of one will, in most cases, warp the vision of the other.

It is Adam's strictly intellectual approach that makes him appear, at the beginning, rigid and hard. And there is only one way, the narrator comments, "in which a strong determined soul can learn" fellow feeling, and that is "by getting his heart-strings bound round the weak and erring, so that he must share not only the outward consequences of their error, but their inward suffering" (p. 214). To share the "outward consequences" is to be given merely empirical evidence of the facts of reality toward the support of an intellectual conclusion; but to share the "inward suffering" no intellect is required, only the receptivity which does not close the self to the experience of another. At first, Adam is closed; he lacks as yet an intimate acquaintance with human weakness such as can cultivate in him an understanding of human temptations and compassion for the consequences of yielding to them. In this respect, Felix Holt is identical to Adam. Both are particularly interesting because they are, in many ways, rather superior people, so much so, in fact, that they have been taken by some as touchstones of the ideal, Eliot's moral parables.[18] This they certainly are not.[19] On the contrary, their rigidity is intentional, involved in the very problem Eliot works out through them, namely, the problem of characters whose self-images have an exclusively intellectual origin.

At the beginning of the novel, Adam is emotionally sterile. The reader's first view of him finds him working, which in itself Eliot clearly approves, but which Adam uses as a substitute for human relationships in the same way that Dinah uses religion. His first words are the lyrics of a song that establishes his character:

"Awake my soul, and with the sun
Thy daily stage of duty run;
Shake off dull sloth . . ." (p. 1).

This, in a sense, is Adam's catechism, and its point is immediately emphasized as the narrator distinguishes between the
brothers. "The idle tramps always felt sure they could get a
copper from Seth; they scarcely ever spoke to Adam" (p. 2).
Idleness, only one item in a very long list, is to Adam a weakness
for which he has no sympathy. For his father, lately become a
drunkard, he has only contempt, although his unhappy mother
urges him to " 'forie thy feyther—thee munna be so bitter again'
him. He war a good feyther to thee afore he took to th' drink' " (p.
39). It is a futile plea, however, for Adam seems only slightly more
sympathetic to her, and the narrator's remark—that "we are apt
to be kinder to the brutes that love us than to the women that
love us" (p. 40)—contrasts Adam's failure in human relationships
with his fondness for his dog, Gyp.

It is surprising that Adam falls in love with Hetty—so inferior
to his lofty standards—only to those who do not recognize
Adam's intellectual posture as a suppression of feeling which,
uncultivated by experience, remains rigidly isolated. Indeed,
Hetty seems Adam's inevitable choice. Like Pentheus in Euripides's *Bacchae,* Adam closes all emotional outlets until he
erupts. The experience, painful though it is for him, is highly
educational. Hetty, immovable in her egotism, requires Adam to
yield everything. Through his love for Hetty, Adam begins to
expand his self to include Hetty's joys and sorrows until he
opens himself to the knowledge of error and frailty. The transformation is slow but pervasive. In newborn sympathy, he begins to substitute understanding for judgment. " 'Ah, I was
always hard,' " he confesses of his earlier view of his father;
" 'the devil *will* be having his finger in what we call our duties as
well as our sins' " (p. 205).

Important as this insight is to Adam's growth, he has yet

143

taken only the first step. The "lesson" itself is "long and hard," and "Adam had at present only learned the alphabet of it" (p. 214). Not until he is able to suspend judgment entirely in a moment of such compassion that he feels the suffering of another almost as his own can Adam be free of the rectitudinal fever his purely intellectual nature had justified to him. Evidence of the final stage of his emotional maturation is heard only later, when he tells Bartle Massey that he will " 'stand by' " Hetty, whatever she has done. " 'We hand folks over to God's mercy, and show none ourselves. I used to be hard sometimes; I'll never be hard again' " (p. 439). Adam's prophecy proves true, for, although difficult, the knowledge is permanent. To Seth, he becomes almost indulgent (see, for example, p. 497), and even Arthur he can come at last to forgive (p. 480). In this more human condition, Adam is able to form a far deeper and more realistic attachment which his earlier rigidity had precluded. "Tender and deep as his love for Hetty had been," the narrator remarks, "—so deep that the roots of it would never be torn away—his love for Dinah was better and more precious to him; for it was the outgrowth of that fuller life which had come to him from his acquaintance with deep sorrow" (p. 541).

This fuller life of which the narrator speaks is brought to Adam through his experience of pain, and it is sometimes tempting to conclude that Eliot reiterates the old view that suffering ennobles. This, however, seems to be neither the case nor the point in Eliot's novels. For one thing, we have far too many examples of characters left entirely indifferent by suffering. Hetty herself, for example. It is often remarked that Dinah has a beneficial effect on Hetty when she visits her in the prison, but it is difficult to find evidence for this. Each of Hetty's actions seems prompted by the same egotism that has impelled her throughout, although some of these might appear redemptive were the narrator and Hetty's own words not telling us otherwise. At first, Hetty keeps her eyes fixed on Dinah's face, like "an animal that gazes, and gazes, and keeps aloof." Soon, however, she allows herself to be clasped in Dinah's arms. Yet, the narrator explains, it "was the human contact she clung to, but she was not the less sinking into the dark gulf." When Dinah introduces the subject of God, His mercy, His perennial watch over the living and the dead, all Hetty understands is that Dinah is confirming the certainty of her execution. " 'Oh, Dinah,' " she blurts out, " 'won't nobody do anything for me? *Will* they hang me for certain? . . . I wouldn't mind if they'd let me live.' " When Dinah persists in giving her "religious comfort," Hetty answers with "sullen sadness" that she can't know anything about what Dinah is saying. Finally, she kneels, but only in obedience to Dinah. " 'I can't feel anything like you,' " Hetty says instead of the prayer Dinah is trying to prompt; " 'my heart is hard.' " At last, Hetty breaks into sobs and offers to tell the story of her child's death. If anywhere, it is here that Hetty is touched at all by the suffering she has undergone. Yet, when all is told, Eliot seems to deny even that minimal possibility by showing us Hetty's motive in the confession had been, not surprisingly, a still entirely egotistic one: " 'Dinah, do you think God will take away that crying and the place in the wood, now I've told everything?' " (pp. 457-465).

Sometimes, indeed, suffering does worse than leave a character no better than before; it actually, at times, hardens him. Feuerbach wrote that pleasure "expands man" but "suffering contracts and concentrates him; in suffering man denies the reality of the world; . . . he is absorbed in himself, in his own soul." [20] Tom Tulliver seems to be proof of this insight. It appears likely that, although he does not begin with much compassion, better circumstances would have made a better man of him. In fact, the point at which he apparently passes his last opportunity to escape permanent hardness is the point of his most acute suffering, and its effect is only to ensure a further narrowing of sympathy. When Mr. Tulliver asks Tom to write his curse on Wakem in the family Bible, Maggie, who had long before been given the "gift of sorrow—that susceptibility to the bare offices of humanity which raises them into a bond of loving fellowship" *(The Mill on the Floss,* p. 170), protests in horror; but Tom, with a determination that sends Eliot to the use of italics and an exclamation point, says " 'Be quiet, Maggie! . . . I *shall* write it' " (p. 236).

Clearly, in these matters, there is no formula. But there is a fact and one which must be known in any action that claims to look at moral ends. There is pain in the world. And this fact cannot be known as an item of tabular information but must be sensed in a living experience. If there is no certainty—and there is not, for in fact the statistics are weighed in the other direc- tion—that feeling pain teaches us about the reality of it in the lives of others with that direct and sharp perception which only experience can yield, there is certainty that without feeling that pain we can never know what another means when he claims to feel it. And if morality must, as well as recognizing cosmic laws, attempt to modify the hard, nonmoral outward pressure of man's existence, it is essential that we learn not merely that there is pain and that it ought to be minimized but what it feels like and what it is to want it minimized in our own lives. Imagination must have a basis in fact, and no one can make the imaginative leap to identifying self with others in matters which the self has not experienced. That is why, indeed, it is so easy for Adam to know that he, unlike Arthur, would have avoided temptation which, of course, he has never felt. That is why, also, it is so easy for Adam to know that he, unlike his father, would not yield to the weakness of drinking, a weakness he doesn't happen to have. We are all of us, Eliot's argument would run, indulgent to our- selves because we know how difficult self-restraint is in our own case; when we become as subjective on behalf of another as we are on our own behalf, the sympathy which is the indulgence of others becomes, if not inevitable, at least possible.

Eliot's emphasis on the necessity of personal experience in the education of feeling leads her to conclude, not paradoxically, that the more sympathy widens, the more it converges on individual human beings. That is the end of moral action, and it is also, for Eliot, the means. The imaginative leap into an objectified subjectivity is impossible except through a personal attachment. Ultimately, such an attachment may act as a catalyst in one's relations to wider and wider circles of general human concerns, but even then the priorities are directly proportional to the immediacy and concreteness of the objects involved. Adam's case is a characteristic example of this process, but Adam himself is not exclusively typical, especially of the resistance that human beings offer to this kind of specific attachment. Resistance there is almost always, for the ego attempts to avoid the dangers of dependence. But such reluctance is not to be found only in such egotists as Hetty, Rosamond, and Gwendolen, although they too exhibit it. It is to be found as well in characters who appear in all ways conventionally "noble." Indeed, it is the very fact that they accept the conventional definition of "moral superiority" that allows them to conceal, under platforms of benevolence, the most primitive fear of rendering themselves vulnerable.

This was, of course, the case with Adam. But the argument against Adam is incomplete without Dinah Morris, a structural parallel to Adam and a character who adds as well a further dimension to this question. In a letter to Sara Hennell, Eliot once wrote that the infirmities of one's friends "touch one's imagination more than the wrongs done by the tyrant of Thibet" *(Letters,* VII, 343). This is, basically, the reality from which Dinah has been trying to escape. Reason alone suggests that the opposite should be the case, but human psychology, not reason, is the heart of this issue. Feeling, Eliot maintains, can be aroused only by the concrete. But when we first meet Dinah, she has evolved only to the second of the three stages. From the kind of total and personal subjectivity that Hetty represents Dinah has long emerged. The world has become for her an objective reality, as it is for Adam, but, like Adam too, she has not yet been able to allow herself to resubjectify in the person of another. Both remain suspended in that impersonal world between self and others.

Yet Dinah, although the reverse at first appears to be true, is more rigid than Adam, and it is for this very reason that Dinah, of all the characters who change in the novel, is the last to arrive at an understanding of her problem. Ironically, her rigidity is inherent in her religion, the very source, Dinah believes, of her moral strength. The religion itself, indeed, is not rigid, at least not if it is accepted in its true terms, which are, for Eliot, the terms in which Feuerbach interprets it, as a means to human ends. But it is those very human ends that Dinah avoids through her religion. This she does very subtly, for in external ways she is careful to fulfill the most minute details of her office: she ministers to the sick and poor in Stonyshire, comforts the suffering—she is the first to appear, for example, at Lisbeth Bede's home when Thias dies—and worries about Hetty constantly. In this last, however, she reveals the detachment of her concern, for it is seldom that she attempts to enter Hetty's concrete world, praying, rather—as Dino does for Romola—for the "poor lost lamb" of Christ's flock. In all this she is entirely sincere, just as Adam is sincere in the self-discipline with which he performs all his duties, and more. Yet her sincerity can be as deep only as her self-knowledge, and self-knowledge Dinah cannot entirely afford.

Her religion, as she views it, allows her to probe only as far as her rational nature, where, indeed, the many have a greater claim than the one. To feel for one more than for another seems to her a narrowing of sympathy such as Christ would not approve. Conversely, Dinah believes that her commitment to causes is a mark of such overflowing feeling that it cannot be contained in a single relationship. This, indeed, is her argument to Seth when he proposes marriage to her. " 'I seem to have no room in my soul for wants and fears of my own,' " she says, " 'it has pleased God to fill my heart so full with the wants and sufferings of his poor people' " *(Adam Bede,* p. 33). It is not, we are to understand, that she rejects Seth specifically but rather that she is beyond earthly love. But Dinah deludes herself. Her ideals are not reasons but excuses; the intellect may be capable of statistics, may understand categories and ideals, but the heart responds only to the individual. And Dinah, although she is too detached to realize it, has responded already.

It is not because God calls her to His service that Dinah refuses Seth but because it is not Seth she wants. Only a character in Dinah's state of suspension could be puzzled by the fact that she always blushes in Adam's presence (p. 117); Lisbeth Bede, as we learn much later, had no doubt from the beginning what Dinah's blushes meant (p. 512). Yet even at the end, Dinah, still blushing, refuses Adam with the same arguments she had offered Seth: " 'all my peace and joy have come from having no life of my own, no wants, no wishes for myself, and living only in God and those of his creatures whose sorrows and joys he has given me to know' " (p. 519). Yet, after a brief concession to her persistent delusion, Dinah does find that Adam, after all, would not be a betrayal of her commitments.

The difference between her rejection of Seth and her first rejection of Adam, although they are virtually identical in form, is that Dinah, despite the fact that she has not yet been able to acknowledge in herself the exclusivity of affection, has been taught by her relationship to Hetty—who is, indeed, the object lesson of the novel—more wisdom of the heart that she had had at the beginning. Dinah calls it " 'Divine Will' " that inspires her to accept Adam at last (p. 544), but we recall that is was the same divine will that forbade her marrying Seth and at first prevented her from accepting Adam. The fact is that in her professed dedication to two great causes, God and Man, she had found an escape from the more difficult commitment to the vigorous demands of a personal relationship. Such a relationship cannot survive even on the generous gifts of time and energy that Dinah willingly grants, but requires rather a giving of the self in compromise, sympathy, and a wide tolerance of error. Compared to the demands of human ties, God and Man are easy alternatives

For very much the same reasons, Felix Holt enters the novel

detached from the concrete human reality. Like Adam, he is a virtual text of platitudes, political as well as moral, and neither does Eliot find acceptable at the beginning of the novel. Jerome Thale, explaining what he considers to be the failure of Felix's characterization, remarks that the problem of the novel is "that the Felix of the novel is, like the Felix of the essay, the author's mouthpiece for her own views, and that she agreed so thoroughly with him that she did not think very critically about his character." [21] But, apart from the fact that an impeccable political taste would not have interfered with characterization necessarily—since personality is far from identical with opinion—both Felix and his politics are, at the beginning, nowhere near perfect. Felix, in fact, takes detachment further than either Dinah or Adam, for he sees human imperfection as thoroughly contemptible. With much pride, Felix confesses that a phrenologist had told him that his " 'large ideality' " prevented him " 'from finding anything perfect enough to be venerated.' " Rev. Lyon reproves him with his usual gentle manner, but his analysis is scathing enough. The " 'temptations,' " he remarks, " 'that most beset those who have great natural gifts, and are wise after the flesh, are pride and scorn, more particularly toward those weak things of the world which have been chosen to confound those things which are mighty' " (p. 68).

In a letter to Charles Bray, Eliot had once written that she disliked "extremely" a passage in his book in which he appeared to consider "the disregard of individuals as a lofty condition of mind." Her own "experience and development," she continues, "deepen every day my conviction that our moral progress may be measured by the degree in which we sympathise with individual suffering and individual joy" *(Letters,* II, 403). Felix is a character who, like Adam and Dinah, finds it easier to sympathize with the common concerns of the group than with the experience of any individual. This is as much a flaw in the politician as in the man. It is not that his political theories, as such, are false any more than Adam's moral abstractions are false as descriptive generalizations. But Felix is immersed in politics as Naumann is immersed in art; the relationships between means and ends become confused, and rather than seeing political ideals as means for achieving human ends, Felix begins to conceive of men as objects to be organized for the achievement of political perfection. Inevitably, politics and human welfare, which should be in harmony, are, in his mind, in conflict.

Felix's personal life is a structural analogy to his political one; it is also the cause and in the end will be the solution. Like Dinah, Felix is split, believing that his calling does not allow him personal attachments which, he thinks, will threaten the integrity of his dedication to "wider" causes. He wonders, unwillingly falling in love with Esther, " 'whether the subtle measuring of forces will ever come to measuring the force there would be in one beautiful woman whose mind was as noble as her face was beautiful—who made a man's passion for her rush in one current with all the great aims of his life' " (p. 268). But he cannot commit himself to anything less. If she is saved, Felix condescends to promise Esther, she might be the woman he is thinking of (p. 269). Esther, indeed, changes, even to the point of accepting the difficult life Felix has chosen for himself; in that sense, she comes to fulfill Felix's requirements. Yet the perfection to which he has unfavorably compared her throughout neither Esther nor anyone else can reach.

That Felix is willing, at last, to tolerate weakness and error is a distinct mark of improvement in his moral sensibility; it is an improvement as well in his political perceptions, which had had, until the end, only abstract validity. The thematic center of the novel, which moves in two converging lines, is found in the integration of public and private lives. As Rev. Lyon had said, characters like Hetty and Esther are necessary to "confound" characters like Adam and Dinah and Felix, to interpret to them, that is, by grounding dogma in specific affections, the empirical meaning of their detached theories.

Integrated Knowledge: The Synthetic Apprehension

Obvious through all of Eliot's implicit arguments on the difference between intellectual and empirical knowledge is the Positivist view that, as she explains in a letter, thought is a formative power and feeling a vitalizing power *(Letters,* I, 265-266).[22] The direct basis of action, which in a causal universe is the ultimate moral test, is in feeling, not in thought. In her notes to *The Spanish Gypsy* Eliot had written that man's difficulty in acquiescing in the dire necessities of his lot arose in feeling "which supersedes reflection." And while it is clear that for man to adjust to those necessities he must know, intellectually, what they are, it is equally clear that his willingness to act in accordance with them is not part of that intellectual knowledge but, rather, a question of will. The collision of forces takes place as much because man is not impelled to do what he knows he should as because he is ignorant of what it is he should do.

Unlike many Utilitarians, with whom she agreed on other points, Eliot argues that even self-destructive errors are not always errors in judgment. Bartle Massey, in *Adam Bede,* seems to subscribe to a Utilitarian view when he suggests that the only way Squire Donnithorne can be convinced to hire Adam, against whom he bears a grudge, is for him to be shown " 'what was for his own interest' " (p. 250). Nothing, however, could be further from psychological truth in Eliot's view, grudges and interests having entirely different planes of existence. As Paris suggests, Eliot's position arises rather in the kind of determinism to which biologists like Huxley and Lewes were committed and which led Darwin to conclude that "man seems often to act impulsively, that is from instinct or long habit, without any consciousness of pleasure." [23] In her delineation of character, Eliot stresses again and again the direct psychological continuum from feeling to action which, even more significantly, excludes thought alto-

gether as an artificial interruption—the very reason it is so difficult to achieve—in the natural sequence of events.

In contrast to those characters whose generous impulses are
thwarted by errors in judgment are characters like Tito Melema
whose shrewdness should be sufficient promise of self-advanta-
geous choices. But Tito makes mistakes at precisely that point at
which feeling issues directly in action before intelligence has time
to intervene. Confronted, for example, by Baldassarre, Tito
reacts by instinct or long habit, Darwin would say. The surprise
of seeing Baldassarre for the first time and the fact that the
meeting takes place in public allow Tito no opportunity to
calculate consequences. When Lorenzo asks who the strange
man might be, Tito replies instantly, " 'Some madman, surely.' "
Consciously, he had not intended to say that. Indeed, the narrator adds that he "hardly knew how the words had come to his
lips." But, the narrator continues, "there are moments when our
passions speak and decide for us, and we seem to stand by and
wonder. They carry in them an inspiration of crime, that in one
instant does the work of long premeditation." For some time
now, Tito had been denying Baldassarre's claim on him, but he
had never before spoken the words that would forever sever the
tie. Yet, when the occasion arises, the words come unsolicited,
and he is surprised into a truth he had not meant to confess.

The question here, from Tito's point of view, is not one of guilt,
for which he has a very shallow capacity; it is almost entirely a
matter of self-interest. While Baldassarre was lost, possibly
dead, the advantage lay in disclaiming him. But a living and
present accuser may threaten his position even among the moral
cynics with whom he has chosen to associate. Later, when he has
time to reflect, this is what Tito himself realizes. "If he had not
uttered those decisive words," he thinks, "if he could have sum-
moned up the state of mind . . . for avowing his recognition of
Baldassarre, would not the risk have been less? He might have
declared himself to have had what he believed to be positive
evidence of Baldassarre's death" *(Romola,* pp. 229 and 231).

Events prove his second thoughts right. But then it is too late for him to alter the situation to which his feelings had committed him in the moment of crisis.

The thrust with which feeling impels the individual into action is, often, an irrefutable force; it is the accumulated determination of the whole character. It is obvious why Eliot considers it so important to moral education that feelings should be trained and cultivated as carefully as thought. The narrator of *Daniel Deronda* remarks that it is in the experiences of childhood, "while our elders are debating whether most education lies in science or literature, that the main lines of character are often laid down" (p. 126). The earliest are the deepest associations for Eliot, and those one acquires in childhood, as well as those one doesn't, are the formative influences of one's life.

This point has been, I think, insufficiently stressed in Eliot's novels, although serious misunderstanding of her analysis of character can result from underestimating Eliot's commitment to this view. In childhood, the habitual emotional ties are fostered which can never be either erased or replaced. Eliot frequently speaks of such childhood associations as the binding roots of feeling. Where these are lacking, we observe a proportionately harder egotism in adulthood. The narrator of *Daniel Deronda* speaks not only of Daniel's unrooted childhood but of Gwendolen's as well; the "blessed persistence in which affection can take root had been wanting in Gwendolen's life," the narrator remarks (p. 13). But, interestingly, it is not merely roots in human affections, although these are most important, that Eliot alludes to. A "human life," the narrator had just explained,

> should be well rooted in some spot of native land, where it may get the love of tender kinship for the face of earth, for the labours men go forth to, for the sounds and accents that haunt it, for whatever will give that early home a familiar unmistakable difference amidst the future widening of knowledge: a

spot where the definiteness of early memories may be in-wrought with affection, and kindly acquaintance with all neighbours, even to the dogs and donkeys, may spread not by sentimental effort and reflection, but as a sweet habit of the blood. (pp. 12-13) [24]

The restless vagueness of Daniel's affections and Gwendolen's coldness presents parallel cases in the novel of dislocated personality. Gwendolen's primitive ancestor in Eliot's first novel shares with Gwendolen feelings which had never been bound to concrete objects. Watching Hetty daydream herself into the center of Arthur's life, the narrator of *Adam Bede* asks, in language and detail remarkably similar to the narrator's in *Daniel Deronda,* whether "any sweet or sad memory" mingles "with this dream of the future—any loving thought of her second parents—of the children she had helped to tend—of any youthful companion, any pet animal, any relic of her own childhood even." "There are some plants," the narrator concludes, "that have hardly any roots" (p. 156).

This recurring metaphor is instructive. Feeling is not merely another necessary factor in moral action but a transforming nurturing of thought. In "Evangelical Teaching: Dr. Cumming," Eliot writes that morality depends on the regulation of feeling by intellect *(Essays,* p. 166).[25] But here Eliot has not yet succeeded in suggesting the full psychological fusion of the two into an organic whole. Again and again, Eliot attempts to find the exact language to convey her idea. In *Daniel Deronda* the relationship is a little clearer. Daniel holds out to Gwendolen as the ideal attainment of wisdom a condition in which the " 'affections are clad with knowledge' " (p. 340). But it is in *Middlemarch,* perhaps, in Will's definition of the special power of the poet, that Eliot states her meaning most precisely. " 'To be a poet,' " Will says, " 'is to have a soul so quick to feel, that discernment is but a hand playing with finely-wrought variety on the chords of emotion—a soul in which knowledge passes instantaneously into feeling, and feeling flashes back as a new organ of knowledge' " (p. 166).

In the moment in which she elopes with Stephen, Maggie Tulliver is undoubtedly the most striking example of the degree to which intellectual and emotional sensibilities may be dissociated. In this incident Eliot makes clear that unless knowledge of what is right is informed by feeling which acquiesces in it, the mere cerebrating faculty can have no compelling power. The event, Eliot would say, is a case in which thought had not been vitalized. And the evidence provided in this example is especially significant because, among Eliot's characters, Maggie is on a relatively high level both intellectually and emotionally.

The question is purely one of psychological integration. Although Maggie is determined not to allow a relationship to grow between herself and Stephen, at the crucial moment she has not yet been able to feel what she believes. This she herself realizes later when she tells Stephen that if " 'we—if I had been better, nobler,' " Lucy's claims on her " 'would have been so strongly present with me—I should have felt them pressing on my heart so continually, just as they do now in the moments when my conscience is awake—that the opposite feeling would never have grown in me, as it has done.' " Maggie's is not a lapse in moral dogma nor even an instance of perverted feeling (such as one finds in characters like Bulstrode), but a momentary failure of the imagination which could have brought, as it later does, to Maggie's emotional consciousness the empirical reality of Lucy's suffering. And that expanded identification would have not merely contended with temptation but would have, as Maggie understands, " 'destroyed all temptations' " (The Mill on the Floss, p. 417). The insight Maggie finally acquires is the same as that with which the narrator of Middlemarch explains the apparent incongruity between Bulstrode's principles and his actions. There is, the narrator remarks, "no general doctrine which is not capable of eating out our morality if unchecked by the deep-seated habit of direct fellow-feeling with individual fellow-men" (p. 453).

Notes

1. In this Eliot affiliated herself once more with those nineteenth-century philosophies (Utilitarianism and Positivism, for example) which spurred a major revolution in ethical theories.

2. Cross, III, 36.

3. *Ibid.,* p. 33.

4. As Jebb remarks, Eliot most closely resembles Sophocles, the most characteristically Greek of the three tragedians (Vernon Rendall, "George Eliot and the Classics," *A Century of George Eliot Criticism,* p. 215). Indeed, Sophocles appears to have been Eliot's favorite, for in "The Antigone and Its Moral," she calls him "the crown and flower of the classic tragedy" *(Essays,* p. 261).

5. Cross, III, 34.

6. Eliot habitually uses Greek terms in English translation without acknowledgments or specific references to sources.

7. Gordon Haight believes that it was Aeschylus "more than any other author" who supplied Eliot with the "background for her doctrine of Nemesis," and cites Eliot's quotation from *The Eumenides* in Chapter 11 of *Romola* as evidence *(Letters,* II, 430, n. 6). In ll. 517 ff. of Aeschylus's play, from which Eliot takes the passage in *Romola,* the Furies speak of the dread ("to deinon") of wrongdoing, foreshadowing the symbolic meaning they will acquire later when they become "the well-intentioned ones." But it is not Nemesis but Justice ("Dika") the Furies invoke. The passage in *Romola* does make a reference to "Divine Nemesis," but the qualitfying adjective is important. There is another Nemesis that is not divine, and both are explored in Eliot's novel. Divine Nemesis does rise to Justice, but its existence is strictly limited to man's perception of Justice; it has no counterpart in the external world. It is the Nemesis that is not divine that is the order of the universe, and that Nemesis is nothing more than the consequences of action. What I am suggesting, in short, is that while

Aeschylus may be the source of the Nemesis that is a human moral perception, the Nemesis that governs the forces of nature for Eliot is the causal one to which the mainstream of Greek culture subscribed.

8. Cross, III, 35.

9. *Ibid.,* p. 33.

10. *Ibid.,* p. 36.

11. I refer again, of course, to the predominantly Apollonian strain in Greek culture.

12. Eliot distinguishes here between random determination, whose end is often inimical to the individual's welfare and to moral action, and that determination which, by fortunate accident, helps to cultivate desirable habits of thought and feeling. I will return to this subject later in this chapter and in the next.

13. There is superb irony in the diction here which reveals the central confusion in Fred's mind between fact and fancy. Fred's delusion so permeates his vision that he conceives of "luck" as part of a natural metaphor, as though it too were part of nature's law, an error quickly questioned by the narrator who substitutes the mathematical metaphor, the calculation by which Fred's anticipation should have been governed. But even this measure of reality is perverted by Fred's subjectivity.

14. (New York: Illustrated Cabinet Edition, n.d.), p. 3.

15. *The Ethics of George Eliot's Works* (Philadelphia, 1885), p.12.

16. Charles B. Cox, *The Free Spirit: A Study of Liberal Humanism in the Novels of George Eliot, Henry James, E. M. Forster, Virginia Woolf, Angus Wilson* (London, 1963), p. 37.

17. Tessa exclaims, in one, that Tito is as beautiful as the people " 'going into Paradise' " (p. 112), a reference the narrator repeats for her a moment later (p. 113), and is later credited by the narrator with the thought that Tito's face "was very much more beautiful than the Archangel Michael" (p. 154).

18. David Cecil and V. S. Pritchett, for example, hold this view.

19. The impression that characters like Adam and Felix are Eliot's paragons of virtue is partly the result of Eliot's aesthetic failure in her characterization of them. These, and others like them (Daniel, for example), are characters more reflected on than imagined. Eliot herself gives us the key, perhaps, to the aes-

thetic problem here when she says, in a letter to Frederic Harrison, that it is her intention to "make certain ideas thoroughly incarnate, *as if* they had revealed themselves to me in the flesh and not in the spirit" *(Letters,* IV, 300; my italics). Sometimes, the translation remains partial. That power which, for example, Dickens had to imagine, as George Henry Lewes writes, "not in the vague schematic way of ordinary imagination, but in the sharp definition of actual perception," a power that approached "hallucination" ("Dickens in Relation to criticism," *Literary Criticism of George Henry Lewes,* ed. Alice R. Kaminsky [Lincoln, 1964], pp. 97 and 95), Eliot never had.

20. *The Essence of Christianity,* pp. 185-186.

21. *The Novels of George Eliot,* p. 94.

22. One of Auguste Comte's briefer discussions of this subject can be found in the first chapter of *A General View of Positivism,* trans. J. H. Bridges (Stanford, n.d.), pp. 23-26.

23. *Experiments,* p. 60. (See Charles Darwin, *Origin of Species* [New York, Modern Library Edition, n.d.], p. 490.)

24. Although the differences in their commitments are many and basic, Wordsworth was one of Eliot's favorite poets, and the closing metaphor here clearly echoes 1. 28 of "Lines": "Felt in the blood, and felt along the heart."

25. This view is one of Comte's fundamental premises, stated, repeated, and implied throughout his works. Although the psychological fusion Eliot believes necessary in integrating emotional and intellectual knowledge is far more complex and subtle than what Comte describes, the concept of a perception of reality unified in feeling is also one of Comte's most important premises. (See, for example, *A General View,* especially Chapter 1.)

CHAPTER IV

Morality and Tragedy

Sympathy

The morality Eliot sees as being required by the collision of will and destiny is in part, as she had written to John Morley, one which attempts as much as possible to mitigate the hard, nonmoral outward conditions by calculating the possible and accepting the inevitable. Yet, paradoxically, even this principle of self-preservation becomes part of the hard outward condition of the cosmic forces against which the individual will struggles insofar as its necessity is dictated not by the instinct of the ego but by the cosmic laws which curb the spontaneous will. There is, in Eliot's world, very little sanctuary for the will. To be is, virtually, to be thwarted.

Yet, if the will cannot realize itself on the level of the reality in which consequences follow causes, it can, does, and should realize itself on the level of the second kind of reality in which man evaluates the nature of the first. It is man's prerogative to resent the universe and an essential moral act to grant the validity of that resentment.

In an important note to *The Spanish Gypsy,* Eliot writes that

a good tragic subject must represent . . . irreparable collision between the individual and the general. . . . It is the individual with whom we sympathise, and the general of which we recognize the irresistible power.[1]

In a very fundamental sense, the knowledge that Eliot judges to be essential for that "adjustment to the dire necessity of our lot" which is a moral requirement is identical with the recognition of the irresistible power, the objective facts of cosmic laws that oppose the individual will. But whether or not man agrees to act within those conditions imposed on him by his own impotence, the will never consents, for man is not "determined entirely by reflection, without the immediate intervention of feeling"; feeling, indeed, "supersedes reflection." To the will, every restriction is a defeat. The collision is irreparable partly because will, to whatever degree it is forced to adjust, must always lose more than it gains, but more because even if it does not lose outright, its success is at best a settlement in which reason may, but passion cannot, acquiesce. Nor, in fact, should it. As I discussed in the last chapter, nothing in Eliot's completely natural (and neutral) cosmic order prevents man from indulging his natural inclination to consider the demands of his ego entirely justified. Consequently, although factual reality interferes with a total expression of will, man is free at least in this, that he may sympathize fully, even as his egotism prompts him to do, with his own powerless condition.

For Eliot, this disjunction of power and sympathy logically entails a tragic perception of life. Equally, it is only in this disjunction that a tragic perception is possible. For where power and sympathy coincide, man must find not tragedy but one of two alternative visions. If he denies, in this matter, the validity of the completely subjective point of view, he commits himself to a cosmic authoritarianism in which power and sympathy coincide in something that is not-man, possibly God. Here, destiny is not only powerful but justified in whatever use it makes of that power. While man remains the object of power, he has no right to claim or be granted sympathy. This alternative Eliot rejects. But she rejects as well the coincidence of power and sympathy in man, the essentially romantic view. As Virginia Woolf remarks, Eliot has "none of that romantic intensity which is connected with a sense of one's individuality, unsated and unsubdued, cutting its shape sharply upon the background of the world." [2] The romantic hero frees himself of all restrictions and asserts his own individual and superb identity; he forces events to his will, conquers obstacles, and is limited only by his limitless imagination.

But if man is free in Eliot's universe to deny to power the justification of its tyranny, he is not free to disregard the fact of that tyranny and envision himself as one able to escape it. Indeed, this romantic mirror is the faulty reflection into which the egotists of Eliot's novels characteristically project themselves. In a passage which I quoted earlier for another reason and which deserves to be looked at again, Fred Vincy sees himself as just such a romantic hero:

> Fred had felt confident that he should meet the bill himself, having ample funds at his disposal in his own hopefulness. You will hardly demand that his confidence should have a basis in external facts; such confidence, we know, is something less coarse and materialistic; it is a comfortable disposition leading us to expect that the wisdom of providence, or the folly of our friends, the mysteries of luck or the still greater mystery of our high individual value in the universe, will bring about agreeable issues. *(Middlemarch,* p. 168)

Here the tone of the narrator is unmistakable. As is often the case in the novels when the narrator reveals the romantic thoughts of erring egotism, we hear, along with Fred's reflections, both the judicial undertone which rejects his mistaken suppositions and the sympathetic undertone that yet justifies him in the validity of his resentment, or what would be his resentment could he know the truth of the situation.

Two narrative voices, in fact, run concurrently through all the novels. There is, first, an analytic narrator who explicates, with neutral accuracy, the facts of existence. He is objective in two related senses. He is nonpartisan, not only in the conflicts among characters, but in the conflicts between men and cosmic laws. And he is objective also in the sense that even as he records the events of the conflicts, he remains, in his very nonpartisanship, outside the experience of the characters. Although he knows, for it is part of his necessary knowledge, the content of each individual consciousness, he remains uninvolved. His is the kind of intellectual knowledge I discussed in the last chapter. The second narrator, quite different in tone, is subjective, again in two related senses. He is subjective, first, because he enters fully into the existence of every character; he is, at one and the same time, the internal consciousness of every individual in the narrative and is capable of seeing with the exclusive optical selectivity that characterizes total egotism. In consequence, this narrator is also subjective in that he knows, with that knowledge that comes only from total identification, the final and unquestionable validity of the egocentric view. In the person of each character, he justifies the self against all encroachments.

It is somewhat a paradox that in the integration of intellectual and emotional knowledge that is essential for morality in Eliot's view, man, in another aspect of the tragic collision of forces, confronts once again a disjunction of incompatible elements, and the perception of what is morally necessary becomes the perception of what is humanly tragic. For the two narrators duplicate the disjunction of power and sympathy. If the irony of the above passage from *Middlemarch* is inevitable in the analytic narrator's knowledge of the indifference with which the universe regards Fred, it is so only because the sympathetic narrator is secretly conspiratorial in his identification with Fred's natural inclination to self-centered vision.

Eliot is not, as Robert Preyer believes, free from the "Byronic yearning for the world after the heart's desire." [3] One could come to such a conclusion only by confusing the same two facts that Fred Vincy confuses. To share and to sympathize with that yearning does not necessarily imply a belief in the possibility of its fulfillment. It would be impossible to grasp the tragedy in which Eliot's characters are involved without a very full sympathy for their delusions, a sympathy which is the very acquiescence in the "heart's desire," a profound wish that it were not necessary for them to do something other than what they prefer. But against the objective and analytic narrator, whose exclusive right it is to record the movement of destiny, the subjective narrator is as powerless as the characters themselves against the pressure of compelling facts.

Between them, Eliot's narrators create what is essentially a very Aristotelian catharsis. Eliot herself claimed, invariably, a place in the classical tradition of tragedy. To Frederic Harrison, for example, she writes that it is her purpose to "urge the human sanctities through tragedy—through pity and terror as well as admiration and delights" *(Letters,* IV, 301). It is also the Aristotelian framework that controls Eliot's presentation of her tragic protagonists. Yet, when we turn to the individual characters of the novels, it is obvious that if we are to accept Eliot's characters as Aristotelian figures, we must first translate the terms of his essential criteria. For while the subjective narrator argues, by example, for the reader's pity (or, to use Eliot's favorite word in this context, sympathy), while the objective narrator discloses the terror in the power of destiny over human affairs, the characters themselves seem to fall short of the traditional expectations of tragic stature. Of this fact Eliot is very much aware; but she asks the reader to abandon all conventional definitions and to yield, instead, to the force of two apparently contradictory but in fact complementary considerations, the first requiring in the reader an expansion of his objective imagination, the second a subjective concentration.

For Aristotle tragedy was to be found in the explosive potential of a particular individual and in the situation that grew out of his character. In a nearly unqualified sense, the character of the protagonist creates the tragedy. For Eliot the tragic drama is already and always in progress. It is "Nature," the narrator of *Adam Bede* characteristically remarks, that is the "great tragic dramatist" (p. 37). The real tragic protagonist is the entire human race, and each individual assumes his tragic role the moment his birth thrusts him onto the tragic stage. Each individual must be seen contextually, as a participant in a collective and indivisible drama.

For Eliot, indeed, tragedy is always the property of the context rather than of the individual, for no single character can ever be found to be the causal origin of the tragic collision. This is inherent in her determinism. Questioning Novalis's pronouncement that character is destiny,[4] the narrator of *The Mill on the Floss* suggests a comparison of Hamlet and Maggie Tulliver:

> Hamlet, Prince of Denmark, was speculative and irresolute, and we have a great tragedy in consequence. But if his father had lived to a good old age, and his uncle had died an early death, we can conceive Hamlet's having married Ophelia, and gone through life with a reputation for sanity, notwithstanding many soliloquies, and some moody sarcasms towards the fair daughter of Polonius, to say nothing of the frankest incivility to his father-in-law. (p. 351)

What is especially interesting here is that Eliot does not attempt to identify Maggie's tragedy with Hamlet's—that would have been the conventional technique of gaining dignity by heroic analogy—but rather that she restates Hamlet's tragedy in the same terms as Maggie's. The categorical distinction between the tragic figure who broods in splendid isolation and Maggie whose frustrated life is cluttered with the coarse reality of circumstance is dramatically obliterated. The tragedy in both cases, we are urged to see, is thoroughly contingent. It is the attribute of the total matrix within which one individual may have been our central focus but not our only protagonist; indeed, the tragic protagonists of the novels are exhausted only with the last name of the dramatis personae. Struggle and agony are not the prerogatives of the few.

The humor of the distorted perspective with which the narrator of *The Mill on the Floss* speculates about another view of Hamlet is characteristic of one of the most persistent techniques Eliot uses to recondition her readers. The heroic figure, Eliot says and implies, will assume very different proportions the moment he is removed from the fictional tradition and brought into the light of realistic analysis. "See the difference," the narrator of *Adam Bede* remarks, "between the impression a man makes on you when you walk by his side in familiar talk, or look at him in his home, and the figure he makes when seen from a lofty historical level" (p. 67). This difference is the language that translates the striding Lear into the stumbling Mr. Tulliver. Not unaware of the comic aspect of the association, the narrator of *The Mill on the Floss* insists, nevertheless, that Mr. Tulliver,

> though nothing more than a superior miller and maltster, was as proud and obstinate as if he had been a very lofty personage in whom such dispositions might be a source of that conspicuous, far-echoing tragedy which sweeps the stage in regal robes and makes the dullest chronicler sublime. The pride and obstinacy of millers, and other insignificant people, whom you

pass unnoticingly on the road every day, have their tragedies too. (pp. 173-174)

Especially in the focus on the clothing of the traditional tragic figure, Eliot expresses the degree to which the stature of the heroic protagonist was invested in the artificial. How inaccurate, and even absurd, this attention to alienating accidents is Eliot suggests in *Adam Bede* where the narrator urges us, in the same metaphor, not to consider Dinah and Seth beneath our interest, although we are accustomed to "weep over the loftier sorrows of heroines in satin boots and crinolines, and of heroes riding fiery horses, themselves ridden by still more fiery passions" (p. 36).

In one scene in *Daniel Deronda,* Eliot draws a direct contrast—which ultimately resolves into comparison—between a traditional moment in heroic tragedy and a similar event in Daniel's life. "In the heroic drama," the narrator remarks, "great recognitions are not encumbered with ... details; and certainly Deronda had as reverential an interest in Mordecai and Mirah as he could have had in the offspring of Agamemnon; but he was caring for destinies still moving in the dim streets of our earthly life, not yet lifted among the constellations" (p. 409). Daniel, still bound to the selective vision of the mind's heroic eye, is almost repelled when he finds the reality of his search for Mirah's brother considerably more sordid than it had appeared to him in anticipation. His enthusiasm adjusts itself uncomfortably to the solid fact of experience. But enthusiasm, the narrator had earlier commented, "we know, dwells at ease among ideas, tolerates garlic breathed in the middle ages, and sees no shabbiness in the official trappings of classic processions; it gets squeamish when ideals press upon it as something warmly incarnate, and can hardly face them without fainting" (p. 284).

It is always with this same edge of irony that Eliot contemplates the heroic vision of man while asserting the truth of her own. Characteristically, she makes her point by juxtaposing the two but reversing their conventional standing. Commenting, for example, on the popular unfavorable opinion of Casaubon in *Middlemarch,* the narrator confesses to some uncertainty: "I am not sure that *the greatest man of his age, if ever that solitary superlative existed,* could escape these unfavourable reflections of himself in various small mirrors; and even Milton, looking for his portrait in a spoon, must submit to have the facial angle of a bumpkin" (p. 62; my italics). Suddenly, Milton appears comic, while Casaubon is raised to a level at which he must claim our serious attention.

The surprising inversion in the angle of vision assures us that "superlative" and ludicrous characteristics inhere not in the men but in the point of view. It is on this principle that Eliot answers the possible surprise of the reader that a provincial surgeon should dream of himself as a discoverer. The narrator suggests we compare Lydgate to Herschel not to convince ourselves that Lydgate is equal to Herschel but rather to disabuse ourselves of the suspicion that a categorical distinction obtains between them. The difference between our impression of the two, in the terms of this argument, arises only in the relative degree of intimacy. "Each of these Shining Ones," the narrator assures us, "had to walk on the earth among neighbours who perhaps thought much more of his gait and his garments than of anything which was to give him a title to everlasting fame; each of them had his little local personal history sprinkled with small temptations and sordid cares, which made the retarding friction of his course towards final companionship with the immortals" *(Middlemarch,* pp. 108-109).

Although the effect here is to deflate the traditional tragic protagonist, it is not deflation but contextualization that Eliot is stressing. To see such a figure without heroic bias is to discover his essential and shared humanity. And in an exactly parallel way, to see without bias the figure to whom tradition has assigned a low and therefore untragic stature is to recognize, equally, his essential and shared humanity. That "element of tragedy," the narrator of *Middlemarch* remarks somewhat bitterly, "which lies in the very fact of frequency, has not yet wrought itself into the coarse emotion of mankind." The burden of guilt is clearly on the reader, although the narrator pretends to offer him a noble excuse: "perhaps our frames could hardly bear much of it." Yet this knowledge, painful as it is, is precisely the knowledge Eliot is determined to force on the reader's awareness. "If we had a keen vision and feeling of ordinary human life," the narrator continues, articulating the very premise on which each man is entitled in her view to tragic consideration, "it would be like hearing the grass grow and the squirrel's heart beat, and we should die of that roar which lies on the other side of silence" (p. 144). Eliot's attack on the reader, therefore, is a charge against his sensibilities which can respond to the rage in *Lear* and the passion in *Othello* but consigns to insignificance the daily burdens and frustrations of routine existence—at least in the lives of others.

This last qualification, Eliot well knew, was the crucial barrier to sympathy. His own "ordinary human life" the reader accepted instinctively as important, indeed, supremely important. But this very egotism, while it functioned in the real life of the reader as the insulating force that closed to him the equally insulated existence of others, could become, through art, the very means of forcing the reader to enter into the consciousness of another self. Not only the moral force but in fact the moral necessity of art Eliot argues from the fact that art can fuse reader and character in such a way that they merge in one identity. Through an exclusive and intense concentration on the innermost subjective reality of the concrete individual character, the artist can enlist that completely egotistical bias the reader feels on his own behalf in the forging of a sympathy that undermines self-centered egotism. And thus what the reader spontaneously grants about his own life—its irreducible significance, its inherently tragic proportion to himself—he is surprised into perceiving about others.

It is clear why, given her view of the necessary influence of art on life which I discussed in my first chapter, Eliot could not choose, even had she wanted to and even had no other considerations compelled her, to portray her tragic protagonist in any but the strictest realistic terms. The "greatest benefit we owe to the artist," Eliot writes in "The Natural History of German Life," "is the extension of our sympathy" *(Essays,* p. 270). But "extension" to what? For the characters of the novels, who are urged on a similar path to sympathy, the extension must be toward other characters, for these are their analogical reality. But the reader's reality is elsewhere, beyond the pages of fiction.

Art, Eliot writes in the same essay, is a mode of "amplifying experience and extending our contact with our fellow-men beyond the bounds of our personal lot" (p. 271). In *Adam Bede,* while arguing that characters of traditionally "low" personal stature must not be excluded from fiction, Eliot explicates her view of the relation between characterization and life. Of the reader who, she expects, will be disturbed by a realistic portrayal of human nature and who will ask her to " 'improve the facts a little' " she asks:

> what will you do then with your fellow-parishioner who opposes your husband in the vestry?—with your newly-appointed vicar, whose style of preaching you find painfully below that of his regretted predecessor?—with the honest servant who worries your soul with her one failing?—with your neighbour, Mrs. Green, who was really kind to you in your last illness, but has said several ill-natured things about you since your convalescence?—nay, with your excellent husband himself, who has other irritating habits besides that of not wiping his shoes?

What is especially striking about this passage is the opening question—"what will you do then?"—implying as it does the logically necessary connection between fiction and life. These fellow mortals, the narrator continues,

> every one, must be accepted as they are; you can neither straighten their noses, nor brighten their wit, nor rectify their dispositions; and it is these people—amongst whom your life is passed—that it is needful you should tolerate, pity, and love; it is these more or less ugly, stupid, inconsistent people, whose movements of goodness you should admire—for whom you should cherish all possible hopes, all possible patience. And I would not, even if I had the choice, be the novelist who could create a world so much better than this, in which we get up in the morning to do our daily work, that you would be likely to turn a harder, colder eye on the dusty streets and the common green fields—on the real breathing men and women, who can be chilled by your indifference or injured by your prejudice; who can be cheered and helped onward by your fellow-feeling, your outspoken, brave justice. (pp. 179-180)

The convictions Eliot expresses in this essay within the novel elaborate, as does the novel itself,[5] the moral-aesthetic criteria she had energetically supported in her review of Riehl and constitute, perhaps, Eliot's reply to Dickens, whom she had cited as a counterexample to Riehl's principles. Dickens's "false psychology, his perpetually virtuous poor children and artisans, his melodramatic boatmen and courtesans," Eliot feels, encourage the "miserable fallacy that high morality and refined moral sentiment can grow out of harsh social relations, ignorance, and want." Were his characters realistic, Dickens would be the "greatest contribution Art has even made to the awakening of the social sympathies." But it is a serious matter "that our sympathy with the perennial joys and struggles . . . in the life of our more heavily-laden fellow-men, should be perverted, and turned towards a false object instead of a true one." "We want to be taught to feel, not for the heroic artisan or the sentimental peasant, but for the peasant in all his coarse apathy, and the artisan in all his suspicious selfishness" ("The Natural History of German Life," *Essays,* pp. 270-273).

Thus, the extension of sympathy can be achieved only in the synthesis of two parallel processes of identification. The perversion of which Eliot speaks here is the result of the writer's focus on only one of these, namely, the reader's identification with the characters of fiction. But this single focus must be a morally truncating experience because the widening movement through which art takes the reader must be able to absorb, if it is not to end in perversion, the reader's simultaneous process of identification with real men and women. Obviously, characterization is the point at which the writer makes this choice. Only in realistic characterization are the two processes synthesized, and only in that synthesis can the writer hope to impel the reader to make the imaginative leap from fiction to life.

The controlling force in the fusion of reader and character is the voice of the thoroughly subjective narrator. It is he who raises the traditionally "low" figure to the same level to which the traditionally heroic figure had been lowered in the process of being contextualized. The techniques, in fact, through which Eliot levels distinctions of inherent significance are complementary aspects of the same vision. Just as the traditionally heroic character, caught in the surprise of a different set of assumptions, may become as ordinary or even absurd as Milton reflected in the distortion of a spoon (p. 168, above), so the ordinary man, suddenly apprehended from a completely subjective point of view, acquires an internal reality whose struggles and sufferings are made so personally real to the reader that he can no longer be judged to be below that absolute standard at which he empirically feels himself to stand.

Casaubon is an excellent example, for he yields easily to caricature and is, at first, presented quite deliberately in a satiric tone. We begin the novel, as Eliot expects her reader will naturally begin it, very much outside the characters. Everything about Casaubon is distasteful. The inner man is so much obscured that he grows ghostlike, an image to which Eliot unerringly directs us with references to Casaubon's sallow complexion, his cavernous eyesockets, and his emaciated bone structure. Even Casaubon conspires to create this illusion by announcing that he lives " 'with the dead' " *(Middlemarch,* p. 13). Celia speaks for the reader when she exclaims, and not only about his appearance, " 'How very ugly Mr. Casaubon is!' " (p. 15).

We are, indeed, encouraged to entertain the false hypothesis, to which the ghostlike imagery contributes, that there is no inner man, that beyond the surface Casaubon is hollow. His proposal to Dorothea, for example, a letter so pompous and unimpassioned that it strikes the narrator like the "cawing of an amorous rook" (p. 37), appears incontrovertible evidence that whatever inner reality nature might have once endowed Casaubon with has long ago withered. Subtle variations on the water imagery of the novel enforce this impression. Casaubon's feelings, Dorothea imagines, " 'his whole experience' " are " 'a lake compared with my little pool!' " (p. 18). But we learn, shortly, when Casaubon determined "to abandon himself to the stream of feeling," that he was "surprised to find what an exceedingly shallow rill it was" (p. 46).

It is with a dramatic shift in point of view that in Chapter 10 the narrator suddenly chastises the reader for accepting the only terms so far presented to him, as though, having patiently waited for a challenge, the narrator can no longer endure the callousness he has encouraged only to test the reader's sensibilities. Has Casaubon been, the narrator asks, "fairly represented in the minds of those less impassioned personages who have hitherto delivered their judgments concerning him?" Suppose, the narrator suggests, advancing Eliot's own criterion,

we turn from outside estimates of a man, to wonder, with keener interest, what is the report of his own consciousness

about his doing or capacity; with what hindrances he is carry-
ing on his daily labours; what fading hopes, or what deeper
fixity of self-delusion the years are marking off within him; and
with what spirit he wrestles against universal pressure, which
will one day be too heavy for him, and bring his heart to its final
pause. *Doubtless his lot is important in his own eyes; and the
chief reason we think he asks too large a place in our consideration must be our want of room for him. . . . Mr. Casaubon,
too, was the centre of his own world;* if he was liable to think
that others were providentially made for him, and especially to
consider them in the light of their fitness for the author of a
"Key to all Mythologies," this trait is not quite alien to us, and,
like the other mendicant hopes of mortals, claims some of our
pity. (p. 62; my italics)

The argument, obviously, hinges on the "too" of the last clause I
have italicized. That Casaubon's lot is important to himself—that he is the center of his own world—is the fact to which
the reader must emotionally acquiesce. Only by reminding the
reader that he must look for the empirical meaning of this claim
in his own similar experience can the narrator hope to elicit that
"pity" which each man's egotism spontaneously releases for
himself.

The same technique is repeated, with equal force, much later
in the novel when the narrator has allowed the reader to identify for a long time with Dorothea and her point of view about
the marriage. Chapter 29 of the third book begins by continuing
this point of view but shifts, suddenly, to a recognition that to
identify with Dorothea is to close the door of sympathy on her
husband. "One morning, some weeks after her arrival in Lowick,
Dorothea—but why always Dorothea? was her point of view the
only possible one with regard to this marriage?" The resentment
the reader had been building against Casaubon's insensitivity to
his wife is suddenly revealed to be nothing more than the same
insensitivity directed against Casaubon. "Mr. Casaubon," the

narrator reminds us, "had an intense consciousness within him, and was spiritually a-hungered like the rest of us" (p. 205).

Nothing suggests so clearly Eliot's perception of the tragedy inherent in ordinary human life as the standard of human heroism implicit in her novels. At nineteen, Eliot writes to Maria Lewis that she believes "it requires more of a martyr's spirit to endure with patience and cheerfulness daily crossings and interruptions of our petty desires and pursuits, and to rejoice in them if they can be made to conduce to God's glory and our sanctification, than even to lay down our lives for the truth" *(Letters,* I, 6). Thirty-six years later she has lost God but not the conviction. To Oscar Browning she writes that she thinks "the most difficult heroism" is "that which consists in the daily conquests of our private demons, not in the slaying of world-notorious dragons" *(Letters,* VI, 126). The grand confrontation of traditional tragedy has at least this compensation, that the greatness of the protagonist, the grandeur of the situation are highly redeeming; and it comes, moreover, once only; the character who can withstand that single conflict has risen to the utmost requirements of the tragedy. But such a test of courage, in Eliot's view, is in the end less demanding than the persistent and less dramatic tests which life in fact imposes.

Maggie Tulliver, indeed, is characteristic when she almost eagerly accepts a course of action which she anticipates will bring her a heroic martyrdom. Converted, as she thinks, by the spirit of Thomas à Kempis, she acquires, the narrator ironically tells us, a "zeal of self-mortification." And we are not surprised, as the narrator knows, that a character like Maggie "threw some exaggeration and wilfulness, some pride and impetuosity, even into her self-renunciation." For Maggie has still not learned to live in the real world; "her own life was still a drama for her, in which she demanded of herself that her part should be played with intensity." It is important that this preparation for a glorious martyrdom Maggie attempts comes not at the end of the novel, where it might have introduced the traditional denouement—thus satisfying the structure of the drama Maggie imagines herself acting in—but in the middle of the novel, where we recognize that Maggie's estimate of the climax is a false one, in direct contradiction to the climax her author is preparing for a much later scene. Between Maggie's climax and Eliot's many "unheroic" tests will disabuse Maggie's romantic vision of martyrdom. Maggie's is "the path we all like when we set out on our abandonment of egoism," the narrator remarks; it is "the path of martyrdom and endurance, where the palm-branches grow, rather than the steep highway of tolerance, just allowance, and self-blame, where there are no leafy honours to be gathered and worn" *(The Mill on the Floss,* p. 257).

Climactic moments, indeed, are never as glorious as the characters imagine; they are quite prosaic, in fact. Cox laments the absence of "new horizons" in Eliot's conclusions,[6] but it is precisely Eliot's point that there are no new horizons, no grand discoveries, only the same fundamental fact, to be recognized and accepted, as has obtained through all human existence: life is an exercise in disappointment and failure, and our best efforts are often those which teach us that "stoical resignation" which Eliot had called, in a letter to Mrs. Ponsonby, "a hidden heroism" *(Letters,* VI, 99).

Perhaps the strictest test of this view is to be found in the character of Kester Bale in *Adam Bede,* a character in no way unique or remarkable. We are told little more about him than that he is a good laborer. Yet the narrator does not quarrel with Bale's sense of the dignity of his contribution and the authenticity of his human struggle, a sense, indeed, of which the narrator is far more aware than Bale himself. Bale's case is, in a sense, analogical. The argument has been, from the beginning, that ordinary men and women such as the novel is concerned with—from the main characters to the rustic chorus—*are* important. It is a paradox only in terms of the heroic vision to state, as the narrator does, that "insignificant"—the word ironically concedes the reader's prejudice—people are, in the end, not inferior to the "great." They "can be shown to affect the price of bread and the rate of wages, to call forth many evil tempers from the selfish and many heroisms from the sympathetic, and, in other ways, to play no small part in the tragedy of life" (p. 66), although, as the narrator also concedes much later, people "in high station are of course more thought of and talked about, and have their virtues more praised, than those whose lives are passed in humble every-day work" (p. 274).

It is in this context that the narrator pauses to comment with affectionate sympathy on Kester and his "humble everyday work." When

> the last touch had been put to the last beehive rick, Kester, whose home lay at some distance from the farm, would take a walk to the rick-yard in his best clothes on a Sunday morning, and stand in the lane, at a due distance, to contemplate his own thatching—walking about to get each rick from the proper point of view.

Then, as though anticipating the reader's impatience, the narrator adds:

> I am not ashamed of commemorating old Kester; you and I are indebted to the hard hands of such men—hands that have long mingled with the soil they tilled so faithfully, thriftily making the best they could of the earth's fruits, and receiving the smallest share as their own wages. (p. 529)

This passage bears a remarkable similarity to two others. In *Felix Holt,* the narrator, speaking of Rev. Lyon, remarks:

> [We] see human heroism broken into units and say, this unit did little—might as well not have been. But in this way we might break up a great army into units; in this way we might break the sunlight into fragments, and think that this and the

other might be cheaply parted with. Let us rather raise a monument to the soldiers whose brave hearts only kept the ranks unbroken and met death—a monument to the faithful who were not famous, and who are precious as the continuity of the sunbeams is precious. (p. 189)

And in the "Finale" of *Middlemarch,* the narrator, looking back to Dorothea's life, says that her

finely-touched spirit had still its fine issues, though they were not widely visible. . . . The effect of her being on those around her was incalculably diffusive; for the growing good of the world is partly dependent on unhistoric acts; and that things are not so ill with you and me as they might have been is half owing to the number who lived faithfully a hidden life, and rest in unvisited tombs. (pp. 612-613)

Most remarkably, the passages commemorate three quite different individuals: Kester Bale, whom not even a romantic vision could raise to the traditionally heroic—at best to the chorus of a rustic idyll—and who might have served, for another author, as comic relief; Dorothea Brooke, in whose restless soul stirred the spark of St. Theresa; and Rev. Lyon, who stands somewhere between the two. Yet for Eliot their lives, ultimately, do not differ so much; if Bale is satisfied to take pride in his work, unconscious of the standing it claims for him, Dorothea must be resigned to reduce her anticipated impact on the world. Writing of the forthcoming last installment of *Middlemarch* in which Dorothea's end was to be described, Eliot anticipates Sara Hennell's distress and warns her that she must expect "to be disappointed with the close of the novel"; she is to remember, however, to "look back at the Prelude" *(Letters,* V, 330). Apparently, Sara Hennell had expected very much what Dorothea herself had imagined: success, or at least a grand failure. Neither is or can be the case, for the actual end of the novel had been implied in the very facts of Dorothea's existence, as the "Prelude" had suggested.

An identical pattern is found in the parallel case of Lydgate who, like Dorothea, had begun the novel with expectations of unusual achievement. Such achievement, of course, is not impossible, as we see in characters like Klesmer, Daniel, Naumann, and others. But these are the exceptions rather than the norm. More commonly, those who dream of becoming St. Theresa must learn to accept a far smaller part; those who hope to pattern their lives after Herschel are forced to resign themselves to a far commoner lot. In an introductory passage which stands as a parallel to the "Prelude" in which Dorothea's story is prefigured, the narrator hints at Lydgate's lot:

in the multitude of middle-aged men who go about their vocations in a daily course determined for them much in the same way as the tie of their cravats, there is always a good number who once meant to shape their own deeds and alter the world a little. The story of their coming to be shapen after the average and fit to be packed by the gross, is hardly ever told even in their consciousness; for perhaps their ardour in generous unpaid toil cooled as imperceptibly as the ardour of other youthful loves, till one day their earlier self walked like a ghost in its old home and made the furniture ghastly. (p. 107)

Like Dorothea too, Lydgate finds no more fulfillment in his personal life than in his professional; the domestic paradise he had envisioned, crowned by the "tender devotedness and docile adoration of the ideal wife must be renounced"; instead, "life must be taken up on a lower stage of expectation" (p. 377). That his concept of the ideal marriage had been vain and egotistical, as had Dorothea's in fact, is of little consequence in the face of the hard fact of his disillusionment. All that matters is that this is not what Lydgate's youth desired, although it is all, or nearly all, which man acquires. Such "ordinary human life," as the narrator of *Middlemarch* had called it, requires a faithful persistence in confronting the sordid fact, a heroism which is for Eliot the essence of the courage that alone can endure the terms imposed on man by his tragic existence.

Fatal Innocence: The Case of Hetty Sorrel

Nowhere does Eliot test more rigorously the power of identification than in the case of Hetty in *Adam Bede*. Here, the disjunction of power and sympathy yields one of the most painful conflicts between the two narrative voices in all of Eliot's fiction, for there is no other character as innocently fatal as Hetty. As the analytic narrator reflects on her fatality and the sympathetic narrator on her innocence, the novel evolves the paradigm pattern which Eliot follows through all her subsequent novels. The principle is simple enough. Against the voice of the analytic narrator who traces the inevitable evolution from cause to effect, the sympathetic narrator calls for that human evaluation of the events which render Hetty's fate an object of compassion.

Harvey, discussing Eliot's handling of her narrators, suggests that the narrative expressions of sympathy are a "form of snobbery," that the author is "inviting the reader to share with her an attitude of lofty condescension towards one of her characters." She is saying to the reader, in effect, " 'poor deluded man,' " and " 'but *we* know better, don't we?' " [7] Such an interpretation confuses, I think, the very important distinction between the two narrators, one perhaps lofty in his distance from the action he records but the other very personally and subjectively involved in that action. Eliot's tone to the reader is often ironic, but it is never condescending. In *Impressions of Theophrastus Such,* Theophrastus remarks that if he laughs at the follies of mankind, he includes himself under his own indignation, for if "the human race has a bad reputation, I perceive that I cannot escape being compromised" (p. 3). The total effect is characterized by a paradoxical sense of the world revealed sometimes in an intellectual perception of absurd juxtapositions but more often in the controlled pathos of the sympathetic narrator's identification with a character suffering consequences which the analytic narrator is powerless to alter.

Fundamentally, the formula never varies: compassion is the absolute right of suffering, regardless of what the cause of that suffering is. There is no question of responsibility here. As far as responsibility is concerned, Hetty is as much a spectator as we are. Indeed, the question of responsibility in Eliot arises only in the voice of the analytic narrator, for here the distinction between the two voices is even more significant. George Levine, in his discussion of this question, suggests that Eliot's form of determinism accepts responsibility; she believes, he claims, that "although every action is caused, few causes are uncontrollable in the sense that no effect to alter them can succeed." Therefore, "as long as the cause is not a compulsion, that is, as long as it is not physically impossible or excessively dangerous to will differently and as long as one is not so mentally ill that one cannot will differently even if one wants to, one is responsible for his actions." [8] Levine's thesis is accessible to an important objection, namely, the typical determinist argument that if our wills are conditioned, we cannot will to will differently any more than we can will differently, nor will to will to will differently, and so on to an infinite, if at some point meaningless, regression. As though in answer, Levine adds that Eliot was concerned with immediate and practical matters—external pressures and internal desires——and not with what had caused the susceptibility long before.[9] But this is not strictly the case, for Eliot is always acutely concerned with early conditioning, even when she does not, as in *The Mill on the Floss* she does, develop the childhood influences in great detail. We are always informed of essential background that tightens the deterministic chain. Paris, disagreeing with

Levine, concludes that it would be a contradiction of Eliot's determinism for her to believe in responsibility for action.[10]

Both critics, I think, respond to a very tangible reality in the novels, for one is always aware that Eliot does and does not hold her characters responsible for what they do. She does not do both, however, on the same level. Responsibility is the demand made by the power whose workings the analytic narrator describes and which imposes consequences on agents who are out of harmony with natural laws, reagrdless of their failings or weaknesses. This is not, obviously, responsibility in a traditional moral sense, although it becomes, in essence, identical with what Eliot considers to be a moral requirement. But the ego, and the sympathetic narrator who assumes its claims, rebels against this natural responsibility and asserts that if nature cannot concede us innocent and so excuse us from suffering the consequences of our actions, man can and must exonerate us, at least in his judgment. For the kind of responsibility that holds us accountable is valid only in the context of "free will," where genuine choice is possible, and can have no application in the determined world of Eliot's novels.

In combination, Eliot's two narrators create, in an irresoluble tension, the deliberately ambivalent attitude to the events and characters of the novels which explicates the relationship between power and sympathy. The statement is made not only through apostrophes to the reader,[11] but in complex symbolic structures as well. In Hetty's case, Eliot already concentrates most of the devices and symbols to which she returns again and again in later novels. Throughout, Eliot's plan is obviously to obliterate guilt and substitute a compassionate identification. This Eliot accomplishes in part by continually reducing Hetty's status as a morally deliberative agent; Hetty becomes a victim, although not of specific circumstances as much as of her own nature and the general human condition. The passage in which she is introduced to the reader is characteristic of the way Eliot will handle her throughout. Her beauty, the narrator says, was like that of kittens, or very small downy ducks making gentle rippling noises with their soft bills, or babies just beginning to toddle and to engage in conscious mischief—a beauty with which you can never be angry, but that you feel ready to crush for inability to comprehend that state of mind into which it throws you. *(Adam Bede,* p. 83)

Almost immediately after, the narrator compares her cheek to a rose petal (p. 83). Although Hetty is, chronologically, a young woman, Eliot identifies her with children, with animals—young ones—and finally with plants.

The symbol of the child is a complex one in Eliot's novels. The child is only, at best, a potential human being, and forms a natural bridge down to the animal at the next level. In "The Wisdom of the Child," Eliot wrote:

true wisdom; which implies a moral as well as an intellectual result, consists in a return to that purity and simplicity which characterizes early youth, when its intuitions have not been perverted. It is, indeed, a similarity with a difference: for the wonder of the child at the material world is the effect of novelty, its simplicity and purity of ignorance; while the wonder of the wise man is the result of knowledge disclosing mystery, the simplicity and purity of his moral principles, the result of wide experience and hardly-attained self-conflict. ("Poetry and Prose, From the Notebook of an Eccentric," *Essays,* p. 20)

Despite the Wordsworthian allusion to unperverted intuitions, it is obvious that Eliot does not acquiesce in the romantic vision of the child as a "seer." The "simplicity and purity" of the child are desirable only when recaptured in knowledge and experience. In a state of nature which precedes both, the child is an ignorant, undisciplined creature.

Eliot's children, in fact, unlike many of Dickens's, are at least

183

mischievous and sometimes malicious. Young Harold Transome, in *Felix Holt,* is a characteristic sample. He is always
compared to animals and, in fact, keeps a menagerie in which he
feels much more at home than in the human world (p. 383). He
also mimics animals with that remarkable ability which springs
from strong similarity: squirrels, sometimes (p. 430), great
tropical birds (p. 430), puppies, when he is in better than
normal humor (p. 467), and—perhaps an evolutionary reference—monkeys (p. 384). He is entirely wild (p. 383), tossing his
black mane in furious fashion (p. 97). His favorite activity is,
characteristically, biting the guests at Transome Court. Nevertheless, young Harold, like his father whom he all too often
resembles, is rather charming, and Hetty, too, as the narrator
had suggested in introducing her, is in some ways enhanced by
the very childlikeness of her nature.

But this kind of charm is implicitly restricted to activities of
the child's world; in the more serious business of adult concerns,
where actions have consequences all too real and pervasive, this
premoral state is potentially explosive. The narrator prepares
us to see the absurdity of Hetty in a world of adult responsibilities by imaginatively projecting her into mother-
hood. The comment is ironic as is the concept of Hetty in an
adult situation because both narrative voices can be heard at
once. "Ah, what a prize the man gets who wins a sweet bride like
Hetty!" exclaims the narrator explicating Adam's thoughts.
"How the men envy him who come to the wedding breakfast."
The lines echo Odysseus's address to Nausicaa in Book VI of the
Odyssey, but Adam, unlike Odysseus who makes up a pretty
speech in the hope of finding some shelter in a strange land,
believes what he is saying. Adam's blindness, sharpened by this
contrast to the epic hero, is even more strikingly revealed by the
sequence of the next two sentences: "How she will dote on her
children! She is almost a child herself" *(Adam Bede,* p. 154).
Here, the exclamation point is a superb subterfuge. For Adam,
and the sympathetic narrator who identifies with him, it stands

for a causal conjunction. But in that fact, the analytic narrator sees the central flaw in Adam's psychological perception. The statements divided by the exclamation contradict one another, for to be a child is to be a primitive egotist, incapable of self-expansion. The mirror in which Hetty is reflected in Adam's mind is as distorted as the one in which Hetty sees herself.

It is the essence of the child not to recognize reality, to take fancy for fact, and to expect the impossible as though it were inevitable. Hetty is, like the baby of the first set of images, totally helpless, and, as the narrator remarks, one cannot be angry with her. As she makes her bewildering and painful journey in search of Arthur, the narrator reminds us that she is blameless even of her hardened egotism. It is what nature made her, something Hetty neither asked for nor understands. For one who finds herself forced to act in a context for which, through no fault of her own, she is entirely unequipped, there can be only sympathy. "Poor, wandering Hetty," the narrator remarks, "with the rounded childish face, and the hard unloving despairing soul looking out of it—with the narrow heart and narrow thoughts, no room in them for any sorrow but her own, and tasting that sorrow with the more intense bitterness!" (p. 397). What is remarkable about this passage—and there are many like it—is the resolution of what would have been, more normally, an antithesis; it is partially suggested in the "and" which joins the "childish face" and the "unloving soul"; one would have expected at least a "but." Yet Eliot passes from the one to the other without comment or transition. By the time we reach "despairing," the juxtaposition seems no longer antithetical at all but quite inevitable. For both aspects are on the same level of neutrality, and Hetty can claim as little merit for the first as blame for the second.

It is this same insight, forced on the reader by the sympathetic narrator, that Adam acquires in his own evolution into compassion. Adam distinguishes between the responsibilities of the adult and those of the child, warning Arthur that " 'things don't lie level between Hetty and you. You're acting with your eyes open, whatever you may do; but how do you know what's been in her mind? She's all but a child—as any man with a conscience in him ought to feel bound to take care on' " (p. 314). Later, when the catastrophe occurs, it is Arthur he blames, and not purely out of bias for Hetty. " 'I want him to feel what she feels. It's his work ... she was a child as it 'ud ha' gone t' anybody's heart to look at ... I don't care what she's done ... it was him brought her to it. And he shall know it ... he shall feel it ... if there's a just God, he shall feel what it is t' ha' brought a child like her to sin and misery' " (p. 432). Here, of course, Adam lacks compassion for Arthur; but the reference to the "just God" who could not hold Hetty responsible for her actions —although natural law destroys her as though she were—provides the reader with a standard for judgment.

The second, animal, level of imagery enforces the effect of the first, but does more as well, for here Eliot removes Hetty from the human world altogether. With an occasional exception, as when Mrs. Poyser calls Hetty a peacock (p. 157), these animal allusions deliberately suspend moral judgment in favor of completely subjective sympathy. Of the animal images introduced in Eliot's first description of Hetty, the image of the kitten is most developed in the novel, and the reader's response is guided into an amused indulgence of the kitten's playful claws. Even Mrs. Pomfret, who sees no practical matrimonial advantage in Hetty's pretty ways, yields grudgingly to her charms (p. 136). By the time the reader arrives at the fateful moment in which the kitten kills its own offspring, he finds it very difficult to dismiss the habit of affection he has been trapped in. Moreover, the animal image discourages moral indignation. Whatever the analytic narrator has to record, the sympathetic one has long before prepared a defense against. At its climax, the imagery culminates in a contrast between Hetty's human tragedy and the picture of the "kitten-like" creature who "till a few months ago had never felt any other grief than that of envying Mary Burge a new ribbon" (p. 378).

Something of Hetty's detachment is already suggested in the image of the kitten, but, on a lower level of animal allusions, the narrator, noting Hetty's indifference to Adam's troubles, remarks that "young souls, in such pleasant delirium" as the anticipation of a glance from Arthur, "are as unsympathetic as butterflies sipping nectar" (p. 101). Both the Olympian and the natural association place Hetty well beyond human culpability and centrally into an amoral state of nature. The image is repeated as the events evolve toward the expected conclusion (p. 136) and climaxes in the sympathetic narrator's full exposition of the discrepancy between Hetty and the human situation in which she finds herself: "it is too painful to think that she is a woman, with a woman's destiny before her—a woman spinning in young innocence a light web of folly and vain hopes which may one day close round her and press upon her a rancorous poisoned garment, changing all at once her fluttering, trivial butterfly sensations into a life of deep human anguish" (p. 256).

Supported by the very important reference to her "innocence," the imagery prepares us for what might otherwise be a surprising emphasis in Hetty's "journey in despair." Here, at the moment when she is most destructive, she is most freed of responsible agency. We are constantly reminded that Hetty is by nature unsuited to anything but pleasure, as when the narrator remarks that she had "the luxurious nature of a round, soft-coated pet animal" (p. 386). She should never have been forced into human conflicts. But cosmic laws make no exceptions, however ill prepared the victim is. And toward the end, Hetty is all victim. Pursued relentlessly by the sequence of events, Hetty's confusion and terror are captured in a sharp transformation of the animal image as we see her now a "wounded brute" (p. 398), shrinking like a "frightened animal" (p. 428), stalking Dinah, in the prison, like an animal at bay (p. 457).

The success of Eliot's vast network of sympathetic devices in this most rigorous test of the reader's compassion is confirmed in the ease with which we accept the implications of the narrator's description of Hetty as a "young blooming girl, not knowing where to turn for refuge from swift-advancing shame; understanding no more of this life of ours than a foolish lost lamb wandering farther and farther in the nightfall on the lonely heath; yet tasting the bitterest of life's bitterness." The thought calls forth an appropriate apostrophe: "No wonder man's religion has much sorrow in it; no wonder he needs a Suffering God" (p. 371). Very early in the novel, Dinah had called Hetty a " 'poor wandering lamb' " (p. 31), speaking, naturally, in her own religious idiom. It is this idiom that the narrator has now taken up, raising Hetty's suffering to a universal condition, something already foreshadowed in the suggestion of Hetty as Adam's Eve, which Eliot has been implying throughout.

But, somewhat ironically, as the passage raises Hetty so it also lowers her, although to the same end; the "blooming" is not a trite description but a strict continuation of the plant imagery which explains, more than any other, why, as the narrator had first said, we cannot be angry with Hetty, whatever she does. It would make as much sense to blame her for what she is as it would to blame a tulip for not being a rose. Like a bud (p. 133), Hetty grows unconsciously from seed to fruition, and it is not her doing that she is a plant that has "hardly any roots" (p. 156). Adam's thoughts about Hetty reveal a dark irony:

> Nature, he knows, has a language of her own, which she uses with strict veracity, and he considers himself an adept in the language. Nature has written out his bride's character for him in those exquisite lines of cheek and lip and chin, in those eyelids delicate as petals, in those long lashes curled like the stamen of a flower, in the dark liquid depths of those wonderful eyes. How she will dote on her children! She is almost a child herself, and the little pink round things will hang about her like florets round the central flower. (p. 154)

An apparent cosmic perversion adorns with charming innocence the deadliest plant and mocks the moralist's sense of propriety. But the narrative voices deny neither reality.

The Moral Code of the Unique Instance

The two narrative voices which speak to the reader of the tragic collision of power and sympathy have resounding echoes in Eliot's definition of moral action. In a sense, morality is the arena in which power and sympathy confront one another in the concrete fact. For morality implements the vision of the narrative voices with a vital difference. In the case of the narrative voices, sympathy and power operate on two distinct levels. As a function of the imagination, sympathy escapes the material tyranny of power and yields to no limitation except the human capacity for compassion. Indeed, by Eliot's very definition of the tragic collision, sympathy is entirely coincidental with the consequences of power, since it is aroused only and precisely when will is defeated by destiny. But to "lighten the pressure of hard non-moral outward conditions," morality must function in the causal world. In morality, power and sympathy must be brought to the same factual level, and here sympathy can operate only where power does not. Thus, morality becomes a concession to sympathy as far as the facts of destiny permit.

Yet it remains always true for Eliot that primary consideration must be yielded to the individual will. In each concrete fact in which will and destiny make conflicting demands, resolutions can be justified only if they have resisted to the last possible degree the tyranny of power. This is the only moral formula Eliot accepts, but it is a formula, obviously, whose very purpose it is to invalidate all formulas. For every event, every moment of time, every individual is unique; and whatever may be the best compromise in one situation will seldom be the exact best compromise in another.

It becomes somewhat inaccurate to speak of Eliot's "morality," except in the collective sense of the term, and essential to distinguish moralities. In perhaps her most radical concession to the individual ego, Eliot asks for ad hoc moralities created for each individual instance, although she despairs of the world ever attaining such a state of perfection. If generalizations on the basis of similarities are possible, or for practical purposes necessary, they must be made provisionally, skeptically, and should be, at least ideally, applied with any degree of flexibility dictated by the specifics of the case. In short, even when a rule can be or is appealed to, it must be evaluated anew; the decision becomes, in consequence, once more an ad hoc decision. The appeal, again, to thought and critical judgment is obvious. Obvious, too, is the fact that this commitment breaks for Eliot another and very crucial tie with Christianity. Differing somewhat from more characteristic nonbelievers of the century, Eliot finds not even for the morality that grew out of religion a very useful place in her concepts. But it is not only or specifically the rules of religious morality that Eliot finds unacceptable. The moral rules of social traditions as well, and even those an individual evolves for himself, are at best insufficient, at worst perversions, as long as they function as rules. All three varieties are prone to a list of errors, the particulars of which Eliot makes clear in the novels through a dialectic of example and counterexample.

On one level, the attempt to live by, or worse still to judge by, rules is an attempt to simplify drastically the complexity of the world. In the infinite variety of reality, there are situations to which such broad generalizations as moral maxims do not apply, or apply only imperfectly, or, more problematic yet, apply in numbers, one conflicting with another, each dictating a different course of action. Each moral crisis in the novels tests the apparently relevant rules and invariably finds them deficient or useless.

We see this, for example, in Silas Marner's dilemma when, confronted with Godfrey Cass's demand for the return of

Eppie, Silas must decide what to do. Although Silas does not articulate them very clearly, the considerations which are involved in his decision are many and complex. Godfrey is asking for the return of what, in a sense, belongs to him, his daughter; but she belongs to Silas as well, and there is no very real guide for settling the question of "ownership" here, particularly since the object of contention is a living creature whose best interests must be centrally considered. But what, indeed, are Eppie's best interests? Godfrey realistically reminds Silas of the advantages he can give her, important advantages such as education, refinement, position, prospects for the future which she cannot possibly have if she remains with Silas. Moreover, Godfrey offers her a home in which she will be loved by himself and Nancy, perhaps no less than she has been loved up to now by Silas. And what of Godfrey himself? His needs are important, certainly. He wants Eppie very much. That he abandoned her years before is not a very convincing argument in itself, for he is, for one thing, not the same man. But if we see Godfrey's claim, we see Silas's too. Eppie is at least as important to Silas as she is to Godfrey; and perhaps he needs her more. At least one suspects he does, but in the matter of needs only the individual character can testify and, in the face of individual isolation, can inevitably do so only to himself.

None of these arguments can lead to a decision. There are no traditional axioms here to ensure a comfortable conclusion to the dilemma. It is significant that Silas's decision is indecision, for the only determining factor is that to which Silas agrees to appeal, Eppie's preference. And it is on this basis, in fact, that Eppie herself makes her decision, or rather her choice, for a decision it certainly cannot be called. She chooses to remain with Silas because he and his world have been the molding context of her identity. " 'I can't feel as I've got any father but one,' " she answers Nancy. " 'I can't think o' no other home. I wasn't brought up to be a lady, and I can't turn my mind to it. I like the working-folks, and their victuals, and their ways' " *(Si-*

las Marner, p. 234). Although she cannot quite articulate it in her idiom, Eppie knows that to leave the environment in which she has been created is to negate the self. In this case, there can be no more pressing consideration. In a situation for which religious, social, even legal, morality could find a large number of rules—but only by dismissing the necessities of the specific instance—Eliot chooses to appeal to the uncodified unique fact. Nancy, indeed, cites some of the traditional rules when she says to Eppie that " 'there's a duty you owe to your lawful father. There's perhaps something to be given up on more sides than one. When your father opens his home to you, I think it's right you shouldn't turn your back on it' " (p. 234). But Eliot obviously sees little merit in such rigid notions of "duty" and "right."

Nancy Cass, throughout the novel, is one of a number of rule-ridden characters in Eliot's works; she names duties for every situation, sifting her rights and wrongs through an iron sieve. In important ways, she reminds one a good deal of Casaubon, even more of Tom Tulliver. On the whole, they are an unappealing lot. Yet, from a conventional point of view, none of them does anything "wrong." Nancy accepts her barrenness as the will of God, although her God is at such a remove from heaven that He is, more strictly, merely the name of ideas she has absorbed from her social environment. On the basis of this view, she forces Godfrey to suffer the perpetual pain of a childless marriage, a pain sharpened by conscience and memory. Yet she acts on what is virtually a communal mandate, and even the reader cannot quite find the traditional name of her sin. Similarly, Tom Tulliver—"Rhadamanthine Tom" *(The Mill on the Floss,* p. 48)—and the world he represents constrict Maggie's larger passions and imagination on the very same argument that confirmed the Capulets and Montagues in their narrow visions. Like Tom, Casaubon confronts a woman of far greater depth and potential than himself and, being in a position to enforce his views, represses much of what is best in Dorothea, although he too has a very valid conventional claim to expect loyalty from his wife.

These characters, and others like them, do little thinking, very little feeling, and find rather their criteria for judgment and action supplied by the mores of their societies. Following, as they generally do, the stale social habits they inherit, they convince the reader that they could as well have followed completely different sets of standards, with equal tenacity, had those prevailed. As repositors of enduring communal conditionings, they are regarded by their equals as highly respectable, far more respectable, indeed, than those who are their antagonists, although they slowly erode the more sensitive lives they touch.

The alternative is not exactly a repudiation of tradition. Eliot generally regards herself as a conservative—obviously in a very etymological sense of the word—and sustains that position partially on the empirical basis that many centuries of experience must provide guidelines that have some practical value, although such guidelines had their origin in informed judgment. In "Evangelical Teaching: Dr. Cumming," Eliot writes that "all human beings who can be said to be in any degree moral have their impulses guided, not indeed always by their own intellect, but by the intellect of human beings who have gone before them, and created traditions and associations which have taken the rank of laws" *(Essays,* p. 166). The question Eliot raises, rather, is what is to be done with this accumulated experience of mankind. Near the end of *The Mill on the Floss,* reflecting with Dr. Kenn on the complexities of the relationships of Maggie, Stephen, Lucy, and Philip, the narrator remarks that the great problem

of the shifting relation between passion and duty is clear to no man who is capable of apprehending it; the question, whether the moment has come in which a man has fallen below the possibility of a renunciation that will carry any efficacy, and must accept the sway of a passion against which he had struggled as a tresspass, is one for which we have no master key that will fit all cases. The casuists have become a by-word of reproach; but their perverted spirit of minute discrimination was the shadow of a truth to which eyes and hearts are too often sealed: the truth, that moral judgments must remain false and hollow, unless they are checked and enlightened by a perpetual reference to the special circumstances that mark the individual lot. (p. 435)

In the concluding part of this passage—I will return to another part of it at a later time—Eliot rejects not the accumulated common sense of the species which a moral maxim may express but its indiscriminate application without regard to the individual case—to those unique considerations that make any implementation of a conventional guideline a newly informed ad hoc decision. Indeed, a significant group of characters in Eliot's novels seem to function in terms of traditional codes but do so armed with a practical sensibility that vitalizes their response to individuals. Mrs. Poyser, Caleb Garth, Mrs. Meyrick, Bob Jakin, and others reveal an almost unconscious susceptibility to the needs of individual situations. Bob Jakin, in fact, seems to have inherited the soul of St. Ogg—after whom the town is so ironically named—whose legend epitomizes the ultimate and justified concession, even against what others call wisdom, to the individual's heart's need, which must be, by its very nature, incomprehensible to all others. For the other ferrymen of the Floss asked to know why the ragged mother wished to cross the river and, on the basis of their own judgment, advised her to take the wiser course of staying the night. Only St. Ogg seemed to understand, with an understanding, indeed, that is a resignation to not understanding; offering his boat, he said " 'it is enough that thy heart needs it' " *(The Mill on the Floss,* pp. 104-105).

For Eliot, it is, in a sense, a question of the allegiances she had dissociated in separating power from sympathy that had confronted St. Ogg in the image of the Virgin. Morality is necessary because man is powerless, but the heart's need has the supreme claim on our allegiance. The morality of rules sides with destiny, and so against man, when it persists in demands not even destiny imposes on every specific situation. It takes an authoritarian attitude that negates the tragedy of human experience by uniting power and sympathy in opposition to human needs. In *Adam Bede,* Eliot constructs what is in effect a debate in the concrete fact between the morality of codified rules, exemplified in Mr. Ryde, and the more flexible morality of sympathy, exemplified in Rev. Irwine. The narrator remarks that until "it can be proved that hatred is a better thing for the soul than love, I must believe that Mr. Irwine's influence in his parish was a more wholesome one than that of the zealous Mr. Ryde" who "insisted strongly on the doctrines of the Reformation" and "was severe in rebuking the aberrations of the flesh" (pp. 182-183).

Mr. Ryde's "hatred" has related existences in two areas, in motive and in effect. In her essay on Young, Eliot had remarked that the poet's "adherence to abstractions, or to the personification of abstractions, is closely allied" to his *"want of genuine emotion" (Essays.* p. 371). The two are, to a large degree, incompatible, the abstraction often serving—as in characters like Adam, Felix, Dinah, and others—as a means of avoiding feeling. Contact with reality is always, for Eliot, contact with the concrete. In her journal of her visit to Ilfracombe, Eliot writes: "I never before longed so much to know the names of things. . . . The mere fact of naming an object tends to give definiteness to our conception of it—we have then a sign that at once calls up in our minds the distinctive qualities which mark out for us that particular object from all others" *(Letters,* II, 251). In Mr. Ryde's mind there are, as it were, only the names of classes. Human beings are not individually real to him but rather a collective entity in God's cosmic architecture. In consequence, his "hatred" becomes, in its effect, an implicit preference for the abstraction over the human being.

Religious morality is more, although not exclusively, prone to this error for it offers characters like Mr. Ryde an alternative to tolerance and compassion, namely, the knowledge that they are serving the "higher" duty in God. Eliot consistently shows that to love God in the formal manner—to accept and approve only the perfection God represents—is to reject, with logical inevitability, man and the frailty he represents, ultimately, as in the case of Mr. Ryde, to hate him. In a view of the world such as Mr. Ryde holds, pity and piety, as Dante had said, are not compatible:

> Here pity, or here piety, must die
> If the other lives; who's wickeder than one
> That's agonized by God's high equity? [12]

In her essay on Young, Eliot continued to say that morality, exclusive of that portion which is the recognition of the cosmic law, exhibits itself "in direct sympathetic feeling and action, and not as the recognition of a rule. Love does not say 'I ought to love'—it loves. Pity does not say 'It is right to be pitiful'—it pities. Justice does not say 'I am bound to be just'—it feels justly" *(Essays,* p. 379). Mr. Ryde is, obviously, the counterexample. He is, in fact, the rigid embodiment of Feuerbach's vision of the degeneration of moral sensibility in religious codifications.

In religion, Feuerbach argues, there are moral actions but there are no "moral dispositions" informing them. "Moral rules are indeed observed, but they are severed from the inward disposition, the heart, by being represented as the commandments of an external lawgiver, by being placed in the category of arbitrary laws, police regulations. What is done is done not because it is good and right, but because it is commanded by God. The inherent quality of the deed is indifferent; whatever God commands is right." This, Feuerbach believes, "poisons, nay it destroys, the divinest feeling in man—the sense of truth, the perception and sentiment of truth." [13] In a letter to Elma Stuart, Eliot had written in very similar terms that the "worst of all privation is not the privation of joy but of ardent sympathy—the finding one's heart dry up, so that one has to act by rule without the tide of love to carry one" *(Letters,* VII, 210).

In this matter, once again aesthetic and moral considerations merge for Eliot. In a letter to Charles Bray, Eliot remarks that she has had "heart-cutting experience that opinions are a poor cement between human souls" and that, therefore, the only effect "I ardently long to produce by my writings, is that those who read them should be better able to *imagine* and to *feel* the pains and the joys of those who differ from themselves in every-thing but the broad fact of being struggling erring human crea-tures" *(Letters,* III, 111). It is for this reason that Eliot finds propaganda and didacticism entirely antithetical to her aims, although she has, ironically, been accused of trying to harass her characters and readers alike into moral rectitude.[14] But against such fiction Eliot argued all her life, and that too in a century in which hers was not the predominant view. As early as "Janet's Repentance," Blackwood was disturbed that the story studied an alcoholic woman sympathetically and wished too that the Bishop of the story "had been a better sample of the cloth" *(Letters,* II, 360). But a picture of sordid life, Eliot argues in reply, need not produce "those miserable mental states" Blackwood feared *(Letters,* II, 362). Dogma merely tells the reader what to do, with the likely result that he will resent the lesson and be provoked in the opposite direction. It is the *"aesthetic"* rather than the "doctrinal teacher" who rouses "the nobler emotions, which make mankind desire the social right" *(Letters,* VII, 44).

Discussing the moral obligations of authorship, Eliot writes that to "lay down in the shape of practical moral rules courses of conduct only to be made real by the rarest states of motive and disposition, tends not to elevate but to degrade the general standard, by turning that rare attainment from an object of admiration into an impossible prescription" ("Authorship," "Leaves From a Note-Book," *Essay,* p. 437). She returns to the topic again, in the same vein, in an essay on Carlyle where she adds that the most effective educator "does not seek to make his pupils moral by enjoining particular courses of action, but by bringing into activity the feelings and sympathies that must issue in noble action" *(Essays,* p. 213). Again, to Frederic Harrison, who urged her to write the Positivist novel, Eliot explained that her moral aim could be fulfilled only aesthetically. "I think aesthetic teaching is the highest of all teaching because it deals with life in its highest complexity. But if it ceases to be purely aesthetic—if it lapses anywhere from the picture to the diagram —it becomes the most offensive of all teaching" *(Letters,* VI, 300).

Ultimately, Eliot's position on this question rests on the same psychological conviction as supports all her moral beliefs. "Appeals," she writes in "The Natural History of German Life," "founded on generalizations and statistics require a sympathy ready-made, moral sentiment already in activity; but a picture of human life such as a great artist can give, surprises even the trivial and selfish into that attention to what is apart from themselves which may be called the raw material of moral sentiment" *(Essays,* p. 270).

As Mr. Ryde's "formal" religion stands for the "diagram" in *Adam Bede,* so Rev. Irwine's more "humanistic" morality reflects the "picture." That Irwine's is not much of a religion in the conventional sense Eliot's narrator confesses in the seventeenth chapter. He thinks of God seldom, and of doctrine even less. Although not irreligious, his concerns are rather secular, his choices somewhat epicurean, his sentiments—reflected everywhere in the imagery Eliot surrounds him with—even pagan. In his ministry, he seems to regard himself more as a kindly neighbor than an officer of God. Mr. Ryde, the reader cannot help reflecting, strikes one as marching at the head of a perhaps heavenly but fearsome militia. Irwine makes errors and some very serious ones.

He fails when, early in the novel, he does not seize the opportunity to speak to Arthur, who seems to have come for advice. Irwine is reticent, dislikes to intrude. Had he felt compelled to press Arthur to the confession the latter apparently came to make, he might have spared many unnecessary suffering. Mr. Ryde, we are certain, would not have been reluctant to lecture Arthur. But Irwine was "too delicate to imply even friendly curiosity" (pp. 176-177), and Arthur leaves in silence. Yet from Mr. Ryde Arthur would undoubtedly have left in rebellion, had he come at all. Irwine's mistake in this instance is very costly. But, imperfect as he is, he is obviously superior to his alternative. When the narrator addresses the reader directly on the subject of Rev. Irwine, he anticipates an argument. "Perhaps you think he was not—as he ought to have been—a living demonstration of the benefits attached to a national church? But I am not sure of that; at least I know that the people in Broxton and Hayslope would have been very sorry to part with their clergyman, and that most faces brightened at his approach" (pp. 182-183). For Rev. Irwine—and higher praise it is difficult to conceive from Eliot— had learned "tenderness for obscure and monotonous suffering" (p. 66).

The same contrast is repeated in *Middlemarch* between Farebrother and Tyke. The former—whose name is a significant hint of his character—confesses to Lydgate what the narrator of *Adam Bede* confesses to the reader of Irwine, that he is not a " 'model clergyman—only a decent makeshift.' " But he speaks, obviously, in a humility already beyond the imagination of Tyke. Neither the narrator nor Eliot seems to quarrel with Farebrother's estimate of Bulstrode and his "set," whom Farebrother characterizes as " ' "narrow and ignorant," ' " doing " 'more to make their neighbours uncomfortable than to make them better.' " It is Farebrother, not Bulstrode—another formal man of God—who gives Lydgate the freedom to vote his conscience for the position at the hospital, saying, as Bulstrode,

Tyke, Ryde, and those like them could never truthfully say, " 'I don't translate my own convenience into other people's duties' " (p. 131).

Sympathy and Utility

The contrast between characters like Ryde, Tyke, and Bulstrode on the one hand and Irwine and Farebrother on the other is, ultimately, a contrast between judgment and compassion. It is repeated, again and again, in the novels, especially at moments of crucial transition, in variations of a fundamental pattern. It is the same pattern as Feuerbach had seen in the parable of the incarnation of God in Christ. Feuerbach distinguishes God the Father as pure intellect, judging according to "the stringency of law," on a purely objective basis. Because God can judge in no other way, Christ is necessary; in Him, man allegorized love, compassion. In Christ, "the heart accommodates itself, is considerate, lenient, relenting, $\kappa \alpha \tau'$ $\mathring{\alpha} \nu \theta \rho \omega \pi o \nu$. . . . The law condemns; the heart has compassion even on the sinner. The law affirms me only as an abstract being,—love as a real being." [15] But to acquire this love, God had to become man. God knows what man is, God knows his weakness, his temptations, for how can a God be conceived who does not? Yet even God can know such things only from His own divine point of view, externally. To "know" man in a subjective, therefore real, way, God had to assume the nature of man. Only in the experience of man can be rooted the compassion man requires which Feuerbach defines, in a striking phrase, as the "justice of sensuous life." [16]

It becomes clear that there are two kinds of justice in Eliot's world, paralleling, again, the two narrative voices: one, like God's justice, is externally fair, demanding—as indeed cosmic law demands—from each the same measure of competence. Yet seen from a subjective point of view, in the keen knowledge that not all men are in fact capable of the same endurance, this kind of

200

justice emerges as curiously unjust, and only a concession to weakness and ignorance seems entirely fair. Indeed, these conflicting concepts of justice are always very central to Eliot's concerns. In *Felix Holt* she seems to anticipate the argument that it is not, somehow, fair to ask more from some than from others. But her determinism implies her answer. "The stronger will always rule, say some," the narrator begins in what seems to be a rebuttal of the moral implications of the theory of evolution,

> But what is strength? Is it blind wilfulness that sees no terrors, no many-linked consequences, no bruises and wounds of those whose cords it tightens? Is it the narrowness of a brain that conceives no needs differing from its own, and looks to no results beyond the bargains of to-day; that tugs with emphasis for every small purpose, and thinks it weakness to exercise the sublime power of resolved renunciation? There is a sort of subjection which is the peculiar heritage of largeness and of love; and strength is often only another name for willing bondage to irremediable weakness. (p. 81)

Felix, Adam, Lydgate, and others are asked to yield, persistently, to the degree that Esther, Hetty, and Rosamond are weaker. If it seems unfair to make such excessive demands on those who can withstand them and to forgo making them on those who cannot, we are quickly reminded that such "unfairness" only attempts to mitigate the irremediable injustice of the universe. Eliot sees a considerable development in the Lydgate who has "almost learned the lesson that he must bend to her nature, and that because she came short in her sympathy, he must give the more" *(Middlemarch,* p. 555). For it is certainly just as unfair that Hetty should be as weak and foolish as she is, that Rosamond should be as selfish as she is. If Lydgate is capable of giving more, he is merely the beneficiary of a cosmic accident. The burden falls to him by default. In a letter to Mme Bodichon, Eliot writes that right "or not right, it is the hard fact, that those who are strong ... have to bear the infirmities of those that are weak" *(Letters,* VII, 215). It is pointless, in Eliot's novels, to look for a concept of justice which takes into account only a hypothetical state of perfection in which we are all equally capable of dealing with reality. It is a "hard fact" that this is not the state of the world. In terms of the "justice of sensuous life," Rosamond and Hetty give as much as Romola and Dorothea, that is, as much as they can. The "renunciation" of which the narrator of *Felix Holt* spoke is, as Eliot's letter to Mme Bodichon (above) states, as much an imposition on man's existence as any other cosmic law; for, strictly, there is no escaping the reality of individual limitations.

It is always this second sense of justice that Eliot favors as conducive to individual and general human welfare—toward which all morality must be directed—in those crucial moments of transition which are the constant moral tests of the novels. In these characteristic test cases, we are often presented with three or more characters who take, essentially, three distinct roles; one stands on the threshold of moral decision or change; the other two speak for the two conflicting concepts of "justice." In just such a situation, at an important point in his life, Fred Vincy is caught between the oppostie opinions of Mr. and Mr. Garth. Characteristically, Fred is a character whose moral future is genuinely uncertain. Although self-centered and thoroughly unaware of the inner reality of others, he is capable, as well, of generosity and affection. The decision the Garths will make about him will help to enforce one or the other capacity in him. Mrs. Garth, not unsympathetic but morally less adventurous, takes a somewhat absolute stand; too often disappointed in Fred, she concludes him a worthless investment and argues against giving him another chance after he had gambled away the money for which Caleb had stood security. Caleb, however, is more forgiving. While Mrs. Garth is "rational and unhopeful," Caleb decides to help Fred one more time. "Which would turn out to have the more foresight in it—her rationality or Caleb's ardent generosity?" the narrator asks *(Middlemarch,* pp. 421-423). It is, of course, Caleb who is right, whereas Mrs. Garth might have condemned to failure a young man who, although standing at the edge of a moral precipice, was, nonetheless, retrievable.

The formula, as Eliot seems to admit in characters like Hetty, Rosamond, and Grandcourt, is by no means an unfailing one; some people, regretfully, are hopeless. Yet even in extreme cases there are relative advantages to be gained and lost, for salvation is never for Eliot a dramatic conversion to purity, and every atom of goodness must be prized as by that much rendering the world more habitable. So hardened an egotist as Tito can never "reform," but there is, even in his case, a better and worse consequence to be considered in an individual event, especially since Eliot always distinguishes between the possible regeneration of the whole man and the distinct acts he may perform for good or ill. Like Fred, Tito finds himself the subject of two very different attitudes. Romola, for all her intelligence, cannot understand that in her persistent judgment of Tito's actions by absolute standards of right and wrong she is "really helping to harden Tito's nature by chilling it with a positive dislike." It is Tessa who, incapable of judgment, offers him the uncritical adoration which keeps "the fountains of kindness" open in him *(Romola,* p. 438).

In these instances, as in all others, it is clear that Eliot's moral vision repudiates deontological ethics and accepts, rather, an ultimately utilitarian criterion.[17] In a passage I quoted earlier from *The Mill on the Floss,* the question, the narrator claims, is "whether the moment has come in which a man has fallen below the possibility of a *renunciation that will carry any efficacy,* and *must* accept the sway of a passion against which he had struggled as a trespass" (p.435; my italics). The alternatives are obvious: renunciation is valuable insofar as it may still have desirable consequences. It is not, therefore—as the religious associations of the word might suggest—a good in itself but a good only if the end it serves is good. But if it is not efficacious, there seems not only no need for it but, as the emphatic word "must" implies, it is to be rejected in favor of something whose end is better.

Maggie's case instantiates Eliot's position very precisely. Bissell, writing about Maggie's dilemma, maintains that when Eliot forces Maggie to "face the uncomprehending wrath of society at the call of moral principle," she is denying the validity of "utilitarian ethics."[18] One assumes that Bissell would have declared Eliot's conclusion utilitarian had Maggie married Stephen on the argument that, first, they loved one another and, second, neither could return to the earlier relationship—although in fact Stephen does return to Lucy. That is, in the choice Maggie makes, no one can be happy, whereas if Maggie had married Stephen at least these two would have been happy and so something of a utilitarian purpose would have been served. But this, I think, is no more true than it is that Eliot suggests the "call of moral principle" in Maggie's decision, if by "moral principle" we understand—as Bissell seems to suggest—a deontological criterion. It is probably true that Bentham, and perhaps the early Mill, would have preferred that Maggie marry Stephen. Yet Eliot makes clear before the novel ends that had this marriage taken place quite the contrary of the utilitarian end would have been achieved; far from happiness, it would have brought Maggie greater suffering than a separation from Stephen does. For while Eliot holds that the end of morality is always the greatest possible degree of happiness man can find in a world ill suited to accommodate man's welfare, she insists that the strict Utilitarian calculus is simply oblivious to the infinite psychological and moral complexities involved in attaining that end. The question "What will make Maggie happy?" cannot be answered be merely citing her passion for Stephen. There are other questions equally or even more important that must be posed.

First, Eliot asks whether Maggie could have been happy with Stephen, not merely for the moment—as in their elopement—but for the less romantic and more taxing relationship of a lifetime. The answer, for a number of reasons, must be that she could not. For one thing, Stephen is too unequal to Maggie. He is less intelligent, less sensitive, less passionate even; in fact, he is rather mediocre. The very fact that he chooses Lucy—a sweet but dull creature—to be his wife suggests the level of his comfort. And the manner in which he arrives at this choice suggests the depth of Stephen's nature. Projecting himself into the character's mind, the narrator asks whether Stephen was not "right in his decided opinion that this slim maiden of eighteen was quite the sort of wife a man would not be likely to repent of marrying?" The element of cool deliberation implicit in the language is quite revealing, as it is when the narrator remarks that Stephen "was conscious of excellent judgment in preferring" Lucy to Miss Leyburn, apparently her nearest rival, and as it is again in the narrator's conclusion that Stephen, taking all things into consideration, "meant to choose Lucy" (p. 323). We are not surprised that Lucy, too much in love to be aware of what she implies, tells Stephen, when they have finished singing a duet, that he does " 'the "heavy beasts" to perfection' " (p. 321).

Such a character is necessary for Eliot's purpose. For what Eliot is showing is not that Maggie has found too late and in the wrong place the love she has searched for all her life but rather that Philip's prediction has finally come true. And that it has come true is, in fact, Eliot's proof that psychological reality will be revenged on deontological principles of renunciation. Unable to confront or escape the practical limitations of her life, Maggie had sought an inner refuge in the teaching of Thomas à Kempis. She had found, she told Philip, " 'even joy in subduing my own will.' " But Philip's analysis of the situation had been much more accurate. " '*You* are not resigned,' " he had told her, " 'you are only trying to stupefy yourself.' " No one, he had maintained, " 'has strength given to do what is unnatural. It is mere cowardice to seek safety in negations. . . . You will be thrown into the world some day, and then every rational satisfaction of your nature that you deny now, will assault you like a savage appetite' " (pp. 286-8).

It is obvious from the first that, apart from the motive I discussed earlier—her desire to replace Lucy—Maggie is attracted to Stephen more sexually than in any other way. How important it is to Maggie that Stephen is handsome we may gauge by her persistent inability to overcome, even with effort, her distaste for Philip's deformity. Perhaps in a twentieth-century novel Eliot would have said more on this subject, but in the idiom of the nineteenth she says enough for the reader to recognize the intense sexuality in Maggie and to know that when Maggie meets Stephen it is the "savage appetite" that erupts. It is precisely the point of Maggie's dilemma, in her fluctuation between flesh and spirit, that she can accept neither Philip nor Stephen, that she must remain torn between one who is inadequate on a spiritual level and one whom her flesh cannot tolerate but who is otherwise far more nearly her equal. Ultimately, we know that Maggie cannot be "happy" whomever she chooses, for each denies a vital part of herself. Thus, in her brief elopement with Stephen she finds that escape from painful sensitivity, from spiritual and intellectual anguish, in an oblivion that is for her an essential respite. But it is, and can be, only a respite. The agon can be interrupted but not resolved.

Yet, even if Stephen were all that he should be, another and very important reason why Maggie could not be happy with him is that Maggie, unlike Stephen, cannot find happiness so easily. For a few days she can forget, harassed as her life has been, all that troubles her and find a kind of pseudo-happiness in being with Stephen. But she cannot feign amnesia the rest of her life. She rejects Stephen not because she has weighed the possible happiness she might have with him against the unhappiness of others but rather because she has realized that her happiness with him would not be sufficient to balance her unhappiness with him, an unhappiness which grows, partially, out of the unhappiness of others.

One might ask, with Bissell perhaps, why Eliot should so construct her fictional world as to show that a character like Maggie cannot, on rationally concluding that neither Lucy nor Philip can again be restored to their happiness, decide to put them out of her mind entirely and make the best arrangement for herself. This question Eliot has very seriously considered and answered in the novel. The answer constitutes, in fact, an explanation of Maggie's behavior in this situation and, generalized, throughout the novel.

Inherent in a deterministic psychology is the unalterable fact that the human mind functions structurally. Maggie is or is not the kind of person who can, without pain to herself, take Lucy's fiancé, abandon her own ties, and run away to satisfy a momentary passion with no memory of those she has hurt. And Maggie is not. In the complex explication of this whole matter, which begins in the fourteenth chapter of the sixth book, the narrator early reminds us that it is Maggie's "nature"—not her "moral principles"—that recoils from the action she has just taken. Recognizing herself as one divided, Maggie significantly identifies her "real" self with this nature that must reject the passionate act. Her soul, she feels, had been "betrayed, beguiled, ensnared," but it could never "consent" to what she has done (p. 413). And this, she tells Stephen, is the irreducible and therefore unassailable foundation of her decision. Stephen argues that they belong together because it is the first time both of them have loved with their whole hearts and souls. " 'No,' " Maggie replies, " 'not with my whole heart and soul.' " " 'I have never consented to it with my whole mind' " (p. 418).

In discussing this question with Stephen, Maggie enters on broader issues. When Stephen presses her to marry him on the grounds that " 'natural law surmounts every other' " (p. 417), he urges implicitly the side of the "hard non-moral outward condition." Maggie is not certain where Stephen's argument has gone wrong, but she is certain of its logical conclusion: if " 'we judged in that way, there would be a warrant for all treachery and cruelty,' " she replies (p. 417). Stephen would follow nature beyond what destiny demands, and would choose to act on the basis of natural law even in those areas where sympathy can make concessions to human welfare. Maggie has found, at last, a position which rejects both the deontological ethics that can conflict with the utilitarian end of human happiness and the narrow utilitarian criterion that considers only the individual's pleasure-pain calculus as though in a temporal and social vacuum. She has discovered that, contrary to her earlier stand on the principles of Thomas à Kempis, the end must be happiness of some sort but that happiness is not, as Stephen's narrow utilitarianism argues, the satisfaction of desire only but rather the satisfaction of the whole human being.

Against the persistently painful temptation to yield to Stephen's entreaties, there is another, a psychological, reality which she cannot escape. She has reached, in the process of the novel, that level of sympathy in which she can completely and subjectively identify with another. The inclination had always been there; we saw it at the very beginning when, in contrast to Tom, she worried whether the baiting worms felt pain (p. 36). Fitful though this power has been in her, it checked her again and again when temptation threatened to overcome her. By her own evaluation, Stephen cannot be for her a "choice of joy," for she could never "cease to see before her Lucy and Philip, with their murdered trust and hopes" (p. 413).

The view to which Eliot has brought Maggie by the end of the novel is one which interprets utility through sympathy in the sense that the happiness principle is invoked not on behalf of the individual only but on behalf of those others whose pain the individual has come to feel as his own. Yet neither the reader nor Eliot doubts that this transition to a sympathetic utilitarian criterion is a difficult and often partial one; nor does Eliot

assure us that all are capable of it. Stephen himself is the instantiating case. His last letter to Maggie is "a passionate cry of
reproach: an appeal against her useless sacrifice of him—of herself: against that perverted notion of right which led her to
crush all his hopes, for the sake of a mere idea, and not any
substantial good" (p. 449). Obviously, Stephen has completely
misunderstood everything Maggie has told him. For him, everything which is not personal utility is prescriptive dogma. He
remains bound, that is, to a narrowly subjective egotism.

In this, he is, although a better version, not essentially different from characters like Hetty, Rosamond, and the other
egotists without imagination in the novels. But they are always
the retarding friction in the world's progress toward that best
compromise with nature in which we try, rather than to deepen
the tragedy, to lighten the burden which is, even at best, all to
close to the limits of human endurance. And this general progress is by no means without its benefit even for those who do not
contribute to it. As the narrator of *Middlemarch,* speaking of
Dorothea, remarks in a passage I quoted earlier in another connection, "the growing good of the world is partly dependent
on unhistoric acts; and that things are not so ill with you and me
as they might have been is half owing to the number who lived
faithfully a hidden life, and rest in unvisited tombs" (pp.
612-613). In this context we must remember that for Eliot the
tragic protagonist is, after all, not the individual in himself but
the individual collectively, the whole human race. In every
sense, men's lives are inextricably bound together.

It is this conviction, ultimately, that Stephen lacks, not so
much intellectually (although, apparently, he lacks that too)
but emotionally, as a conditioning element in his feeling. In
contrast, it is to the concrete social tie that Maggie finally
appeals in justifying her actions. Maggie does not return, as
Bissell claims, to an "uncomprehending society," for this she
would be happy enough to escape from. She returns to the
society of St. Ogg's, to which she belongs, and accepts its being

uncomprehending as an inevitable if regrettable fact. The past, as both time and place, is the foundation of her identity. The force that draws her to Stephen " 'would rend me away from all that my past life has made dear and holy to me,' " she explains. " 'I can't set out on a fresh life, and forget that: I must go back to it, and cling to it, else I shall feel as if there were nothing firm beneath my feet' " (p. 420).[19] Maggie speaks here of feeling, not belief. Maggie is not bound because she holds to moral convictions such as Stephen ascribes to her in his last letter, convictions which she could choose to violate or about which she could change her mind. She is bound because her own feelings are deeply contextualized, because she feels herself organically integrated in a social existence.

Thus, Maggie's decision is not a Christian renunciation of happiness but a concession to the fact. If anything, Maggie's life, like the lives of all of Eliot's characters, is an attempt at fulfillment. In one of their earliest conversations, Will Ladislaw says to Dorothea that the " 'best piety is to enjoy—when you can.' " " 'I suspect,' " he adds, " 'that you have some false belief in the virtues of misery, and want to make your life a martyrdom' " *(Middlemarch,* p. 163). Both in his analysis of Dorothea and in principle, Will has more than half of Eliot's vision of truth on his side. There is no virtue in misery and unnecessary martyrdom. Where Will is wrong here is in his having as yet failed to recognize that while we may be thoroughly entitled to demand happiness, our expectations must be conditioned by the tragic reality from which none can escape. It is precisely because man feels that he is born for something better, deserves to have it, and yet cannot find it except in fleeting moments that Eliot sees human life as tragic, and, moreover, irretrievably tragic.

Eliot was, as she claims, a meliorist (see *Letters,* VI, 333). She believed, as did others (like Comte and Mill), that man could, by accepting the inevitable, alter the variables of his condition. She presses her meliorism, always, as the preferable alternative to complete hopelessness in the face of that much larger share of destiny which remains forever unalterable. But the tragic agon goes on. In a letter to Clifford Allbutt, Eliot writes that never "to beat and bruise one's wings against the inevitable but to throw the whole farce of one's soul towards the achievement of some possible better, is the brief heading that need never be changed, however often the chapter of more special rules may have to be re-written." But, although she reminds herself of this every day, she cannot hold off the thought of a "past which widens more and more in the consciousness of a wasted good," or the "visibly narrowing future." "All the devices," she concludes, "which men have used under the name of consoling truths, to get rid of this need for *absolute* resignation, are in my deep conviction false and enfeebling. But I know through the experience of more than two thirds of my life the immense difficulty, to a passionate nature, of attaining more than a fitful exercise of such resignation" *(Letters,* IV, 499). The best one may hope for is morality, but even in that the will has lost the contest.

Notes

1. Cross, III, 33.
2. *The Common Reader: First Series* (New York, 1953), p. 170.
3. "Beyond the Liberal Imagination," p. 34.
4. W. G. Yuill argues that Eliot misunderstood Novalis (" 'Character Is Fate': A Note on Thomas Hardy, George Eliot, and Novalis," *MLR,* 57 [July 1962], 401-402), a point which, however, has no bearing on Eliot's purpose in this passage.
5. See Pinney's introduction to "The Natural History of German Life," *Essays,* p. 266.
6. *The Free Spirit,* p. 16.
7. *The Art of George Eliot,* pp. 85-86. This interpretation leads Harvey to conclude that Eliot's editorial comments on Hetty are an attack on her and that "this sense of intrinsic unfairness adds to our sense of unjustified hostility on the part of the author" (p. 87). As I will show shortly, Eliot both intends and achieves, I think, the exact opposite effect.

8. "Determinism and Responsibility," p. 275.

9. *Ibid.,* p. 276.

10. Bernard J. Paris, "George Eliot's Religion of Humanity," *ELH,* 29 (December 1962), 440.

11. Eliot uses, for example, diminutives, endearing names, and, even more, the adjective "poor" (in the sympathetic sense) to entice the reader to share with her a compassionate attitude to the characters.

12. *The Divine Comedy: Hell,* trans. Dorothy L. Sayers (Baltimore, 1963), p. 196.

13. *The Essence of Christianity,* p. 209.

14. David Cecil and V. S. Pritchett, for example, are particularly prone to this view.

15. *The Essence of Christianity,* pp. 47-48.

16. *Ibid.,* p. 49.

17. This is not to say that Eliot is, in the strictest sense, a Utilitarian, and certainly not a Benthamite, although some critics speak of her views as Utilitarian subject to qualifications (see, for example, H. V. Routh, *Towards the Twentieth Century: Essays in the Spiritual History of the Nineteenth* [New York, 1937], p. 274; Paris, "George Eliot's Religion of Humanity," p. 421; Bourl'honne, p. 82; Arnold Kettle, *An Introduction to the English Novel: Defoe to George Eliot* [New York, 1960], p. 187). I think it more accurate to conclude that, as usual, Eliot prefers to remain eclectic. Yet the affiliation with the criteria of Utilitarianism is inevitable in a morality that evolves out of a secular and scientific view of the world and whose ultimate aim is to mediate between the conflict of will and destiny.

18. "Social Analysis in the Novels of George Eliot," p. 165.

19. In his recent article, "A Reinterpretation of *The Mill on the Floss" (PMLA,* 87 [January 1972], 53-63), John Hagan, rightly I think, stresses that Maggie's decision to return to St. Ogg's is based on Maggie's deep emotional ties to family and place.

Bibliography

(As well as sources cited in the text, this bibliography includes works I have found useful in my study.)

Adam, Ian W. "Restoration Through Feeling in George Eliot's Fiction: A New Look at Hetty Sorrel." *VN,* No. 22 (Fall 1962), 9-12.

Allen, Walter. *George Eliot.* New York, 1964.

Anderson, Quentin. "George Eliot in *Middlemarch.*" *From Dickens to Hardy,* ed. Boris Ford. Baltimore, 1963. Pp. 274-293.

Appleman, Philip, William A. Madden, and Michael Wolff, eds. *1859: Entering an Age of Crisis.* Bloomington, 1959.

Baker, Ernest. *From the Brontes to Meredith: Romanticism in the English Novel. The History of the English Novel,* Vol. 7. New York, 1960.

Beaty, Jerome. *Middlemarch from Notebook to Novel: A Study of George Eliot's Creative Method.* Urbana, 1960.

———. "Daniel Deronda and the Question of Unity in Fiction." *VN,* No. 15 (Spring 1959), 16-20.

Bedient, Calvin. *Architects of the Self: George Eliot, D. H. Lawrence, and E. M. Forster*. Berkeley, 1972.

Bennett, Joan. *George Eliot: Her Mind and Her Art*. Cambridge, 1962.

Bissell, Claude. "Social Analysis in the Novels of George Eliot." *Victorian Literature: Essays in Criticism*. Edited by Austin Wright. New York, 1961. Pp. 154-171.

Blind, Mathilde. *George Eliot*. Boston, 1883.

Blotner, Joseph. *The Political Novel*. New York, 1955.

Bourl'honne, P. *George Eliot: Essai de biographie intellectuelle et morale, 1819-54*. Paris, 1933.

Bray, Charles. *The Philosophy of Necessity or Law in Mind as in Matter*. 3rd ed. revised and abridged. London, 1889.

Brown, John Crombie. *The Ethics of George Eliot's Works*. Philadelphia, 1885.

Browning, Oscar. *The Life of George Eliot*. London, 1892.

Buckler, William E. *Novels in the Making*. Boston, 1961.

Buckley, Jerome H. *The Victorian Temper: A Study in Literary Culture*. New York, 1964.

―――. *The Triumph of Time: A Study of the Victorian Concepts of Time, History, Progress, and Decadence*. Cambridge, Mass., 1966.

Bullett, Gerald. *George Eliot: Her Life and Books*. New Haven, 1948.

Carroll, David R. "An Image of Disenchantment in the Novels of George Eliot." *RES*, n.s., 11 (February 1960), 29-41.

———. "The Unity of *Daniel Deronda.*" *Essays in Criticism,* 9 (October 1959), 369-380.

———. *"Felix Holt:* Society as Protagonist." *NCF,* 17 (December 1962), 237-252.

Cecil, Lord David. *Victorian Novelists: Essays in Revaluation.* Chicago, 1961.

Cockshut, A. O. J. *The Unbelievers: English Agnostic Thought, 1840-1890.* London, 1964.

Comte, Auguste. *A General View of Positivism.* Translated by J. H. Bridges. Stanford, n.d.

———. *System of Positive Polity.* Translator not named. 4 vols. London, 1875-77.

———. *The Positive Philosophy of Auguste Comte.* Translated by Harriet Martineau. 2 vols. New York, 1853.

———. *The Catechism of Positivism: or Summary Exposition of the Universal Religion.* Translated by Richard Congreve. London, 1858.

Cooper, Lettice Ulpha. *George Eliot.* New York, 1960.

Coveney, Peter. *Poor Monkey: The Child in Literature.* London, 1957.

Cox, Charles B. *The Free Spirit: A Study of Liberal Humanism in the Novels of George Eliot, Henry James, E. M. Forster, Virginia Woolf, Angus Wilson.* London, 1963.

Cross, John Walter. *George Eliot's Life as Related in Her Letters and Journals.* 3 vols. New York: Illustrated Cabinet Edition, n.d.

Daiches, David. *George Eliot: Middlemarch.* London, 1963.

Diekhoff, John S. "The Happy Ending of *Adam Bede*." *ELH,* 3 (September 1936), 221-227.

Eliot, George. *Adam Bede*. Edited with an introduction by Gordon S. Haight. New York, 1957.

———. *The Mill on the Floss*. Edited with an introduction by Gordon S. Haight. New York, 1961.

———. *Silas Marner*. Edited with an introduction by Q. D. Leavis. Baltimore, 1967.

———. *Romola*. With an introduction by Viola Meynell. New York, 1949.

———. *Felix Holt, The Radical*. Edited with an introduction by George Levine. New York, 1970.

———. *Middlemarch*. Edited with an introduction by Gordon S. Haight. Boston, 1956.

———. *Daniel Deronda*. Edited with an introduction by F. R. Leavis. New York, 1961.

———. *Essays of George Eliot*. Edited by Thomas Pinney. New York, 1963.

———. *Impressions of Theophrastus Such: Miscellaneous Essays*. New York: Illustrated Cabinet Edition, n.d.

———. *The George Eliot Letters*. Edited by Gordon S. Haight. 7 vols. New Haven, 1954-55.

Feltes, N. N. "George Eliot and the Unified Sensibility." *PMLA,* 79 (March 1964), 130-136.

Ferguson, Suzanne C. "Mme. Laure and Operative Irony in *Middlemarch:* A Structural Analogy." *SEL,* 3 (Autumn 1963), 509-510.

Feuerbach, Ludwig. *The Essence of Christianity.* Translated by George Eliot. New York, 1957.

Gregor, Ian. "The Two Worlds of *Adam Bede.*" Ian Gregor and Brian Nicholas, *The Moral and the Story.* London, 1962. Pp. 13-32.

Hagan, John. "A Reinterpretation of *The Mill on the Floss.*" *PMLA,* 87 (January 1972), 53-63.

Haight, Gordon S., ed. *A Century of George Eliot Criticism.* Boston, 1965.

———. *George Eliot: A Biography.* New York, 1968.

Hardy, Barbara. "The Moment of Disenchantment in George Eliot's Novels." *RES,* n.s., 5 (July 1954), 256-264.

———. "Imagery in George Eliot's Last Novels." *MLR,* 50 (January 1955), 6-14.

———. *The Novels of George Eliot: A Study in Form.* London, 1959.

———. *The Appropriate Form: An Essay on the Novel.* London, 1964.

———. ed. *Middlemarch: Critical Approaches to the Novel.* New York, 1967.

Harvey, W. J. *The Art of George Eliot.* London, 1961.

———. *Middlemarch.* Baltimore, 1965.

———. *Character and the Novel.* New York, 1965.

Henley, William Ernest. [On George Eliot]. *A Century of George Eliot Criticism.* Edited by Gordon S. Haight. Boston, 1965. Pp. 161-162.

Hennell, Charles. *Christian Theism.* London, 1839.

————. *An Inquiry Concerning the Origin of Christianity,* 2nd ed. London, 1841.

Holloway, John. *The Victorian Sage: Studies in Argument.* New York, 1965.

Hough, Graham. "Novelist-philosophers. XII. George Eliot." *Horizon,* 17 (January 1948), 50-62.

Hutton, R. H. [Review of *Romola*]. *George Eliot and Her Readers: A Selection of Contemporary Reviews.* Edited by Laurence Lerner and John Holmstrom. London, 1966. Pp. 56-66.

Hyde, W. J. "George Eliot and the Climate of Realism." *PMLA,* 72 (March 1957), 147-164.

Kaminsky, Alice R. "George Eliot, George Henry Lewes, and the Novel." *PMLA,* 70 (December 1955), 997-1013.

Kettle, Arnold. *An Introduction to the English Novel: Defoe to George Eliot.* New York, 1960.

Knoepflmacher, U. C. *Religious Humanism and the Victorian Novel: George Eliot, Walter Pater, and Samuel Butler.* Princeton, 1965.

Leavis, F. R. *The Great Tradition.* New York, 1963.

Lerner, Laurence. " 'The Cool Gaze and the Warm Heart': Laurence Lerner on George Eliot's 'Middlemarch.' " *The Listener* (September 29, 1960), pp. 518-519, 522.

————. *The Truthtellers: Jane Austen, George Eliot, D. H. Lawrence.* New York, 1967.

———— and John Holmstrom, eds. *George Eliot and Her Readers: A Selection of Contemporary Reviews.* London, 1966.

Levine, George. "Intelligence as Deception: The Mill on the Floss." *PMLA,* 80 (September 1965), 402-409.

————. "Determinism and Responsibility in the Works of George Eliot." *PMLA,* 77 (June 1962), 268-279.

Lewes, George Henry. *Literary Criticism of George Henry Lewes.* Edited by Alice R. Kaminsky. Lincoln, 1964.

————. *The History of Philosophy from Thales to Comte,* 4th ed., corrected and partly rewritten. 2 vols. London, 1871.

Murphy, Howard R. "The Ethical Revolt Against Christian Orthodoxy in Early Victorian England." *The American Historical Review,* 60 (April 1955), 800-817.

Paris, Bernard J. "George Eliot's Religion of Humanity." *ELH,* 29 (December 1962), 418-443.

————. "Toward a Revaluation of George Eliot's *The Mill on the Floss.*" *NCF,* 11 (June 1956), 18-31.

————. *Experiments in Life: George Eliot's Quest for Values.* Detroit, 1965.

Parlett, Mathilde. "George Eliot and Humanism." *SP,* 27 (January 1930), 25-46.

————. "The Influence of Contemporary Criticism on George Eliot." *SP,* 30 (January 1933), 103-132.

Pond, E. J. *Les Idees morales et religieuses de George Eliot.* Paris, 1927.

Praz, Mario. *The Hero in Eclipse in Victorian Fiction.* Translated by Angus Davidson. New York, 1956.

Prest, John. *The Industrial Revolution in Coventry.* New York, 1960

Preyer, Robert. "Beyond the Liberal Imagination: Visions and Unreality in *Daniel Deronda.*" *VS,* 4 (September 1960), 33-54.

Pritchett, V. S. *The Living Novel.* New York, 1947.

Rendall, Vernon. "George Eliot and the Classics." *A Century of George Eliot Criticism.* Edited by Gordon S. Haight. Boston, 1965. Pp. 215-226.

Robinson, Carole. "The Severe Angel: A Study of *Daniel Deronda.*" *ELH,* 31 (September 1964), 278-300.

Routh, H. V. *Towards the Twentieth Century: Essays in the Spiritual History of the Nineteenth.* New York, 1937.

Rubin, Larry. "River Imagery as a Means of Foreshadowing in *The Mill on the Floss.*" *MLN,* 71 (January 1956), 18-22.

Simon, W. M. "Auguste Comte's English Disciples." *VS,* 8 (December 1964), 161-172.

Stang, Richard. "The Literary Criticism of George Eliot." *PMLA,* 72 (December 1957), 952-961.

Steinhoff, William R. "Intent and Fulfillment in the Ending of *The Mill on the Floss.*" *The Image of the Work: Essays in Criticism.* Edited by B. H. Lehman and others. Berkeley, 1955. Pp. 231-251.

Stephen, Leslie. *George Eliot.* New York, 1902.

Strauss, David Friedrich. *The Life of Jesus, Critically Examined.* Translated from the 4th German ed. by George Eliot. London, 1846.

Stump, Reva J. *Movement and Vision in George Eliot's Novels.* Seattle, 1959.

Thale, Jerome. "Image and Theme: *The Mill on the Floss.*" *University of Kansas City Review,* 23 (March 1957), 227-234.

———. *The Novels of George Eliot.* New York, 1961.

Van Ghent, Dorothy. *The English Novel: Form and Function.* New York, 1953.

Wagenknecht, Edward. *Cavalcade of the English Novel: From Elizabeth to George VI,* 1954 ed. New York, 1954.

Woolf, Virginia. *The Common Reader: First Series.* New York, 1953.

Yuill, W. G. " 'Character is Fate': A Note on Thomas Hardy, George Eliot, and Novalis." *MLR,* 57 (July 1962), 401-402.